How to Analyse Talk in Institutional Settings

How to Analyse Talk in Institutional Settings

A Casebook of Methods

Edited by
ALEC McHOUL and MARK RAPLEY

Continuum
The Tower Building, 11 York Road, London SE1 7NX
370 Lexington Avenue, New York, NY 10017–6503

First published 2001

British Library Cataloguing-in-Publication Data

A catalogue record for this book is available from the British Library.

ISBN 0-8264-5463-1 (hardback)
0-8264-5464-X (paperback)

Library of Congress Cataloging-in-Publication Data

How to analyse talk in institutional settings: a casebook of methods / edited by Alec McHoul and Mark Rapley.

p. cm.

Includes bibliographical references and index.

ISBN 0-8264-5463-1 (hardback) — ISBN 0-8264-5464-X (pbk.)

1. Conversation analysis. 2. Discourse analysis. 3. Social interaction. I. McHoul, Alec II. Rapley, Mark.

P95.45 .H69 2001
302.3′46—dc21

2001017347

Typeset by CentraServe Ltd, Saffron Walden, Essex

Printed and bound in Great Britain by MPG Books Ltd, Bodmin, Cornwall

Contents

Contributors

Charles Antaki is Reader in Language and Social Psychology at Loughborough University. His research interest is conversation analysis as it illuminates the interactions of everyday life and work. He has recently co-published with Susan Widdicombe *Identities in Talk* (Sage).

Martha Augoustinos is Associate Professor in Psychology at Adelaide University where she teaches social psychology. Her current research interests include discursive studies of racism and political rhetoric. She is co-editor with Kate Reynolds of *Understanding Prejudice, Racism and Social Conflict* (Sage).

Helena Austin teaches at undergraduate and postgraduate levels in the School of Education and Professional Studies at Griffith University. Her current research investigates theories of the child and childhood as they are enacted in institutional practices.

Carolyn Baker is Associate Professor in the Graduate School of Education at the University of Queensland. She has written on language and social interaction in classrooms, meetings and interviews. Current research projects include analyses of helpline calls by children, the telling of marriage and courtship narratives, and talk, interaction and difference in primary classrooms. She is also preparing *Conducting and Analysing Interviews* (Sage).

Bronwyn Dwyer completed her PhD in Education at Griffith University in 1997 and is now working as a research officer within the Attorney General's Department in Canberra. Her research interests include ethnomethodology and the enactment of childhood within school classrooms.

Derek Edwards is Professor of Psychology at Loughborough University. His main interests are in the analysis of discourse and conversation, and especially in discursive psychology. He is author or co-author of several books including *Common Knowledge* (Routledge), *Ideological Dilemmas* (Sage), *Discursive Psychology* (Sage) and *Discourse and Cognition* (Sage).

Michael Emmison is Associate Professor of Sociology at the University of Queensland. He has published articles on language and social interaction as well as cultural consumption and the mass media. He is co-author of *Accounting for Tastes* (Cambridge University Press) and *Researching the Visual* (Sage) and co-edits the *Journal of Sociology*.

Norman Fairclough is Professor of Language in Social Life at Lancaster University. His previous publications include *Language and Power* (Longman), *Discourse and Social Change* (Polity), *Critical Discourse Analysis* with L. Chouliaraki (Longman), *Discourse and Late Modernity* (University of Edinburgh) and most recently *New Language, New Labour?* (Routledge).

Alan Firth is Associate Professor in the Department of Languages and Intercultural Studies at Ålborg University. He has published articles on negotiation discourse, English as an international language, ethnomethodology, and language and culture. He is currently preparing *Discourse and Culture* (Sage) and *Studying Language as Social Interaction* (Macmillan), and has edited *The Discourse of Negotiation* (Elsevier).

David Francis is Senior Lecturer in Sociology at Manchester Metropolitan University. He is co-author of *Perspectives in Sociology* (Routledge) and co-editor with Stephen Hester of *Local Educational Order* (Benjamins). He has written numerous articles in the fields of ethnomethodology and conversation analysis, and is currently working on *Language, Society and Social Interaction* (Sage).

Peter Freebody is Professor of Education and Director of the Centre for Literacy and Language Education Research at Griffith University. His research and teaching interests are literacy education, government policy on literacy, and interaction analysis in relation to disadvantage, health and literacy. Among other books, he is co-author of *Children's First School Books* (Blackwell) and co-editor of *Knowledge, Culture and Power* (Taylor & Francis).

Karen Herschell is a PhD candidate in the Graduate School of Education at the University of Queensland. She is tracing the discursive construction of single-parent mothers in Australia through governmental welfare policies. Currently, she is a Senior Policy Officer with Education Queensland.

Stephen Hester is Reader in Sociology at the University of Wales (Bangor). His main research interests are in ethnomethodology, conversation analysis and membership categorization analysis. He is co-author of *Deviance in Classrooms* (RKP), *A Sociology of Crime* (Routledge), *The Montreal Massacre* (Wilfrid Laurier University Press, in preparation), and is co-editor of *Culture in Action* (University Press of America) and *Local Educational Order* (Benjamins).

Christina Howard is a doctoral student and graduate assistant in the School of Psychology at Massey University. She is currently undertaking research into discursive aspects of the recovered memory/false memory syndrome debate.

Ann Kelly is a doctoral candidate in the Graduate School of Education at the University of Queensland. Currently she is interested in using conversation analysis to explicate how work and vocational training are enacted. She is the President of the Queensland Council for Adult Literacy and has published in the areas of adult literacy and vocational education and training.

Amanda LeCouteur is Senior Lecturer in the Department of Psychology at Adelaide University where she teaches in the areas of qualitative research methods, gender and metapsychology. Her research interests include discursive studies of racism, and of medicine and women's health.

John Lobley is Head of the Research and Development Department of the Calderstones NHS Trust. He is involved in management development and in research in services for people with intellectual disabilities in the British NHS. He has previously published articles on 'quality of life' measurement and on leadership in human services.

David McCarthy is a graduate student in the School of Psychology at Murdoch University. His interests are in discursive work as applied to 'mental illness', in particular in professional accounts of the experiences of people who hear voices.

Alec McHoul is Professor of Communication Studies at Murdoch University. He has published in the areas of discourse analysis, cultural theory, literary studies and technology. His most recent books are *Semiotic Investigations* (University of Nebraska Press) and *Popular Culture and Everyday Life* with Toby Miller (Sage). His current research project involves a reconsideration of the meaning of the concept of culture.

Maurice Nevile is a PhD candidate in the School of Language Studies at the Australian National University. Previously he was an academic advisor to university students, and he has published articles on the nature and acquisition of academic literacy. He is joint author of a reference book for students, *Making the Most of Your Arts Degree* (Longman).

Angela O'Brien-Malone completed her PhD in 1999 at the University of Western Australia. Since then, her research interests have included the relationship between methodology and theory in psychology and, in particular, how method constrains the way we think about theory. Recent publications include chapters (with Murray Maybery) in *Implicit and Explicit Mental Processes* (Erlbaum).

Jonathan Potter is Professor of Discourse Analysis at Loughborough University. His most recent book is *Representing Reality* (Sage) which provides a systematic overview, integration and critique of constructionist research. He is co-editor of the journal *Theory and Psychology*.

Mark Rapley is Senior Lecturer in Psychology at Murdoch University. His current work applies discursive psychology to questions of power. Other work has examined the interactional and rhetorical production of persons with intellectual disabilities, the 'mentally ill' and Aboriginal Australians. Two books are in preparation: *The Social Construction of Intellectual Disability* (Cambridge University Press) and *Quality of Life Research in the Social Sciences* (Sage).

Kathy Roulston recently completed her PhD in Education at the University of Queensland and is now Post-doctoral Fellow at the University of Georgia where she teaches in the Qualitative Research Methods program. Her research interests include conversation analysis, ethnomethodology and the application of qualitative research methods in music education.

Paul ten Have is Associate Professor in the Department of Sociology and Anthropology at the University of Amsterdam. He has published work in conversation analysis and on computer-mediated interaction. His most recent book is *Doing Conversation Analysis* (Sage). He edits the website, *Ethno/CA News*, at: <http://www.pscw.uva.nl/emca/index/htm>.

Keith Tuffin is Senior Lecturer in the School of Psychology at Massey University where he teaches critical social psychology and discursive psychology. His research interests include political discourse, and constructionist approaches to emotion, culture and identity. He is currently working on *Understanding Critical Social Psychology* (Sage).

Rhyll Vallis is a PhD candidate in the Graduate School of Education, University of Queensland. She has published on several aspects of social interaction in internet chat rooms.

Preface: with a little help from our friends

Alec McHoul and Mark Rapley

Most of the prefatory work in this book is achieved by the three guest-expert introductions (Chapters 1 to 3) and by the editorial prefaces to each of the other chapters. For that reason, we omit the normally obligatory blow-by-blow preface and instead offer a sketch of our 'analytic mentality' (as Jim Schenkein used to call it) along with some technical preliminaries.

The book aims to provide models, templates and perspicuous case studies for beginning researchers in the fields of conversation analysis (CA), discursive psychology (DP) and critical discourse analysis (CDA) as those – we think convergent – approaches apply to 'institutional' settings. We take the term 'institutional' loosely so that it can refer to a broad range of settings: from airline cockpits to schools; from computer helplines to personality testing; from political speeches to organizing concerts. 'Institutional', then, is not intended to carry important analytic or theoretical weight – at least, that is, until the very last chapter of the book where the term (or concept) is opened to thoroughgoing criticism (Chapter 17).

We begin with a section called 'Approaches', where three leading experts in the fields listed above (applied CA, DP and CDA) provide introductions to them. We then move on to ten 'Applications', our core demonstrations. Finally we have included a short section on questions of 'Theory and Method'. Apart from the 'Approaches' section, as noted, each chapter is separately introduced by the editors.

All contributions to the book are new and original; none has been published previously. Contributors range from interested professionals (political speech-writers and clinical psychologists, for example), to world experts in various types of discourse analysis, to postgraduate students who are themselves beginning to explore the fields of CA, DP and CDA. In particular, the book showcases the work of newly emergent women analysts, including many from Australia.

What we are attempting, above all, is to introduce readers to applied CA, lay a specific emphasis on its fairly recent uptake in DP and, then, show how some of the resultant work closely approaches CDA – even if it sometimes departs from the specific version of that field as outlined in Norman Fairclough's chapter (Chapter 3). That is, as we note below, CDA has a very distinctive orientation to data and analysis; nevertheless it strongly informs Chapters 9 to 13, where the impetus is as much towards criticizing and changing social practices as it is towards describing and understanding them.

As Paul ten Have notes in the first chapter of the book, applied CA usually comes in two varieties: 'the application of the findings of "pure" CA to study what is often called "institutional interaction"' vs. the application of 'CA findings and/or specific studies to advise people and organizations how specific practical problems might be handled in order to facilitate smooth and effective practice'. Both of these are exemplified in the book, but our movement in the direction of CDA effectively foreshadows a third variety: applying CA as a critical window on institutional procedures and aiming at what Fairclough calls 'emancipatory change'.

For us, there are important similarities and differences between applied CA (including its DP arm) and CDA; and these show up in Fairclough's chapter. The crucial difference is the *inversion of starting points*. Applied CA begins with prima-facie evidence of actual talk and builds its findings on that foundation. By contrast, for Fairclough:

> CDA analyses texts and interactions, but it does not *start* from texts and interactions. It starts rather from social issues and problems, problems which face people in their social lives, issues which are taken up within sociology, political science and/or cultural studies.

Yet, as Fairclough also notes, 'there is no party line' in CDA; instead it is 'transdisciplinary' and open to influence by any 'disciplines which are concerned with linguistic and semiotic analysis, and between a range of other disciplines and particular theories'. In this case, after closely reading and editing the contributions to this volume, we see no reason to exclude applied CA/DP from that range. In fact, CA/DP may be especially contributive to CDA given that the latter also works with 'close analysis of texts and interactions' and 'cannot take the role of semiosis in social practices for granted' because 'it has to be established through analysis' (Fairclough). Another point of contact is that CDA 'seeks to establish non-obvious connections' and, as ten Have argues, 'Applied CA [also] requires a distance from practical interests because . . . an important part of its discoveries might be that things are *different* from what established ideas suggest'. This is what conversation analyst George Psathas (1995) calls 'the intuitively non-apparent'. And this is precisely what each one of our chapters, whatever approach informs it, aims to *make* apparent.

In terms of topics, the approaches are also strikingly similar. That is, just as applied CA forms around institutionally located interactions, so CDA analyses 'social practice', defined as any 'relatively stabilized form of social activity'; 'examples would be classroom teaching, television news, family meals and medical consultations' as well as 'everyday conversation, meetings in various types of organization, political and other forms of interview, and book reviews' (Fairclough). All of these would be familiar territory in applied CA where there is, as Fairclough says of CDA, a central focus on 'the active . . . work that people are doing on specific occasions'. It is no coincidence, then, that Fairclough's own illustrative analysis is of an appraisal situation in which 'the skills of the appraiser are reminiscent of the counsellor' and that several contributions to this volume take up the analysis of counselling/helping situations, starting with Edwards and Potter's introduction to DP itself (Chapter 2).

Throughout the book then, but especially in Part III, we want to open up some current debates in the field with regard to questions of theory and method. That is, assuming the reader has worked through the approach-guides in Part I and the demonstrations of them in Part II of the book, the controversial nature of questions raised in Part III will be relatively self-evident. Example problems include the following. As Angela O'Brien-Malone and Charles Antaki ask: How does the newer DP sit with respect to more traditional cognitivist concerns in psychology? Do Tuffin and Howard's policies for *how to actually do* discourse analysis sit well with Edwards and Potter's version of DP? Does Austin *et al.*'s intervention open up new possibilities for analysing the *relations* between text and talk? Can the division into 'pure' vs. applied CA – which is where Paul ten Have begins the book – still stand after Hester and Francis's methodological rethinking of the field (in the last chapter), where they even go so far as to question whether there *can be* such a phenomenon as 'institutional talk'?

These two chapters, then, form our bookends. However, they are not uniform ones and offer a deliberate message: read these and make up your own mind, but most of all do so on the basis of your own experiments with actual data collections and analyses. Our casebook of methods will, we hope, provide templates for your own efforts in the field. But we do not mean them to be followed slavishly – far from it. As it were, once they have allowed you to climb up, they can, like Wittgenstein's famous ladder, be kicked away.

* * *

At this point we must move on to some essential technical information. With some minor exceptions, all contributions work with the Jeffersonian transcription notation. This is so standard today that we have not felt the need to include all its details. The canonical source for this is Heritage and Atkinson (1984) and a simplified form can be found in Psathas (1995). What is important is that readers grasp the importance of the accuracy of this transcription system. An earlier draft of one of our chapters – by Carolyn Baker, Michael Emmison and Alan Firth (Chapter 4) – contained as succinct a discussion of this as we have seen. We reproduce it below with our thanks to those three friends and colleagues:

> We have used the transcription notation system developed by Gail Jefferson, the standard form used in CA. This system is particularly sensitive to the sequential order of turns, to gaps, pauses and overlaps, and to properties of turn delivery such as emphasis, prolonged vowels, and stretches of louder, softer, faster or slower talk relative to the surrounding talk. This transcription system can be seen to attend to turns and timing as main dimensions of the talk. A silence or pause of (0.4) – four-tenths of a second – is barely noticeable in the ordinary course of conversation *unless* one is looking for a place to insert one's own turn without cutting into the middle of

a word or phrase being delivered by the current speaker. The places where this self-insertion can be done include these micro-pauses, which is why they are included in CA transcripts. They are places where a next speaker *could* possibly begin to speak, and if next speaker does not start to speak in these possible places, then it can be interpreted as (intendedly) leaving the floor to the current speaker:

C	I've recently installed microsoft office pro:
	(0.4)
CT	yeah

These places or slots in ongoing talk are known as 'transition-relevance places' (Sacks *et al.*, 1974), tiny slots (or longer ones) where starting to speak may be hearable as not-an-interruption or at least not-a-rude-interruption. When we are very anxious to enter into a (fast-moving) conversation without interrupting, we all listen for these tiny slots. We listen prospectively for them (retrospectively would be too late) by orienting to when a phrase, sentence or some other chunk of talk is likely to be finished. That is, we listen for the upcoming, imminent end of the 'turn-constructional units' currently being delivered. Sometimes we underestimate when the turn-constructional unit will be finished and we end up overlapping. (This is shown in transcripts with square brackets at the beginning of two speakers overlapping.)

We also use underlining to show emphasis on words or parts of words: for example, 'some form of ma:sking'. The transcript looks something like a drama script but is much more detailed. Not only are the very words (and non-words like 'erm') captured, so is their pronunciation (for example, 'wanna' instead of 'want to'). The character of the delivery and the character of the turn-by-turn coordination of turns are central to CA because of the analytic interest in words as parts of utterances (equivalent with turns or turn components), and utterances as activities such as 'eliciting information' or 'making a proposal'. In this sense, CA is an exercise in studying social inter-activity or interaction.

Transcription extracts such as this, of course, are usually referred to by analysts according to individual lines. In this book, numbers in brackets – (7), (22), (126), etc. – are used for this purpose. Readers should also note that the following abbreviations are used consistently throughout the book:

CA	Conversation analysis
CBA	Category-bound activity (or predicate)
CDA	Critical discourse analysis
DP	Discursive psychology
EM	Ethnomethodology
IT	Institutional talk
ITP	Institutional talk program
MCA	Membership categorization analysis
MCD	Membership categorization device
PDS	Perspective display series
SRP	Standard(ized) relational pair

Acknowledgements

The idea for this book grew out of the first Murdoch Symposium on Talk-in-Interaction (23–24 September 1999) where we were pleased and surprised to find such widespread and mutual interest in CA, DP and CDA applied to institutional talk. In particular we thank Susan Hansen for all her organizational efforts at the symposium (and for advice on this book), as well as the Centre for Research in Culture and Communication and the School of Psychology (both at Murdoch University) for funding. Professors Tom O'Regan (CRCC) and Mike Innes (Psychology) are especially to be thanked for arranging this funding. A grant from the Division of Social Sciences, Humanities and Education in 2000 greatly helped in the production of the final typescript.

PART I

Approaches

1 Applied conversation analysis[1]

Paul ten Have

INTRODUCTION

Conversation Analysis (CA), as developed by Harvey Sacks and his collaborators and students, most notably Emanuel Schegloff and Gail Jefferson, was originally an effort at 'pure science'. Its purpose was to build a formal science that would provide for the interactional organization of conversation or, in Schegloff's later formulation, of 'talk-in-interaction'. This can be contrasted with an applied CA which, as I have argued elsewhere (ten Have, 1999), can be conceived of in two more or less independent ways. On the one hand, it can be used to denote the application of the findings of 'pure' CA to study what is often called 'institutional interaction', as in interviews, medical consultations, court sessions, and so forth. But on the other hand, it can also refer to efforts to apply CA findings and/or specific studies to advise people and organizations how specific practical problems might be handled in order to facilitate smooth and effective practice. Both kinds of application can, of course, be combined in one project; but for my purposes here, I want to separate them, as they raise distinct problems of conception and analysis.

TALK IN INSTITUTIONAL SETTINGS

Although Sacks's and Schegloff's early studies were based on data of an institutional kind, their major analytic efforts were not directed at elucidating the relationship of that talk to its setting, but rather to explicate the endogenous organization of talk-in-interaction as such. The turn-taking paper (Sacks *et al.*, 1978), originally published in 1974, makes that very clear. It is suggested that conversation, since it is locally managed by the parties themselves, is substantially different from other forms of talk-in-interaction – such as debate or ceremony – which are constituted by imposing various kinds of 'restrictions' on a purely local allocation of turns and turn types (Sacks *et al.*, 1978: 45–7). Their suggestion is that conversation represents a more basic format from which various institutional formats can be derived. While they concede that they have 'barely been looking into' those other systems, they do offer some interesting overall observations, suggesting that the various speech-exchange systems might be 'linearly arrayed':

> The linear array is one in which one polar type (which conversation instances) involves 'one turn at a time allocation'; that is, the use of local allocational means, and the other pole (which debates instance) involves 'preallocation of all turns', and medial types (which meetings instance) involve various mixes of preallocational and local allocational means. (Sacks *et al.*, 1978: 46)

Finally, they remark:

> While we have referred to conversation as 'one polar extreme' on the linear array, and 'ceremony' as possibly the other pole, we should not be understood thereby to be proposing the independent, or equal status of conversation and ceremony as polar types. For it appears likely that conversation should be considered the basic form of speech-exchange system, with other systems on the array representing a variety of transformations on conversation's turn-taking system to achieve other types of turn-taking systems. In this light, debate or ceremony would not be an independent polar type, but rather the most extreme transformation of conversation, most extreme in fully fixing the most important, and perhaps nearly all, of the parameters that conversation allows to vary. (Sacks *et al.*, 1978: 47)

By so forcefully arguing for the original status of informal conversation and by showing how some of its most important features could be analysed in a systematic and empirical fashion, this can be taken as an invitation to start a *comparative* investigation of speech-exchange systems. This has been taken up now and then, although largely with a broader focus than just turn-taking, and including the setting-specific use of sequencing, as with, for example, questioning (Atkinson and Drew, 1979: 34–81; Greatbatch, 1988; McHoul, 1978; Peräkylä, 1995: 37–102). The general idea is that, for some institutional systems, there is a pre-established system of *turn allocation*, and quite often of turn-*type* allocation:

> In debates, for example, the ordering of all turns is preallocated, by formula, by reference to 'pro' and 'con' positions. In contrast to both debates and conversation, meetings that have a chairperson partially preallocate turns, and provide for the allocation of unallocated turns via the use of the preallocated turns. Thus, the chairperson has rights to talk first, and to talk after each other speaker, and can use each such turn to allocate next speakership. (Sacks *et al.*, 1978: 45)

Important initiatives for the overall programme of applying CA to institutional interaction have been taken by researchers from the UK such as Max Atkinson, Paul Drew and John Heritage. Their general purpose is to use the acquired knowledge of conversational organization in order to show how institutions are 'talked into being', to use Heritage's much-quoted phrase (1984b: 290). In an overview of this field, Heritage has written:

> There are, therefore, at least two kinds of conversation analytic research going on today, and, though they overlap in various ways, they are distinct in focus. The first

examines the institution *of* interaction as an entity in its own right; the second studies the management of social institutions *in* interaction. (Heritage, 1997: 162)

I will refer to the first type as 'pure CA', while the latter represents the first kind of 'applied CA', as distinguished above.[2] It is remarkable that most of the studies in this tradition deal with agent/client contacts or interviews, ranging from more formal types (Atkinson, 1982) like court sessions (Atkinson and Drew, 1979; Drew, 1992), to more improvised ones like news interviews (Greatbatch, 1988; Heritage, 1985; Heritage and Greatbatch, 1991).[3]

As noted, the underlying idea in this type of research is that institutional forms can be seen as being more 'restricted' than those found in conversation, in the sense of having one or more kinds of actions, forms or sequences, that could be observed in conversation, excluded from the specific institution's repertoire, or from a particular type of party's expected or tolerated range of available options. The asymmetrical distribution of questions and answers is but one example of such a 'restriction'. This overall approach to the study of institutional interaction has been criticized from a number of different perspectives. On the one hand, some tend to view such 'restrictions' as a dependent phenomenon, stressing the power of professionals over (specific categories of) clients, while others object to the formalistic tendencies that seem to be implied in it, ignoring the specific local circumstances and relevances of the participants.

One crucial point in all this seems to be where one locates the 'centre of gravity' for understanding interactional phenomena: in the local interaction and its procedural infrastructure itself, in the general institutional arrangements, or in the institutionalized power of one category of participants over another (see Schegloff, 1991, 1992; Wilson, 1991). An ethnomethodological take on these issues, on the other hand, would start from the locally relevant aspects of the task-at-hand, the situated work that the parties are involved in, rather than merely issues of turn-taking and sequencing (see Bjelic and Lynch, 1992: 54, 76). I will return to these issues in a later part of this chapter, but first I will discuss some aspects of the general approach elaborated by Drew and Heritage in their various writings.

In their overview of analyses of institutional interaction, Drew and Heritage (1992a) emphasize that CA studies activities as interactional products and takes a dynamic view of context, both the local context of consecutive utterances and the larger context of institutional frameworks (1992a: 16–19).[4] They note:

A clear implication is that comparative analysis that treats institutional interaction in contrast to normal and/or normative procedures of interaction in ordinary conversation will present at least one important avenue of theoretical and empirical advance. (Drew and Heritage, 1992a: 19)

Such a comparative approach is not as simple and straightforward as one might wish, however, since:

> CA researchers cannot take 'context' for granted nor may they treat it as determined in advance and independent of the participants' own activities. Instead, 'context' and identity have to be treated as inherently locally produced, incrementally developed and, by extension, as transformable at any moment. (Drew and Heritage, 1992a: 21)

Against this background, CA studies of institutional interactions will not produce hard and fast distinctions between institutional and non-institutional realms. Rather, little more than a set of 'family resemblances among cases of institutional talk' (Drew and Heritage, 1992b: 21) is to be expected.

Drew and Heritage (1992a: 21–5) also elaborate on three themes that have emerged from such efforts: 1) institutional talk is goal-oriented in institutionally relevant ways; 2) it often involves 'special and particular constraints' on 'allowable contributions to the business at hand'; and 3) it may be 'associated with inferential frameworks and procedures that are peculiar to specific institutional contexts' (1992a: 22). In other words, participants in such interactions assume and demonstrate their overall 'instrumental' orientation, leading to specific withholdings, and also, as Drew and Heritage note, positive preferences or allowances while, at the same time, providing specific interpretive frames to account for such 'departures' from conversational practice.

QUESTIONING AND 'CONTROL'

One particular aspect of institutional interaction which has probably been most consistently in focus in applied CA studies is that of agents questioning clients. As noted above, the idea is that there is, in many situations, a pre-established system of *turn allocation*, and quite often of turn-*type* allocation. Drew and Heritage (1992a: 39) summarize the findings of a number of studies of relatively formal kinds of institutional interaction (including courtroom interaction, formal teaching, news interviews and mediation) as follows: 'All of these studies focus on turn-taking systems which, in their different ways, are organized through the preallocation . . . of questions and answers'. And one frequently noted upshot of such preallocation is that, because the question*er* has a pre-given *right* to a questioning turn, he or she can easily build a quite long, multi-unit turn, until a recognizable question is finally produced. The one being question*ed*, on the other hand, runs the *risk* of being interrupted as soon as a minimally adequate answering component has been uttered. This demonstrates that turn allocation and turn-type allocation are intimately related; but other aspects of interactional organization also need to be taken into account.

It is an empirical fact that in many (if not most) interactions between institutional agents and the lay persons with whom they talk, the dominant interactional format, at least for an important part of the encounter, is one of questioning. The analytically important point, however, is whether this empirically obvious division of interactional labour between a questioning agent and an answering client is an effect of an *institutional* pre-allocation of questioning rights and answering duties, or whether it is implied in general *sequential* properties of activity organization, irrespective of the institutional embeddedness of such an activity. This issue is discussed by Schegloff (1991) under the heading of 'Social structure or conversational structure?'. A 'focus on social structure' and a 'focus on conversational structure in studying talk-in-interaction' could be 'complementary', but 'they can also be alternatives in a more competitive sense', for: 'Each makes its own claims in organizing observation and analysis of the data, and one can preempt the other. In particular, the more familiar concerns with social structure can preempt new findings about conversational phenomena' (Schegloff, 1991: 57).

For instance, the distributional fact that doctors ask patients more questions than patients ask doctors can be discussed in institutional terms, as an aspect of 'professional dominance', but it can also be analysed in terms of the overall sequential organization of the encounter. Such an encounter ordinarily takes off from a request for assistance; that is, for a professional diagnosis and/or treatment, which requires additional information before it can be given. This information can be acquired in various ways, including questioning. In other words, the sequential structure of such encounters tends to consist of a request/service pair, with *a series of insertion sequences* between the two parts of the pair. This structure is evident not only in medical consultations (ten Have, 1989), but also in other kinds of service encounters, such as calls for police assistance (Wilson, 1991; Zimmerman and Boden, 1991), and even in non-institutional situations when one party asks a complicated service of another (see Schegloff, 1991: 59). It is a fact, of course, that service requests and their disposal in interaction tend to occur mostly in specialized institutional settings. So it is the institutional specialization of *activities*, rather than the conventional institutional *format* (like questioning), that is the crucial point here (see Wilson, 1991: 37–9). The questioning of patients by doctors, or of callers by complaint takers, would *not* then be an issue of *turn-type pre-allocation*, but rather of a sequential-organizational *effect* of an institutional *activity allocation*. In other institutional situations, however, *turn-type pre-allocation* does play a role in having professionals question lay persons, as in job interviews (Button, 1987, 1992; Komter, 1991), news interviews (Clayman, 1988, 1992; Greatbatch, 1988, 1992; Heritage, 1985; Heritage and Greatbatch, 1991), or various kinds of research interviews (Houtkoop-Steenstra, 1995, 1996, 2000; Mazeland, 1992; Mazeland and ten Have, 1996; Suchman and Jordan, 1990).

ON THE USABILITY OF CA FINDINGS

I now turn to a short discussion of the second sense of the term 'applied CA' as distinguished at the start of this chapter. That is, I will discuss ways in which CA might be useful with reference to the concerns of people who have a practical, moral and/or political interest in the practices studied, in terms of the situations, organizations and/or institutions that are co-constituted by those practices. In certain respects, this is a dangerous enterprise, as people with such interests quite often have a pre-conceived idea about what is important or relevant, and what is not. For CA, however, it is essential to bracket such preconceptions and take a fresh look at how things are actually done *in situ*, or more specifically, how talk-in-interaction is actually and locally organized.

Following James Heap in his essay on applied ethnomethodology (1990), we can say that applied CA is effectively the study of the *local rationality* of members' practices. That is, we have to ask why it makes sense, for participants, locally, in their practical context, to do things as they are done, even if this is at odds with how these practices are planned, evaluated or accounted for 'elsewhere', 'in theory', or at higher hierarchical levels in an organization. In this way, I think, Heap's sketch is a useful basis for a reflection on applying CA to various topics that may have a practical interest for lay members.

Applied CA requires a distance from practical interests because, as Heap argues, an important part of its discoveries might be that things are *different* from what established ideas suggest. This difference, however, should also not be presupposed or hunted for, in itself, but rather should be allowed to emerge from the analysis. All this seems to be implied in the notion of 'ethnomethodological indifference' (Garfinkel and Sacks, 1970: 345–6; see also Lynch, 1993: 141–7). Within CA, this policy has been formulated as one of 'unmotivated looking' (see the discussion in ten Have, 1999).

The important point is that both practitioners and managers tend to look at actual practices via the general purpose, plan or function of some activity, in terms of which the activity is both projected beforehand and accountable afterwards. Such a view may, at the same time, obscure aspects of the organization of the activity which are *not* pre-planned, and which tend *not* to be reported in any official *post hoc* account. Research based on audio or video recordings of actual instances of interaction-at-work, possibly supplemented with some ethnographic background explorations, may produce both 'bad' and 'good' news from a practical point of view. For instance, in research on standardized interviewing (such as Houtkoop-Steenstra, 1995, 2000; also ten Have, 1999: 170–81), one can find that interviewers depart significantly from the instruction to 'read the questions as worded'. This would not be allowed, officially, because it could influence answers in unpredictable ways and therefore bias the results. At the same time, however, such research can show that departures from the pre-given plan have a local rationality in that they may be useful in the job of keeping the respondent motivated to cooperate and to produce sensible answers.

In an early discussion of applied directions in CA, George Psathas (1990) has taken a slightly different tack, in that he suggests that applied CA might be useful to supply a description of competencies required for particular types of professional conduct:

> The interactional phenomena which are discovered across and within the varieties of settings will enable us to state, with greater certainty, what interactional competencies are requisite to participation in those systems. As such requisites are discovered, we should be able to say what preparation, training, or prior interactional performative skills are vital for new entrants into these systems. And, if members are lacking in particular, identifiable, and describable interactional skills, we should be able to develop methods for teaching, demonstrating, or training those deficient in the requisite skills. (Psathas, 1990: 21)

But he is careful to add a warning that this may also be a dangerous enterprise and that one should, in each case, consider its ethical effects.

> The promise for a humanistic science of human interaction is considerable. But the possibility also exists, as is the case in the use and application of any findings in the human sciences, for efforts to control, manipulate, and deliberately structure interaction so as to enable certain parties (and/or organizations) to advance their own ends and interests at the expense of others. (Psathas, 1990: 22)

Linda Tapsell (2000) has provided a description of an actual project along these lines, in which novice dieticians were trained in efficient 'history taking'. In a first phase, the research focused on competencies displayed by a number of student dieticians who were considered to do well. This analysis was not only informed by the canonical findings of the CA tradition, but also by a thorough consideration of the institutional task, and by looking at CA studies of different, but in some ways comparable, situations – including Rod Watson's (1997c) study of murder interrogations. In the second phase, a next generation of students was trained using the results of the first phase, with special emphasis on structuring the management of the dietary history. And finally the results of the training were investigated by inspecting recorded instances of dietary interviewing by these trained students. The results seemed to demonstrate that the training was successful in having the student manage the interview in a professional manner – that is, generating useful histories within a limited time frame, and leaving enough time for the required nutrition counselling.

While these studies of interviewing are mostly based on audio data, recent applied CA tends to be based on video recordings, most often supplemented with ethnographic research (see Heath, 1997 for suggestions and arguments). The resources of traditional CA are extended to include visual aspects of interaction, such as gaze direction, gesture and the manipulation of various kinds of objects. In this way, one can, for instance, study the interactional life of people with impaired communicational capacities, such as the deaf (McIllvenny, 1995) and those with cerebral palsy (Collins *et al.*, 1997), to the benefit of those who have to deal with such people or design training programs or supportive technology for them and their care-givers (see ten Have, 1999: 189–92).

WORKPLACE STUDIES

Perhaps the most vibrant sub-field of applied CA these days is that devoted to workplace studies. In the USA, this tradition has emerged from Lucy Suchman's work at the Xerox Palo Alto Research Center (Suchman, 1987; Suchman and Trigg, 1991, 1993), and especially from her collaboration with the Goodwins and others in the 'Workplace Project' (Brun-Cottan, 1990/1991; C. Goodwin, 1996; Goodwin and Goodwin, 1996; M. Goodwin, 1995, 1996; Suchman, 1992, 1996). In the UK, Christian Heath has been and continues to be the major inspiration and organizer of similar work. In the 1980s he was using video analysis to study medical consultations (Heath, 1986, 1988, 1992) but he later turned to studying workers using information technology in medical practices, London Underground control rooms and other settings (Greatbatch *et al.*, 1995; Heath and Luff, 1997, 2000). What these studies show, among many other things, is the importance of 'silent coordination' among colleagues working at different locations in a room. This is achieved by following each other's verbal contributions in relation to their gaze direction (at different screens) and their manipulation of various artefacts (such as keyboards, switches or intercoms). While grounded in the study of verbal interaction, as in traditional CA, such studies make it abundantly clear that understandings and analyses of talk-in-interaction in such settings require a simultaneous consideration of non-verbal aspects of workers' conduct and work situations. What is demonstrably relevant for the participants *in situ* should not be ignored in a full analysis.

These studies are having a specific impact on the course of recently emerged disciplines like Human–Computer Interaction and Computer Supported Collaborative Work which have tended to be dominated hitherto by technological and individualistic perspectives. These new approaches, however, have demonstrated the immensely detailed, sensitive and contextual ways in which collaboration is achieved from moment to moment. As Heath and Luff write (1997: 125):

> It is not simply that work within the Line Control Room is 'collaborative'; it is rather that personnel, even within the accomplishment of apparently individual tasks, are sensitive to and participating in the activities of colleagues, and this participation is an intrinsic part of the organization of the task. The use of the various tools and technologies in the Line Control Room features in the accomplishment of these various activities and their coordination and provides resources through which potentially 'private' actions are rendered visible within the local milieu. The various and complex ways in which the accomplishment of specialized tasks within the Line Control Room and other working environments . . . is embedded in and inseparable from interaction with the concurrent actions of colleagues may lead us to question the usefulness of traditional approaches to the development of requirements for new technologies, approaches that place a single individual user with a relatively circumscribed set of tasks at the forefront of the analytic domain.

In short, by providing a corrective to the traditionally individualistic approaches that dominate current thinking about technologies as used, workplace studies also contribute to more effective design practices.[5]

CONCLUSION

This chapter has tried to provide a summary overview of some of the possibilities, problems and results of efforts to apply CA to institutional data and/or in the service of 'practical' interests. I hope that I have been able at least to give an impression of the many prospects that have been explored for the last twenty years or so. The major challenge in this field seems to be to keep one's mind open amidst the 'lower' interests that pre-structure one's perceptions and insight, while at the same time letting oneself be informed by the doings and sayings in the practical institutional situations under study.

Notes

1. This chapter is partly based on Chapters 8 and 9 of my *Doing Conversation Analysis* (ten Have, 1999). A parallel but different discussion of these issues, touching on some of the same themes as this chapter, can be found in Hutchby and Wooffitt (1998: 145–257).
2. See Drew and Heritage (1992b) for an introduction and examples, as well as Drew and Soronjen (1997) and Heritage (1997) for recent overviews. Boden and Zimmerman (1991) offer a slightly different take, discussions and examples from a larger variety of perspectives.
3. Exceptions to this strong focus on agent–client interactions do exist, as in Boden (1994) on talk in business contexts, and Meier (1997) on work meetings.
4. See Duranti and Goodwin (1992) for an elaborate discussion of the issue of 'context' in analysing talk and for a collection of papers displaying a variety of positions on these issues.
5. At the time of writing this chapter, Luff *et al.*'s (2000) collection, *Workplace Studies* – which includes a number of essays on the implications of workplace studies for design – had not yet appeared.

2 Discursive psychology

Derek Edwards and Jonathan Potter

INTRODUCTION

Discursive psychology (DP) is the application of discourse analytic principles to psychological topics. In psychology's dominant 'cognitivist' paradigm, individuals build mental representations of the world on the basis of innate mental structures and perceptual experience, and talk on that basis. The categories and content of discourse are considered to be a reflection, refracted through various kinds of error and distortion, of how the world is perceived to be. In contrast, DP *begins with* discourse (talk and text), both theoretically and empirically. Discourse is approached, not as the outcome of mental states and cognitive processes, but as a domain of action in its own right.

In DP, it is the business of talk and text to define the nature of the world under description, including the mental states, perceptions, motivations, dispositions, thoughts, prejudices, and so on, of any persons involved, whether as actors in described events or as the producers and recipients of descriptions (Edwards and Potter, 1992a). Both 'reality' and 'mind' are constructed by people conceptually, in language, in the course of their performance of practical tasks (Edwards, 1997; Potter, 1996a; Potter *et al.*, 1993). Because of this emphasis, shared with ethnomethodology (EM) and conversation analysis (CA), on the situated, action-performative nature of talk, DP favours the analysis of records of natural interaction, or textual materials produced as part of life's activities (newspaper reports, medical records, written testimony, etc.), rather than using experiments, surveys and interviews to generate research data.

For theoretical, methodological and empirical reasons, DP takes discourse to be central to everyday life. Most social activity involves or is directly conducted through discourse. Furthermore, even where activity is 'non-verbal' (embodiment, physical actions and their settings, and so forth), its sense is often best understood through participants' discourse. Discourse is the prime currency of interaction, and if we are studying persons embedded in practices, including institutional settings, then discourse will be central to that study. Let us consider in turn three features of discourse that relate closely to how it has to be analysed: it is *situated*, *action-oriented* and *constructed*.

Discourse is situated

DP focuses on discourse, which it regards as 'situated' in two ways. First, it is *occasioned* in the CA sense of this term (see ten Have, in this volume). That is, talk and texts are embedded in sequences of interaction, and in various kinds of mundane and institutional activity. This is not a mechanical contextual determinism; talk is *oriented to*, but not *determined by*, its sequential position and setting. Thus a 'question', say, sets up the normative relevance of an 'answer', but an answer is not inevitable or necessary, and things do not break down if one is not forthcoming. Answers may be deferred or withheld altogether (Heritage, 1984b). Likewise, the fact that talk appears in a school or a doctor's surgery does not mean that it must thereby be pedagogic or medical. Rather than being made presumptively omni-relevant by the analyst, institutional activities and identities are made relevant by participants themselves, by being invoked and oriented to, or indeed subverted and ignored (Schegloff, 1997).

Second, DP considers discourse to be pervasively *rhetorical* (Billig, 1987, 1991). Claims and descriptions offered in talk are often designed to *counter* potential alternative versions, and to resist attempts (whether actual or potential) to disqualify them as false, partial or interested (Edwards and Potter, 1992a). That is, they can have both a defensive and an offensive rhetoric (Potter, 1996a). For example Billig (1991) argues that when people offer evaluations of something (an activity that social psychologists might call 'expressing an attitude'), they are typically countering some other evaluation. This means that evaluative discourse is shaped not merely by how people generally think about things, but by the contingencies of argument and the alternatives in play at the time that an evaluation is produced (see Pomerantz, 1984).

Analysis therefore takes into account the sequentially occasioned, situationally oriented and rhetorically designed nature of discourse. DP's particular focus when approaching discourse in *institutional* settings is on how psychological matters are introduced, defined, and made relevant to the business of those settings. Psychological themes are generally pervasive in how such settings work, as they are in mundane talk, but they are sometimes also part of an institution's official normative goals or agenda, such as in educational and therapeutic settings, where how people think and feel are a central focus of concern.

Discourse is action-oriented

Discourse performs actions or practices of various kinds – agreements, blamings, invitations, displays of neutrality, and so on. 'Action' or 'practice' (the precise term is not meant to carry weight here) invokes the vast range of practical, technical and interpersonal tasks that people perform while doing their jobs, living their relationships, and participating in heterogeneous cultural domains. It is central to people's lives, and therefore central to understanding those lives. Following the convention in CA, DP uses the notion of *action-orientation* to emphasize that actions are pervasively being done even in ostensibly factual, descriptive discourse, and to distance itself from a 'speech act' approach that assumes that some discrete set of words corresponds to a discrete act.

The corollary of DP's focus on discourse as action is its respecification of cognition. Instead of cognitive entities and processes being the principal *analytic* resource, as they are in mainstream psychological research, they are approached empirically as participants' *ways of talking*. The focus is on the way cognitions are constructed in talk, and how their implications are oriented to. Taking 'attitudes' again as an example, rather than treating these as inner entities that drive behaviour, in DP attitudes are evaluations that are studied as part of discourse practices (Potter, 1996b, 1998). Such an approach might consider the way evaluations are organized interactionally, as in Pomerantz's (1978) study of compliments; it might consider how attitudes are interactionally produced through social psychological methods (Myers, 1998; Puchta and Potter, in press); or it might consider the way negative evaluations of minority-group members are turned from potentially accountable personally held 'attitudes' or 'prejudices' into more 'safely sayable' factual descriptions (e.g. Edwards, 2000a; Potter and Wetherell, 1988; Wetherell and Potter, 1992).

This non-cognitivist reformulation of 'attitudes' avoids the circularity of many social psychological studies, where evaluative *discourse* (in response scales) is turned into underlying *cognitive* entities (attitudes), which are in turn used to explain *actions* (involving more discourse). It avoids the uncomfortable blurring of everyday and technical notions in the attitude and belief domain, by taking peoples' evaluative terminology (attitude, belief, opinion, position, view, etc.) as a *topic* rather than as a competing but less adequate theory of behaviour (see Edwards (1997) on psychology and common sense in general). It makes sense of the troubling variability in people's evaluative talk, which stems from the fact that people produce evaluations as parts of various discourse practices and their 'occasions', rather than expressing pre-formed, all-purpose mental entities when asked to do so by a researcher. It focuses attention on life as a practical realm where evaluations are part of getting things done, rather than existing as disembedded assessments waiting to be produced in moments of reflection.

Discourse is constructed

DP is constructionist in two senses. First, it studies the way *discourse itself is constructed.* Words, metaphors, idioms, rhetorical devices, descriptions, accounts, stories, and so on, are drawn on, and built, in the course of interaction and in the performance of particular actions. For example, descriptions may be assembled in ways that present some piece of conduct as orderly and required by the circumstances, as just what anybody would have done, or else as unusual, specially motivated, and implicative of the actor's particular psychology (Edwards, 1994, 1997). Second, it studies the way discourse *constructs versions of the world.* That is, it studies how versions of inner life, of local circumstances, of history and broader social groups and structures are produced to do particular things in interaction. In DP, then, discourse is both construct*ed* and construct*ive*.

Although DP is a constructionist approach, its emphasis on the construction of *versions in discourse* distinguishes it from cognitive constructionisms ranging from Neisser (1967), to Moscovici (1984), to Berger and Luckmann (1966). The essence of DP is to study construction – how versions are assembled and stabilized as factual and independent of their producer – as a discourse activity. Whereas cognitive constructionism tends to guide the researcher away from considering people's practices, DP's emphasis on the construction of specific versions encourages the researcher to consider the practices that those versions are part of, and the particular work that they are performing.

At the centre of DP there is an inversion that, initially, appears counterintuitive. In traditional psychology there is *reality* on the one hand, that is the setting – the 'stimulus conditions' that enclose actors – and there is *cognition* on the other, conceived as something existing and quietly computing inside the actors. Activity is treated as something secondary, the output of this system. DP inverts this. Activity is treated as primary, and reality and cognition are secondary. That is, DP focuses on what people are doing and how, in the course of their discourse practices, they produce versions of external reality and of psychological states. It asks how people categorize and formulate the world, establishing certain particulars as relevant, characterizing its moral flavour, and it asks how people at the same time formulate a relevant 'inner' world of beliefs, values, emotions and dispositions, that make their actions accountable. The notion that actions take place within a kind of play-off between an outer reality and an inner world of thoughts and experiences, is one of a range of ways that people talk and account for themselves. DP's task is to study how people do that, and what they do with it, rather than to adopt or reject it as our own explanatory framework. In EM terms, mind and reality, and their interplay, are DP's topic rather than resource (see Wieder, 1988).

DISCURSIVE PSYCHOLOGY: RESEARCH EXAMPLES

Much of the research literature in discursive psychology has reworked standard psychological topics such as causal attribution (Antaki, 1994; Edwards and Potter, 1992a, 1993); attitudes (Billig, 1987; Potter, 1996b, 1998; Potter and Wetherell, 1987); memory (Edwards *et al.*, 1992; Edwards and Potter, 1992b; Middleton and Edwards, 1990); classroom learning (Edwards, 1993; Edwards and Mercer, 1987); prejudice (Edwards, 2000a; Gill, 1993; Speer and Potter, 2000; Wetherell and Potter, 1992); identity (Antaki, 1998; Edwards, 1998; Widdicombe and Wooffitt, 1995); script theory (Edwards, 1994, 1997); emotion (Edwards, 1997, 1999; Frith and Kitzinger, 1998; Harré and Parrott, 1996; Locke and Edwards, forthcoming); and violence and aggression (Auburn *et al.*, 1999; Clarke *et al.*, forthcoming; McKinlay and Dunnett, 1998; Hepburn, 2000).

It has also introduced topics new to psychology, such as the relation between interaction, mental state attributions and social institutions (Edwards, 1995; te Molder, 1999), and the construction and establishment of factual accounts (Edwards and Potter, 1992a; MacMillan and Edwards, 1999; Potter, 1996a; Wooffitt, 1992).

Rather than attempt to review this and other related work, we offer two brief illustrations of these strands of DP. We focus briefly on 'prejudice', and then examine how talk in a counselling setting, including how relationship problems are defined, orientates to various normative and interactional requirements of that setting.

DP and prejudice

We have noted that people construct versions of the world that attend to their factual status, to the psychology of participants in reported events, and to the current interaction in which versions are offered. These moves are often done simultaneously (Edwards and Potter, 1992a). For example a mental state (belief, certainty, fear, doubt) may be produced as determined by the external world, which may itself be produced as known through repeated experiences (Edwards, 1994). Another way of grounding factual claims is to offer them as reluctantly arrived at, or as counter to one's presumptions and biases (Edwards, 2000a; Potter, 1996a). These (and other) *ways of talking* counter the possibility, which may be at stake in the current interaction, that you believe what it suits you to believe, or what you believed before you looked, that your beliefs are a function of mental predisposition rather than external reality – that is, they attend rhetorically to a possible dismissal as pre-judgement, or prejudice.

Extract 1 is taken from an interview from the early 1980s (R is the interviewee; I is the interviewer) in New Zealand concerning a controversial South African rugby tour, prior to that country's abandonment of apartheid (see Edwards, 2000a, for an extended discussion of this and other examples).

Extract 1

R Uhm (1.2) I would li:ke to see apartheid done away with
(1.0) but can anybody come up with a- [a (.)
I [Mm mhm
R positive way of saying 'This is how it can be done'
I Mm mhm
R It's all very well to turn round and say 'Give 'em a vote'
I Yes
R I mean the majority of them (1.0) don't know what a vote is
I Mm mhm

R's argument for apartheid occurs in the context (not reproduced here) of justifying his support of the controversial rugby tour. He offers his position as one that is forced by practical realities. The notion that the speaker might be talking out of some kind of preference or liking for apartheid – that is, because of psychological disposition (prejudice) rather than worldly reality – is further countered by locating his preferences as precisely the opposite. He would *like* it done away with (1), if only that were realistically possible. This *counter-dispositional construction* is a feature of talk about sensitive and controversial issues, but it draws on a general device in factual discourse, which is making a version or conclusion factually robust by formulating it as reluctantly arrived at. The same device is used in Extract 2:

Extract 2

I (. . .) d'you think there should be res- (.) restrictions
on immigration?
(.)
I How do you [feel about
R [Oh yes.= There's got to be.
I Ye[:h
R [Unfortunately,
I my [e:h
R [I would love to see the whole wor:ld y'know,
jus' where you: (.) go where you like,

R appeals to necessity in contrast to personal preference or desire, a disposition formulated as an emphatic, even extreme counter-preference ('would love', 'whole world' (9)) for a world where people can 'go where you like'. Note the symmetrical appeal to both sides of the psychological equation, to an external known world ('there's got to be' (5)) that constrains a reluctant belief or opinion ('unfortunately' (7), 'would love' (9)). R's reluctance is not a free-standing indication of his attitude, but deals with the interviewer's specific framing of the questions (both 'do you think . . .' (1) and 'how do you feel . . .' (4)), and to the possibly unwelcome inferences about him that would be available were he simply to support apartheid (see Antaki and Wetherell, 1999).

It is important to emphasize that this kind of analysis entails no commitment to the genuineness or falsity of R's reluctance, preferences, nor any other mental state that might be conceptualized, managed by, or at issue in the talk. DP analyses it all as *ways of talking* that can be unravelled through a detailed analysis of how specific descriptions are constructed in ways that perform discursive actions within sequential, rhetorical sequences of talk.

DP and institutional settings: couple counselling

Cognitive social psychology attempts to generate social-cognitive explanations that link underlying variables to outcomes. This effectively directs attention away from the specific structural organizations that make up any culture, such as factory production lines, doctors' surgeries, family meal times, and so on. In emphasizing the occasioned, action-oriented and constructed nature of discourse, DP is required to pay attention to such specifics. In this emphasis on talk-at-work, it picks up from the success of CA in productively explicating relations between discourse and social organization (Drew and Heritage, 1992b).

Extract 3 indicates some potentially intricate relations between lexical selection and the situated activities that are being done. It comes from early in a couple's first relationship counselling session, and starts with the counsellor asking about their first separation (see also Edwards, 1997; Potter, 1996a). C is the counsellor, W the wife, and H the husband.

Extract 3

C Was that the time that you left?=
W =He left the:n that was- [nearl]y two years ago.
C [Yeh.]
W He walked out then.
(.)
W Just (.) literally walked out.
(0.8)
C Okay. So, (0.5) for me listenin:g, (.) you've
got (0.5) rich an:d, (.) complicated lives,
I nee:d to get some his[tory to put-]
W [Yyeh. Mmm,]
H [Mmm. (.) Ye:h. (.) Oh ye:h.]
W [Yeh. (.) That's (.) exactly wha]t ih um

Let us focus on the counsellor's formulation of what he takes W and H to have been saying about themselves, that they have 'rich and complicated lives' (9). A number of analysts have observed that *formulations* – providing gists and upshots of what people are saying (Heritage and Watson, 1980) – play an important role in counselling talk (Buttny and Jensen, 1995; Davis, 1986). Indeed they seem to index counselling talk in much the way that Initiation–Response–Evaluation sequences suggest classroom interaction (Mehan, 1979). So, what might such formulations be *doing* in counselling talk? Let us open up some lines of investigation to illustrate DP's approach.

First, 'rich and complicated' converts a rather painful account of trouble and conflict into something positive or, at the very least, into something interesting. In this it may contrast with critical or anxious responses that the couple might have had from friends or relatives. The counsellor presents himself via this formulation as neither judging nor made anxious by talk about difficult relationship problems. Quite the reverse, 'rich and complicated' looks forward to the exploration of these complexities.

Second, it is an impartial formulation, neither criticizing nor supporting either party. This, of course, is an issue for relationship counselling where trust might easily be broken if the counsellor is seen as aligning with one party against the other. In its particular sequential placing, following the wife's criticisms of her husband, this turn neither disagrees nor agrees with the criticisms. They are left on the table, as it were, for possible later discussion. The interactional outcome of this can be seen in the couple's joint and emphasized agreement with the formulation (11–13).

Third, and less obviously perhaps, this avoidance of taking sides, and the treatment of the events as neither bad nor worrying, can be part of a broader emphasis on how the couple can constructively work toward repairing their relationship. One step will be to become more relaxed about discussing their problems and less fearful of its consequences. Moreover, 'complicated' is a descriptive term that sets up relationship problems as a kind of puzzle that can be unravelled via counselling. That is, it provides for the counselling which is to come, as a sensible option where the technical skills will be put to enthusiastic work sorting out complications. These latter orientations of the formulation 'rich and complicated lives', and of its specific location in the talk, are rather speculative on their own, and with regard to just this one extract, but could be part of a larger analysis of how participants' psychological states, personalities, dispositions, pathologies, motivations, emotions, intentions, and so on, are formulated in ways that orient to the nature and business of counselling, as an activity setting.

One interesting feature of our couple-counselling materials is how people *display* themselves as, say, making efforts at understanding the other, or as hopelessly opposed. Conflicting perceptions, thoughts, feelings and evaluations, for example, are *produced as* conflicting, at loggerheads despite all efforts, and therefore ready for, and in need of, intervention. Opposition and impasse are not merely psychological preconditions for counselling that couples find themselves in, but are actively produced in how they talk, particularly at the outset when telling the counsellor why they have come (this being routine first-session business). The conventional notion of couples who do not properly understand each other, or who suffer from an inability to communicate, although effective as an *account* for relationship failure, can be a poor description of couples whose conflicting stories may be exquisitely designed to display conflict, and may be closely oriented to, and predictive of, each other's alternative perspective.

It is a feature of counselling at work that the couple undergoing counselling make themselves available for it (or sometimes resist it), in how they talk. Their display of mutual opposition and impasse provides for the counsellor's even-handed, neutral treatment of them, as a couple with 'rich and complicated lives' for example, and as a kind of puzzle awaiting solution. Extract 4a is close to the start of the same couple's first session, coming a short time after Extract 3.

Extract 4a

C Whe:n:::, (.) before you moved over here, h how was
the marriage.
(0.4)
W Oh.
(0.2)
W I- (.) to me: all alo:ng (.) right up to now, (0.2) my
marriage was rock solid.
(0.8)

9	W	Rock solid.= We had arguments like everybody else
10		had arguments, (0.4) but hh (0.2) to me there was no
11		major problems. Y'know? That's (0.2) my way of
12		thinking but (0.4) Jimmy's thinking is very very different.

The idea that W's version of their marriage not only conflicts with H's (examined below), but is *produced as* conflictual, making conflict hearable or visible as such, is supported by various details. Note the use of extreme case formulations in how W defines her version of their marriage: 'all along', 'right up to now', 'rock solid', like 'everybody' else (6–9). These extreme expressions maximize W's position, and its distance from H's. Pomerantz (1986) has shown how extreme formulations of this kind tend to occur when claims are being strengthened against doubt or disagreement. They can also be used to signal the speaker's commitment and investment in those claims (Edwards, 2000b).

Note also how W overtly acknowledges H's opposition (11–12), while attending rhetorically to what H may say; they have presumably argued about this already, of course, and H is sitting next to W ready to say his piece. W designs her version with regard to H's opposed version, yet to be produced, and in strong contrast to it. Note small details such as the latching in line 9 – how W immediately attaches the disclaimer about their 'arguments' to the description of extreme stability, 'rock solid'. This is rhetoric in action, orienting to H's opposed version which, as we see in Extract 4b, makes much of those 'arguments' they have been having.

H's disagreement is not far away. As W acknowledges (11–12), this is her version, and H's 'thinking' is 'very very different'. H's versions of their marriage focus on its extreme *lack* of solidity, as evidenced by the frequency and severity of their arguments, which H upgrades to 'fights' (19), and (not included here) in how he had actually left W a couple of times.

Extract 4b (continuing from 4a)

12	W	(. . .) but (0.4) Jimmy's thinking is ve[ry very different.]
13	H	[Well (1.0)]
14		Bein: (0.8) a jealous person, (0.8) u:m, (0.6) we go back-
15		(.) back to: (0.6) when we were datin' (1.0) when we
16		were dating first (0.8) well we met in this: particular pub.
17		(1.0)
18	H	>When we start'd datin' we was in there,<
19		<EV'ry single week> we'd fight.
20		(0.2)
21	H	We were at each other the who:le time.

Again H's account does not just find itself in contrast to W's, but is designed in ways that point up and maximize that opposition. What W called 'arguments' have become 'we'd fight' (19), so it was both *severe* (fights rather than arguments) and *recurrent*, again deploying extreme case formulations in 'every single week' (19) and 'the whole time' (21). Like W's picture of a rock solid marriage, H's picture of perpetual and severe conflict stems right from the start of their relationship, from when they first started dating (15–18). The extreme case formulations are important because they index both W and H *going to* extremes discursively, in depicting not just the nature of their relationship, but the extent of their disagreement about it (Edwards, 2000b).

H's preface 'being a jealous person . . .' (14) looks a bit strange where it is placed, but it refers to something W had said a couple of minutes previously (not included here, but see Edwards (1997)) when she identified a major problem of their marriage as H's excessive and long-term proclivity to fits of jealousy. Its placement here, at line 14, displays H's uptake of W's account in Extract 4a as relevant to that accusation – that theirs was an essentially solid marriage suffering from H's being an unreasonably 'jealous person' – and provides it as a preface to his own account of a marriage characterized from the start by mutual and pervasive antagonism. The thing of special interest for DP is how mental and emotional and dispositional state descriptions such as 'jealous' or 'jealous person' figure not merely as actual psychological states, nor even as participants' all-purpose cognitive understandings of their psychological states, but as parts of situated descriptions, to be analysed for their production at a specific point in the talk, as oriented to a particular rhetorical alternative alive in that talk, and to the counselling setting in which it occurs.

We can begin to see that these are not merely different and inconsistent accounts produced by W and H, the stuff of communication failures and misunderstandings, for instance. They are contrasting accounts constructed precisely in opposition to an actual alternative, in that they display an orientation to that alternative and its evidential and rhetorical grounds. They are constructed in extreme terms, maximizing differences and opposition. We take this not merely as an indication of how opposed this couple is, but as a performance of some kind, a display for the counsellor and for counselling, of two persons at an impasse and in need of help. This kind of talk sets their problems up as counselling-appropriate and counselling-ready. It shows, in answer to the counsellor's inquiry, why they have come.

To summarize, W's and H's opposed versions display the following features: extremity, displaying strong commitment to a position and maximizing opposition; acknowledgement, a clear orientation to the other person's opposed version; symmetry, in which the opposition is direct, counterpointed, detailed; and reformulation, where specific alternative descriptions are offered.

Extract 5 comes from a different couple and counsellor, again close to the start of their first session. W is the first to respond to C's request to tell 'why you went to Relate in the first place', and Extract 5 is how she ends her account:

Extract 5

W And then: (.) u:m: (2.8) 'n that's when I decided to: (.)
uhh w- we tried to sort it out ourselves didn't we, (0.6)
a:nd (0.7) we seemed to be going round in cir:cles.

H-he: had his thoughts I had my thoughts (0.6) and
we just didn't come to an agreement on anything.
(.)
W And that's when we decided we ought to come (.)
to Relate.

In Extract 5, W explicitly formulates a kind of stand-off or impasse as their reason for seeking counselling ('Relate' is the counselling organization). Having tried to solve their own problems (2), W and H have hit an impasse, and these are offered as explanatory precursors for now seeking help. As in Extracts 4a and 4b, W's description of relationship troubles, whatever its basis in fact, is shaped as a motivational account for being here, as an account of troubles that is oriented to normative preconditions for counselling – they are opposed, stuck, having tried and failed to help themselves. The expression 'going round in circles' (3), defines their problems as *relationship* troubles of an idiomatically familiar kind, recurrent and unresolved. It captures the sense of impasse that, in Extracts 4a and 4b, was produced by extreme and opposed versions. Note also the precise symmetry of 'he had his thoughts I had my thoughts' (4), repeating the same verbal formula while at the same time defining their troubles as psychological, opposed ways of thinking. Again, there is the use of extremity ('on anything' (5)), emphasizing the size of the gulf between them. Finally, there is the performative relevance or upshot of these descriptions, their availability as an answer to C's inquiry – their reason for being here (7–8).

In addition to making explicit descriptions of their relationship, the couple in Extract 5 *display* their opposition in the way they describe and narrate events in their lives, using extreme case formulations, symmetrically opposed versions and reformulations of what each other says. In doing so, they display an acute orientation to what the other has said or is likely to say, and an orientation to the requirements of counselling and the prospects of receiving help. There is no space to go into that detailed choreography of versions properly here, but Extract 6 illustrates how the counsellor picks up features of clients' versions and formulates them as (in this case) directly opposed, systemic, and symmetrical. At the same time, their problems are defined as *relationship* stuff, rather than a matter of individual persons and their faulty characters, and as problems of a *recognisable kind*, and thus potentially tractable to counselling.

Extract 6

C I'm say:in::g you come here:, (0.2) becau:se (.) >y'r
marriage is in a mess:.<
(0.5)
C It was: (0.4) what you ((referring to W)) would (.)
descri:be as rock solid. Then all of a sudden,
you've((referring to H)) gone off, (0.2) the thing
you fear:, (1.2) of: (.) Connie, (.) you actually wen'
off (.) and did, (0.2) be[cause of the pain-]
W [That's another thing] (.) I

used to say to myself (.) y'know, (.) my husband
would never have an affair because he is so: (0.2)
strict and such HI:gh MOrals an' everything else
about what I would do:, (0.3) he has gone o:ff and
done eXACtly, (0.4) y'know, (.)
C But what's happened is there's a kind of vicious
circle that's going around.

Note various features of the counsellor's interventions here. The expression 'because your marriage is in a mess' (1–2) is reminiscent of the other counsellor's 'rich and complicated lives' in Extract 3. In the same way, it dissolves the two conflicting versions into a description of *relationship*, and avoids alignment with either party's opposed and extreme position. The counsellor picks up and formulates their troubles as *symmetrical*; H has, ironically, gone and done just what he feared W might do (5–8). W takes this as an opportunity for extrematized criticism of H; note again her use of the extreme terms 'never', 'everything else', 'exactly' (11–14). The counsellor once again resists being recruited into alignment with W against H, formulating their troubles as something that has 'happened' – a nicely non-agentive *process* rather than *action* verb – and glossing it as 'a kind of vicious circle that's going round' (15–16). (Note that this is not the same counsellor and couple as in Extract 5, where W also uses the expression 'going round in circles'.)

The counsellor's formulation of the clients' troubles as symmetrical, circular and systemic (relationship stuff rather than individuals) sets up those troubles as recognizable-to-counselling. She spells that out in Extract 7, in the form of an emblematic pattern of symmetrically opposed perspectives:

Extract 7

C it's it's what I call the Jack and Ji:ll situation, that (.)
Jack will say I go to the pu:b (.) because Jill nags.
(0.6)
C Jill will say: no:, (1.8) I only na:g because he goes
to the pu:b.
(0.5)
C And he'll say no: I go to the pub because you nag
(0.2) so it's this sort of (.) up and d[ow:n situation,
W [°Mm (.) that's
(the way it is isn't it°)

Extract 7 formulates a kind of *generalized script or schema* (see also Edwards, 1995) into which H's and W's pattern of conflict can be fitted, one that is potentially applicable to any number of actual relationship problems, and *recognizable* as such to C ('it's what I call the . . .' (1)). Clearly the example of going to the pub and nagging is just that – an *example*, for a wide range of possible actual disputes. The character names 'Jack and Jill', from the nursery rhyme, help identify them as generalized rather than actual persons. Note also the orientation to opposed versions produced in talk; it is a pattern in which Jack and Jill *say* that the other nags or goes out – not that they actually do it (2, 4, 7). It is a matter of ways of seeing and understanding – a *ways-of-seeing or patterns-of-talking* kind of conflict – rather than the facts of the matter (how much they actually go out or nag). This sets it up for the talking cure, for working things through in counselling.

Again, as with the term 'happened' in Extract 6, troubles are formulated as a non-agentive 'situation' (1, 8) that couples may find themselves in. 'Situation' descriptions typically provide for less blaming kinds of actions by actors (Edwards and Potter, 1993). Systemic *reciprocity* is again built into the relationship, via a precise symmetry; the nagging causes the going out, and the going out causes the nagging. So the reciprocating recriminations of relationship troubles talk are transformed into a recognizable-as-standard, and potentially tractable-by-counselling, 'situation'.

DISCURSIVE PSYCHOLOGY AND INSTITUTIONAL SETTINGS

In Wieder's (1974b) EM terms, the descriptions and formulations we have looked at here are multiformulative and multiconsequential, just as they are in any kind of discourse. They formulate the world and the identities of the participants in a range of different ways, and they have a range of practical upshots. Our general point has been to show the value of treating discourse as *occasioned* (in this sequence, in counselling talk), as *action-oriented* (addressing a range of practical counselling tasks), and as both construct*ed* (from particular terms and devices) and construct*ing* (of the clients' problems in ways that prepare them for counselling work).

Discursive psychology's interest in institutional settings is in how the psychological is worked up and recruited for various kinds of institutional business and orientations. Sometimes, as in schools and counselling settings, there is an obvious, official concern with matters of 'mind', with what people feel, think, know and understand. But psychological matters are pervasive in all kinds of discourse and social interaction, given the general relevance of intentions, motives, thoughts, plans, memories, and so on, to life's accountability. We find psychological themes across a very broad range of studies of situated talk, even when those studies are concerned with ostensibly sociological rather than psychological problematics. Examples include Pollner's (1987) classic study of how 'reality disjunctures' are resolved in traffic courts; Wieder's (1974b) treatment of motives and understandings in accounts of rule-following in a half-way house; and Lynch and Bogen's (1996) studies of the uses of 'memory' in the Iran-Contra hearings (see Edwards and Potter, 1992b). The ways that discourse categorizes and attributes mental states, competencies, dispositions, character, emotions, motives, and so on, are part of the fabric of public accountability. It is the project of discursive psychology to study how that works, alongside related studies of talk in mundane and institutional settings.

3 Critical discourse analysis

Norman Fairclough

INTRODUCTION

Critical Discourse Analysis (CDA) is the name given to and accepted by a rather diverse and loosely affiliated group of approaches to language (and, more broadly, to semiosis – including visual images, body language, and so forth). These approaches have in common a concern with how language and/or semiosis interconnect with other elements of social life, and especially a concern with how language and/or semiosis figure in unequal relations of power, in processes of exploitation and domination of some people by others. Representative of this are works by: Chouliaraki and Fairclough (1999), Fairclough and Wodak (1997), Fowler *et al.* (1979), Kress (1985), Lemke (1995), Scollon (1998), van Dijk (1993), van Leeuwen (1993) and Wodak (1996).

The work that goes on within CDA is very diverse, ranging from engagements with a wide range of scientific and social theory (Lemke, 1995; Chouliaraki and Fairclough, 1999; Scollon, 1998) to direct political interventions,[1] to detailed analysis of texts and interactions – and generally it involves a combination of these. The range of issues addressed is extremely broad. It includes: race and racism (van Dijk, 1993; Wodak, 1996), gender and sexism (Barát, 1999; Lazar, 1998; Talbot, 1998), media representations (Chouliaraki, 1999; Fairclough, 1995; Scollon, 1998), bureaucracy (Sarangi and Slembrouck, 1996), language in relation to education (Chouliaraki, 1998; van Leeuwen, 1993), the restructuring of capitalism and neo-liberalism (Fairclough, 2000).[2]

It is important to begin by stressing this diversity, and the loose grouping of people doing sometimes very different research within CDA. There is no 'party line', as others sometimes seem to think, and no unification of theories or methods. What holds the field together is the shared concerns referred to above. My aim in this short introduction is not to try to cover this entire field – I could not do so in the space – but rather to give an idea of the field by putting forward my own position within CDA.

CDA has drawn upon a variety of theoretical and analytical traditions, and different positions within CDA are characterized by different configurations of influences. 'Western Marxism', including theorizations of ideology, hegemony, and so forth (Althusser, 1971; Gramsci, 1971; Pêcheux, 1975), has been an important influence, as has the critical theory of the Frankfurt School and especially the work of Habermas (1984/1987). Other more-or-less critical social theories (Bernstein, 1990; Bourdieu, 1984; Giddens, 1993), and 'post-structuralist' theories, especially that of Foucault (1977), have also influenced the field. Views of language within CDA have both drawn upon and tried to 'operationalize' such theories in ways of conceptualizing and analysing semiosis, and drawn upon particular traditions in language analysis, especially those following Bakhtin (1986) and Halliday (1994).

CDA analyses texts and interactions, but it does not *start* from texts and interactions. It starts rather from social issues and problems, problems which face people in their social lives, issues which are taken up within sociology, political science and/or cultural studies. CDA looks at these issues and problems in terms of their semiotic dimensions. The assumption is that semiosis is one element in social life which is interconnected with other elements. Accordingly, the aim is to specify how semiosis figures in interconnection with other elements in particular cases, in connection with particular issues or problems such as institutional forms of racism. This means that CDA is inherently interdisciplinary. It sets up dialogues between those disciplines which are concerned with linguistic and semiotic analysis, and between a range of other disciplines and particular theories. I would prefer to say it is 'transdisciplinary', meaning that, in the process of such dialogues, CDA develops through, so to speak, internalizing the logics of other disciplines and theories and, in the process, elaborating its own theory, analytical categories, and methods (Chouliaraki and Fairclough, 1999; Fairclough, 2000).

CDA analyses semiosis as 'discourse', meaning precisely that it sees semiosis as just one element of the social, but one which is dialectically interconnected with others (see below on 'dialectic'). It is 'critical' in the sense it seeks to establish *non-obvious* connections between semiosis and other elements of social processes, including connections which contribute to unequal relations of power. It is also 'critical' in the sense that it is a form of research and analysis which is committed to changing people's lives for the better – although there are usually no simple answers as to what is 'better'; rather, this is a matter of ongoing debate and assessment. The commitment to change means that CDA is concerned not only with a 'negative' critique of semiosis in social life (semiosis within processes of domination) but also with a more 'positive' analysis and an exploration of new and resistant forms of semiosis – with semiosis taken as one element in social struggles.

DISCOURSE ANALYSIS IN SOCIAL RESEARCH

The category of 'discourse' and the analysis of discourse have become increasingly prominent in a wide range of social research and analysis. What CDA has to contribute is what is often missing in some other forms of social critique – namely, close analysis of texts and interactions. CDA sees texts and interactions as part of the material processes of social life, or as materialities in which social life is ongoingly produced, reproduced and changed. Social analysis therefore should include analysis of the complex processes which go on in texts and interactions, and CDA offers ways of analysing the latter which connect them to the wider social process, as other traditions within semiotic analysis generally do not.

Why have discourse, language and semiosis come to be such prominent concerns in social theory and research? Because there is a sense in which they have come to be more prominent elements of social life. Take for instance the widespread interpretation of recent economic change as a move towards a 'knowledge-based' economy. A 'knowledge-based' economy means an economy that is also 'discourse-based' – in the sense that new knowledges are produced, circulated, and applied in production as new discourses (such as the discourse of 'teamwork'). We can say that knowledge, and hence language and other forms of semiosis, become commodities (Lyotard, 1986/1987). For instance, knowledge of how to conduct appraisals in workplaces, including the language to use in appraisal interviews, is produced and sold as a commodity by management consultants. New communication technologies have transformed the means of semiotic production, producing a new articulation between older and newer communication technologies (that is, new ways of using them in combination). In so doing, they have transformed the order of discourse: the relative salience of semiosis in relation to other elements within the network of social practices, and the relation between language and other forms of semiosis (such as the visual). This is how we can approach the apparently increasing importance of 'communication' in contemporary social life.

A THEORETICAL FRAMEWORK FOR CDA

CDA is based upon a view of semiosis as an irreducible element of all material social processes (Williams, 1977). We can see social life as interconnected networks of social practices of diverse sorts (economic, political, cultural, family, and so on). The reason for centring the concept of 'social practice' is that it allows an oscillation between the perspective of social *structure* and the perspective of social *action and agency* – both necessary perspectives in social research and analysis (Chouliaraki and Fairclough, 1999). By 'social practice' I mean a relatively stabilized form of social activity (examples would be classroom teaching, television news, family meals and medical consultations). Every practice is an articulation of diverse social elements within a relatively stable configuration, always including semiosis. Let us say that every practice includes the following elements:

- productive activity
- means of production

- social relations
- social identities
- cultural values
- consciousness
- semiosis

These elements are *dialectically* related (Harvey, 1996). That is to say, they are different elements but not discrete, fully separate, elements. There is a sense in which each 'internalizes' the others without being reducible to them. So, for instance, social relations, social identities, cultural values and consciousness are in part semiotic, but that does not mean that we theorize and research social relations, for instance, in the same way that we theorize and research language – they have distinct properties, and researching them gives rise to distinct disciplines. (Although it is possible and desirable to work across disciplines in a 'transdisciplinary' way, as noted above.)

CDA is analysis of the dialectical relationships between semiosis (including language) and other elements of social practices. Its particular concern (in my own approach) is with the radical changes that are taking place in contemporary social life, with how semiosis figures within processes of change, and with shifts in the relationship between semiosis and other social elements within networks of practices. We cannot take the role of semiosis in social practices for granted; it has to be established through analysis. And semiosis may be more or less important and salient in one practice or set of practices than in another, and may change in importance over time.

Semiosis figures in social practices in broadly three ways. First, it figures as a part of the social activity within a practice. For instance, part of doing a job such as being a shop assistant is using language in a particular way; and this applies equally well to practices such as governing a country. Second, semiosis figures in representations. Social actors within any practice produce representations of other practices, as well as ('reflexive') representations of their own practice, in the course of their activity within the practice. They '*recontextualize*' other practices (Bernstein, 1990; Chouliaraki and Fairclough, 1999); that is, they incorporate them into their own practice, and different social actors will represent them differently according to how they are positioned within the practice. Representation is a process of social construction of practices, including reflexive self-construction; representations enter and shape social processes and practices. Third, semiosis figures in ways of being, in the constitution of identities; for instance the identity of a political leader such as Tony Blair in the UK is partly a semiotically constituted way of being.

Semiosis, as part of social activity, constitutes genres. Genres are diverse ways of acting, of producing social life, in the semiotic mode. Examples are: everyday conversation, meetings in various types of organization, political and other forms of interview, and book reviews. Semiosis, in the representation and self-representation of social practices, constitutes discourses. Discourses are diverse representations of social life which are inherently positioned; differently positioned social actors 'see' and represent social life in different ways, different discourses. For instance, the lives of poor and disadvantaged people are represented through different discourses in the social practices of government, politics, medicine, and social science, *and* through different discourses within each of these practices corresponding to the different positions occupied by social actors. Finally, semiosis, as part of ways of being, constitutes styles; for instance the styles of business managers, or political leaders.

Social practices, networked in a particular way, constitute a social order; for instance, the emergent neo-liberal global order referred to above or, at a more local level, the social order of education in a particular society at a particular time. The semiotic aspect of a social order is what we can call an *order of discourse*. This is the way in which diverse genres and discourses are networked together. So an order of discourse is a social structuring of semiotic difference – a particular social ordering of relationships amongst different ways of making meaning in the form of different discourses and genres. One aspect of this ordering is dominance: some ways of making meaning are dominant or mainstream in a particular order of discourse, others are marginal, oppositional, or 'alternative'. For instance, there may be a dominant way of conducting a doctor–patient consultation, but there are also various other ways, which may be adopted or developed to a greater or lesser extent in opposition to this dominant way. The dominant way probably still maintains social distance between doctors and patients along with the authority of the doctor over the way interaction proceeds; but there are other ways which are more 'democratic', in which doctors play down their authority. The political concept of 'hegemony' can be usefully used in analysing orders of discourse (Fairclough, 1992; Forgacs, 1988; Laclau and Mouffe, 1985). That is, a particular social structuring of semiotic difference may become hegemonic, become part of the legitimizing common sense which sustains relations of domination, but hegemony will always be contested to a greater or lesser extent, in hegemonic struggle. An order of discourse is not a closed or rigid system, but rather an open one, which can be put at risk by what happens in actual interactions.

Discourses, genres and styles are interconnected through a dialectic of 'rematerialization' – they constitute different semiotic materialities which are connected by the processes of operationalization, inculcation and representation. First, discourses can become *operationalized* as ways of acting and interacting, including in their semiotic aspect; that is, as genres. Secondly, discourses can become *inculcated* as ways of being, including in their semiotic aspect; that is, as styles or, in a different theoretical terminology, as 'habituses' (Bourdieu, 1984). Thirdly, genres and styles (along with other, non-semiotic, elements of social practices) can be *represented* as discourses. An example of this dialectic of rematerialization would be the workplace discourse of 'teamwork', which not only circulates as a discourse but becomes operationalized as ways of interacting, including genres, and can become inculcated as ways of being, including styles.

'Can be', because there is no necessity in the dialectic of rematerialization – discourses can and often do fail to become operationalized or inculcated and, to that extent, may in certain circumstances be deemed to be 'empty', or purely 'rhetorical' in one sense of that word.

AN ANALYTICAL FRAMEWORK FOR CDA

The analytical framework sketched out below is more fully elaborated in Chouliaraki and Fairclough (1999). This is a version of what Bhaskar (1986) calls 'explanatory critique' and involves four stages.

Stage 1: Focus upon a social problem which has a semiotic aspect. Beginning with a social problem rather than the more conventional 'research question' accords with the critical intent of this approach: namely, to produce knowledge which can lead to emancipatory change. Of course, this raises the question: a problem for whom? There is no ready definition of what constitutes a social problem, even from the perspective of particular groups and, as I said above, there is no 'party line'. It is an inherently and continually contested issue. CDA is not value-neutral: practitioners work from particular social and political values, and different practitioners have different values. It is not a matter of my personal judgement of what is a social problem; however, it is a matter of my interpretation of what constitute problems for people whose position and perspective I associate myself with (for example, targets of racism, rather than racists), and such interpretations are rightly open to being questioned and contested.

Let me give an example, with reference to the appraisal training material in the Appendix at the end of this chapter. This is taken from a two-hour appraisal training session conducted by a member of a University Higher Education Development Centre and attended by academic and assistant staff from one department. The material includes the overheads used by the trainer, plus a summary of what was said about preparation for the appraisal interview, plus some comments made by the trainer about the overheads.

The context for the pervasive spread of appraisal is a shift in the regulation of work from authoritative to non-authoritative control systems. Work is increasingly organized around teams pursuing defined goals in a relatively autonomous fashion, where control over individual team members comes more from peer pressure than from authority or hierarchical control, and depends upon members 'owning' the goals of the team; that is, internalizing them as their own goals. Non-authoritative control systems are one aspect of the move towards 'flexible' organizations better able to respond quickly to the fast-shifting demands of the market. Flexible organizations need flexible employees.

Universities are a special and interesting case. They are caught up in the changing relationship between the economy and non-economic areas of life, and in the tendency of the former to colonize the latter. Universities are not only expected to be increasingly responsive to the research and employment needs of the economy, they are more and more drawn into what is becoming an intensely competitive educational market on an increasingly global scale. They are competing for students and research money, and they are increasingly subject to changes in the regulation of work similar to those experienced in other sectors. However, their history is rather distinctive. Although they once had (and still partly retain) certain features of hierarchical organizations, there is also a strong tradition of individual academic freedom which is at odds with the emergence of a flexible competitive organization oriented to shared goals. Appraisal has been operative on paper in British universities for a decade or so, but it has not been systematically implemented in many of them. There is a great deal of resistance to it, much of which is based upon a sense that it undermines academic freedom.

In the example, appraisal is located within the University's 'quality assurance/enhancement process'. 'Quality' is one of the buzz-words of the new capitalist organization, be it a private business or a public service. In an intensely competitive environment, organizations compete on 'quality', and are ongoingly audited at all levels down to the individual employee through 'quality assurance' programs. In the case of universities, there is a Quality Assurance Agency responsible for auditing teaching, and a Research Assessment Exercise which audits research.

The new discourse represents departments in the University as pursuing 'goals and objectives' which are set in accordance with the more general 'goals and objectives' of the University, and are open to periodic revision, and subject to a 'quality assurance/enhancement process' which evaluates 'performance' against agreed 'goals and objects' and seeks to enhance 'performance'. This process is carried out at institutional and departmental levels through regular internal and external audits, and is projected down to the individual employee through appraisal. Individuals are also represented as having 'objectives' which are 'negotiated' and 'agreed' in the appraisal process and which should be 'clear' and 'measurable'. Their 'progress' and 'performance' in meeting these objectives is 'evaluated'; they receive 'feedback' on it; and meeting these objectives may require 'development' (for instance, through training) which the institution may provide, subject to 'available resources'. The negotiation of 'objectives' and the evaluation of 'performance' are part of an 'annual cycle of events' within the University's 'quality assurance/enhancement process'.

The application of 'quality management' to higher education gives rise to the set of problems I have alluded to above – the clash between its market-oriented values and its academic values. I shall focus on one particular aspect of this, in my comments below, which arises in the case of appraisal: the way in which appraisal puts pressure on academics to adjust their work to the organizational and market-oriented goals of the University, and how that is widely seen as glossed over by the representation of appraisal as oriented to the development and needs of individual academics.

Stage 2: Identify obstacles to the problem being resolved in the way in which social life is constituted. The objective here is to understand how the problem arises and how it is grounded in the way social life is organized, by focusing on the obstacles to its resolution – on what makes it more or less intractable. This involves analysis of: (a) the network of practices within which the problem is located; (b) the relationship of semiosis to other elements within the particular practices concerned; (c) the discourse, the semiosis itself. The analysis of the latter has a structural facet – the analysis of the order of discourse – and an interactional facet – the analysis of particular texts and interactions. Whereas the analysis of orders of discourse tries to specify the semiotic resources available to people (the social structuring of semiotic diversity), interactional analysis is concerned with how those resources are worked through in interactions, the active semiotic work that people are doing on specific occasions using those resources. It is in the process of being used and worked through that these resources come to be transformed.

Interactional analysis includes both 'interdiscursive' analysis, and linguistic and other forms of semiotic analysis. CDA claims that what is going on *socially* is in part what is going on *interdiscursively* in texts and interactions; that it is a question of how they work together particular genres, discourses and styles, and that the interdiscursive work of the text or interaction materializes in its linguistic and other semiotic features. Notice that even written texts are seen here as forms of interaction; they are always written for a particular readership and oriented to reader response. Linguistic and/or semiotic analysis of interactions is 'multi-functional' (Halliday, 1994) – interactions, that is, work simultaneously on representations of the world (forms of consciousness), on social relations, on social identities and on cultural values. It is concretely and locally in interactions that the dialectic between semiosis and these other elements of social practices is played out.

Let me make some brief comments on the appraisal material in terms of Stage 2. First, the application of quality management, including appraisal, to universities is part of a shift in the networking of social practices. What makes the market logic of quality management difficult to contest is the way in which universities, like other sectors of education and like the public sector more generally, are now locked into a network of practices with government and business. Second, we need to consider the relationship of semiosis to other elements of the practices concerned. One issue here is the rematerialization dialectic. Quality management comes into higher education as a discourse recontextualised from other more overtly economic and market-oriented domains, mediated by governmental agencies such as the Quality Assurance Agency.[3] The transformative effects of such powerful discourses, which increasingly move across diverse domains of social life and internationally across states and cultures, is a characteristic of the knowledge-based economy – knowledges, as I noted above, are constituted, circulate, and are consumed as discourses. But their effectivity depends upon them being operationalized as ways of interacting (including genres), and inculcated as ways of being (including styles). In so far as these rematerializations take effect or 'go through', contestation becomes increasingly difficult; though, as I note below, there are reasons for doubting how far they do go through. The appraisal material in the Appendix includes the specification of a new genre, the appraisal process itself, which 'operationalizes' the new discourse, and projects a new consciousness for employees, a new identity, which employees, it is hoped, will internalize and 'own'.

Third, we need to consider the discourse itself. The 'marketization' of higher education, as of the public sector more generally, is in part a restructuring of its order of discourse which involves a new articulation of market and managerial discourses, genres and styles with academic and educational ones. In so far as this restructured order of discourse achieves a degree of stabilization and normalization, resources for resistance are diminished.

Stage 3: Consider whether the social order (network of practices) in a sense 'needs' the problem; and whether, therefore, the resolution of the problem entails a radical restructuring of the social order. One aspect of the current restructuring of capitalism is the restructuring of the relationship between conventionally economic and non-economic domains, and the subordination of the latter to the logic of the former (Jessop, 2000), and therefore to the order of discourse of the former. It would seem that the new capitalism depends in particular on locking universities into the market as part of the institution of a knowledge-based economy.

Stage 4: Identify possible ways past the obstacles. This stage in the framework is a crucial complement to Stage 2 – it looks for hitherto unrealized possibilities for change in the way social life is currently organized. It focuses on the gaps, the contradictions, in the way things are, seeing these as constituting a potential for resistance and change. In terms of the networking of practices, one might point, for instance, to the contradictory positioning of higher education within networks: the networking of higher education into a configuration of practices with government and business (which I alluded to above) coexists with a still-vigorous academic network which especially links academic research in universities internationally, and is sustained by an apparatus of scholarly journals, academic publishing, conferences, networks on the internet, and so forth.

In terms of the relationship of semiosis to other elements within the practices of higher education, one might note that the rematerialization dialectic of the quality management discourse only goes through to a limited degree. As I noted earlier, for instance, although appraisal systems have existed on paper in British universities for quite some time, appraisal has been widely 'forgotten about' after its initial introduction. Moreover, discussion at the appraisal training session (represented in the Appendix) was indicative of the very limited degree to which quality management has been inculcated as a new way of being – for instance, the 'appropriacy' of appraiser 'skills', such as giving 'constructive feedback', was questioned. The department concerned has operationalized its suspicion of appraisal by adopting a policy of training all its staff as appraisers to avoid what is seen as a division between appraisers and appraisees which is potentially damaging to collegiality. To a degree, one might say that the discourse of quality management has not gone beyond being a rhetoric in one sense of that term – its representations have not been fully rematerialized as ways of acting and ways of being; there is a gap between rhetoric and reality.

Let me come to some brief comments on the interactional analysis of the material in the Appendix. Appraisal is widely resented on the grounds of perceived contradictions between the apparent orientation to individuals and the actual dominance of organizational motives and interests. The contradiction is evident in the first two 'purposes' of appraisal as they were defined in the training session, which constitute different discourses:

- to provide all employees with the opportunity to evaluate their work and to receive constructive and informed feedback on their performance;
- to clarify a department's goals and objectives and to agree personal objectives related to those goals. (See Appendix)

The contradictions are somewhat obscured by the elision of agents for verbs ('evaluate', 'clarify', 'agree', and so forth), but they are clear enough. The first purpose represents appraisal as an 'opportunity' which is 'provided' for employees, and 'evaluation' as something they do themselves ('employee' is the implicit subject of 'evaluate') with 'feedback' from others. The process is represented as institutional support for self-evaluation, with the employee as the main agent. But the second purpose represents appraisal as adjusting 'personal objectives' to institutional 'goals and objectives' – where the main (implicit) agent is the appraiser, constructed as representative of the institution, and as educator ('clarify'). The agency of 'agree' is ambivalent: are 'personal objectives' agreed to *by* the appraiser, or agreed to *between* appraiser and appraisee? This ambivalence makes possible a variety of more or less authoritarian implementations of appraisal.

The contradiction in the discourse of appraisal carries over into its envisaged operationalization as a genre in these materials. It is the appraisal discussion that is particularly interesting. The appraisal discussion is seen as a skilled performance by people who have received training as appraisers or appraisees. It is to be 'managed by someone trained to lead the process'. The skills of the appraiser are reminiscent of the counsellor – they include '(active) listening', and 'reflecting back' (in the sense of mirroring back to the appraisee what she or he has said). The appraiser is advised to give 'constructive feedback', which includes 'starting with the positive' and 'leaving the appraisee with a choice'. The appraisal discussion itself is seen as having a three-stage structure – discussion of the current situation, identifying a different and better 'preferred-scenario', and working out a 'plan of action' to get there. In short, the appraisal discussion is talk strategically designed and inculcated through training which operationalizes the discourse of appraisal; a technology for evaluating performance, setting objectives, and devising a 'plan of action' to achieve them. It is an example of subjecting discourse to organizationally and instrumentally motivated processes of design (called 'Taylorism') which have long been applied to machinery and the bodies of workers in modern industry, but which are now being widely applied to discourse. And it belies the representation of appraisal as a process carried out for the benefit of, and under the control of, the appraisee.

Appraisal is represented, as I have indicated, as 'skilled', or as based upon the training of appraiser and appraisee in a range of 'skills'. The concept of 'skill' is important and pervasive in the new capitalism. Skilled work used to be understood as the facility of a worker in applying tools or techniques to objects and materials in the production process – for instance, the skills of the carpenter or the stonemason, and by extension the skills of the footballer. The decisive shift in the concept of 'skill' is its extension to social relations between people, to interaction and communication. It entails an objectification and commodification of people – treating people as analogous to the objects and materials which are worked upon in production. Skills training is a means for inculcating new discourses into the dispositions and identities of people, for getting them to 'own' them. Central to the restructuring of education in the new capitalism is the idea of 'lifelong learning' conceived in terms of 'reskilling', a capacity for an openness to the internalization of new discourses through training in new skills.

'Skills' are superficially ethically neutral techniques which can be construed as benefiting people in various domains of social life, not only in work but also in citizenship and personal relationships. However, the application of skills in the conduct of social relationships is ethically objectionable in a fundamental way. It incorporates and legitimizes a manipulative and instrumentalist relationship to others. Take for example the injunction 'start with the positive'. This may be legitimized and neutralized with banal claims that there are always positive things to say about people, that people's contributions should be recognized whatever their flaws. Yet 'starting with the positive' is an instrumental and manipulative move designed to set the tone of an appraisal discussion in a way which enhances the likelihood of effectively achieving the organizational goals of appraisal. It is an injunction which treats the appraisee as an object to be worked upon.

The hostile response in the appraisal training session to 'starting with the positive', which I referred to above, is indicative of how contradictions can give rise to resistance. However, one needs to go beyond the text in the Appendix and beyond the training session to appreciate properly the contradiction involved and its effects in terms of resistance. Contradictions within particular texts or interactions are effective through evoking contradictions experienced at a more general level within the practices of higher education – including the contradiction between experienced collegiality in many aspects of university work and the instrumental and manipulative social relations of quality management.

Notes

1. For instance, Wodak's activity in campaigns against the presence of Haider's FPO in the Austrian government.
2. See also the 'Language in New Capitalism' website at: <www.uoc.es/humfil/nlc/LNC-ENG/lnc-eng.html>.
3. Although, according to Boltanski and Chiapello (1999), the discourse of 'New Management' is itself a recontextualization of the discourse of 1960–70s 'artistic critique' of capitalism, in terms for instance of its construction of social relations in work as non-hierarchical.

APPENDIX

The purposes of staff appraisal:

- to provide all employees with the opportunity to evaluate their work and to receive constructive and informed feedback on their performance;
- to clarify a department's goals and objectives and to agree personal objectives related to those goals;
- to support individual development to meet the needs of current and future roles, within available resources.

'Key features' of staff appraisal:

- all staff should receive feedback and have the opportunity to discuss their progress and development as part of an annual cycle of events;
- all staff should negotiate clear and measurable objectives for the review period;
- all staff should receive written confirmation of feedback and of the agreed objectives for the following review period;
- appraisal should be managed by someone trained to lead the process;
- all staff should be properly prepared for appraisal via training or briefing;
- appraisal should become a logical and effective part of the University's quality assurance/enhancement process.

The trainer added that 'the process should be mostly owned by the appraisee'.

The main stages in appraisal are:

- preparation
- discussion
- recording
- dissemination

'Two principles' govern selection of appraisers:

- the choice of appraiser shall be made by the appraisee;

- appraisers shall be experienced members of staff with knowledge of the work of the appraisee.

Preparation involves the appraisee sending the appraiser an up-to-date CV (academic staff) or job description (assistant staff), plus other relevant material such as feedback from colleagues or students, and a list of topics for discussion (a 'reflective document, showing how you see things or how you feel', the trainer added). The content of this documentation 'should be up to the appraisee', the trainer commented. A meeting is then arranged, and 'both parties agree the agenda before starting discussion' – the trainer commented that it 'shouldn't include something the appraisee isn't happy about'. The 'general focus' of appraisal discussion should be 'teaching, research and publication, administration, other professional activities' (academic staff), and 'headings in job description' (assistant staff).

A three-stage appraisal discussion should:

- review appraisee's current situation and the issues arising from it;
- develop 'preferred-scenario' possibilities and how these might be translated into viable goals (the trainer clarified these preferences as the appraisee's);
- determine how to get to the 'preferred scenario' – develop a plan of action.

Skills used by the appraiser include:

- listening (specified as 'active')
- questioning
- summarizing
- reflecting back (specified as echoing back the appraisee's own words to him/her)
- challenging (justified because 'they might be underselling themselves')

Appraisers should give 'constructive feedback' (glossed by the trainer as 'helping individuals get a clearer view of themselves and how they are seen by others'):

- start with the positive
- be specific
- offer alternatives
- refer to behaviour that can be changed
- own the feedback
- leave the appraisee with a choice

The appraisal report is 'a summary written up by the appraiser and agreed with the appraisee' covering:

- areas discussed
- conclusions arrived at as a result of discussion
- agreements made

- goals identified
- any development required by the appraisee

The report 'is confidential to the appraisee, the appraiser and the Head of Department'.

PART II

Applications

4 Discovering order in opening sequences: calls to a software helpline

Carolyn Baker, Michael Emmison and Alan Firth

EDITORIAL

As computers and computing become increasingly part of everyday experience, and since computers are by no means trouble-free systems, so the experience of problems naturally increases. In response, a number of hardware and software companies have set up helplines which computer users can call to help resolve their problems. But how can and should such new forms of institutional dialogue take place? No one has set out and formulated pre-specified rules for these new types of encounter. Nevertheless, as Carolyn Baker, Michael Emmison and Alan Firth show in this detailed analysis, there is still overwhelming order to these calls. What is that order and how is it brought into effect in actual helpline calls?

Most importantly, by focusing specifically on the openings *of the calls – where, among other things, problems are described and initial diagnoses made – Baker, Emmison and Firth show those new to applied CA their working method, adducing their findings as they go along with that methodological display. Beginning with hypothetical structures and orderings to the talk in question (and, interestingly, as with John Lobley's analysis later in this book, working with a variant of Maynard's (1991) 'perspective display series'), the authors bring in several more data sets to effectively test their initial considerations of the orderly nature of these call openings.*

What transpires is a fascinating instance of applied CA; for it turns out that not just (expert) call takers but also (less expert) callers actually co-produce the orderly structure of these calls. They work up, and then work with, what the authors call 'a general sequential framework'. Moreover, at certain points in this sequential framework, it turns out to be crucial that the callers *know – and display that they know – how such interactions ought properly to proceed. For example, in order for any caller to get any help at all 'he or she must first* help the call taker*'. In so displaying conversational competence, callers also – and thereby – display their competence in matters of computing. This then allows the 'expert' call takers to gauge exactly what sorts of talk-about-computers are pertinent to (or 'recipient designed' for) particular callers in any given case.*

In the early days of EM and CA, Garfinkel and Sacks (1970) showed that everyday 'practical actions' (here, calls to a helpline) do indeed have 'formal structures' (here, 'a general sequential framework'). But this does not mean we can read off pre-specified rules from looking mechanically at what participants do. Instead, again following Garfinkel and Sacks, participants orient *to rules and ostensibly display those orientations* in and as *their talk with one another. This makes any 'formal structures' both context-sensitive* and *context-independent. In this chapter, Baker* et al. *then offer us a remarkable instance of this phenomenon: participants working up (in real time) sets of orderly and orientable structures of talk which are observable in large numbers of cases (and regardless of personnel) and yet which are also highly sensitive to the specific problems and levels of expertise thereby displayed in the talk.*

INTRODUCTION

This chapter presents an account of how we found regularities in the opening sections of calls to a computer software technical assistance service. Like others working with similar interactional data, we have accumulated a large volume of audio- and video-taped materials. After some time spent re-viewing and re-listening to many of the tapes, where we found a wealth of possibilities for systematic analysis, we needed to make a decision as to where to begin detailed analysis. We chose to focus on the beginning of the calls – that is, to look at how the telephone calls were begun by the parties to the telephone talk. Research has shown that a number of language-based activities are undertaken in the opening sections of calls (Schegloff, 1986), and this was very evident in our data. So our initial task was to describe, in detail, the interactional character of the opening sections of calls to the helpline.

To set the scene for our analyses, we first present some relevant ethnographic details about the particular workplace we were studying. Following this, we introduce the telephone talk-based data and analyse four transcripts to show how we moved from first noticing regularities in the structure of the openings of the calls, to elaborating and refining our descriptions of these regularities as component parts of a general sequential framework that applies to most calls. The structure that we found shows how callers and call takers coordinate their way into the main business of the call: the problem-diagnosis and its solution. We comment on how this structure provides not only for coordinated entry into the main business of the call, but also for the caller to display, and the call taker to gauge and assess, his/her (that is, the caller's) computer- and software-related competence. As we show, there is a great deal of social-interactional work done early in the call that informs how the 'technical' work of diagnosis and problem-solution may be done.

The chapter concludes with a brief commentary on how the call openings we study here are embedded in a chain of organizational practices. Although we have isolated the *openings* to the calls for our current investigation, these are clearly only one point in a much more complex set of interrelated organizational practices that rely variously on talk, texts and computers.

THE SETTING

The telephone calls we initially examine here are calls made by users of a range of computer software packages to a technical support line that offers assistance with any problems involved in installing or running the software. The technicians work in a large open-plan room where they have their own cubicle with a computer, a telephone and, often, a second computer that can be used for consulting systems, programs, specifications, or the organization's database on problems.

Call takers can see and overhear their colleagues working in their immediate group of cubicles and occasionally consult these colleagues. As soon as they pick up the phone to begin the call, they ask for and enter, via their keyboard, the caller's 'customer number' on their computer, so that, near the very beginning of the call, they have on screen all the caller's details, including (if applicable) the history of the caller's previous contacts with the support service. The call taker makes various notations on the current call in the customer's computer file so that a next call on the problem – which will most likely be directed to a different technician – can be followed up from the point that was reached in the first call.

THE CALL OPENINGS

We audio- and video-taped a large number of calls over a period of approximately ten working days. The calls in our corpus range widely in terms of their duration (between five minutes and three hours; most calls, however, lasted around fifteen minutes). To begin our detailed work on the recordings, we transcribed approximately 50 calls from this corpus. We were faced first with the question of where to begin our detailed analysis; for it was clear to us that many aspects of the calls were potentially fruitful areas for detailed investigation. After some deliberation, we reached the conclusion that the natural place for us to begin was the opening segments. The following extract contains the opening sequence of one call. CT is the call taker, C is the caller:

Extract 1

CT welcome to Microsoft technical support, this is Leena,
can I start with your customer number please
C yes that's three five oh (.) six four four
(1.8)
CT it's Benny is it?
C yeah that's right
CT how can I help you?
C I've recently installed Microsoft office pro:
(0.4)

CT yeah
C and in the access part of the thing I've- I wanna use
the membership (.) but I've got those Americanized
dates an' phone numbers an' erm there's some form of
ma:sking on them?
CT yes there's an input mask on them?
C yeah I wanna- how do I get that bin to an Australian
sta:ndard?
CT you need to edit the ma:sk

As we transcribed, we identified some broad interactional patterns, such that, even after looking closely at only 2–3 calls, we tentatively observed what appeared to be regularities in the talk. First there was a sequence of turns where the call taker ascertains the caller's customer number and first name (1–6). Although this sequence precedes the problem-talk proper, these first turns can contain detail that is important for what comes later. It can be seen, for example, that the call taker establishes a preference that first names be used in the conversation. It can also be seen that the CT 'packages' the three parts of the first turn as one continuous stream of talk, which 'constrains' the caller's first words to answering the question that came last – by giving a series of six numbers. The customer number, logged in, has provided the CT with the information that the caller is Benny, and Benny can take it that the CT has found this and other information by logging in the number, rather than, for example, psychically.

The second 'phase' begins with the call taker's 'how can I help you' (7) and continues through to the point where the caller has completed the description of the problem (17). At line 15, the call taker makes a first substantive comment on the problem: 'yes there's an input mask on them'. The caller then proceeds to formulate the problem more precisely at lines 16–17. This, then, is a first example of finding phases in the call. One of the methods of CA is to locate regularities in the data in the form of identifiable phenomena. We elaborate on this throughout the chapter.

FIRST FINDING A STRUCTURE OF REGULARITIES

In our work with opening segments, we first noticed the 'open' character of CT's first turn. CT does not use 'can/may I help you?', as one hears in many service encounters in shops and offices, but '*how* can I help you?' The following segment is another example of this. (A brief prior sequence dealing with customer number and name has been omitted.)

Extract 2

CT how can I help you?
(0.4)
C erm I've installed (.) office ninety-seven?

(0.8)
.hh and (.) erm my negative figures are different
(0.8)
in excel (.) from this time=an' I think it's
somewhere in the setup that I haven't-
(0.8)
selected something
(0.5)
CT the- when you have negative numbers in your cells? (.)
erm how are they displayed

As a first turn, the hypothetical 'can I help you?' in face-to-face service encounters leaves open the question of whether the service person can help you, or whether you want to be left alone to browse, for example. In calls to technical support, the assumption is that the caller is seeking help, and that this help-seeking is the reason for calling. This seems an eminently reasonable assumption on the call taker's part, and is treated as such by the caller, who responds to the inquiry by revealing his or her reason for calling. Also the '*how* can I help you?' format truncates the exchange so as to go straight into the problem-description. The problem-description that is offered by the caller *is* the answer to the question 'how can I help you?'. We have never heard 'you can help me by doing such-and-such'. Notice that this direct entry into the problem-description is a joint accomplishment of both C and CT.

A next thing we noticed in many callers' initial descriptions was the presence of brief pauses, place-holders such as 'um', and phrases ending in interrogative intonation in their descriptions. These give their talk the hearable qualities in various combinations of (a) being more-or-less composed on the spot, even though some of them have waited a very long time to get connected to a technician; (b) being unsure exactly how to describe the problem; (c) making places for the CT to offer tokens that the CT is listening – tokens like 'yeah' or 'umhum'; and/or, relatedly, (d) making places for the CT to begin speaking. Any of these features of initial turn-design by C can be heard as sensitive to and, at the same time, constitutive of a 'lay-to-expert' relationship.

A further thing we noticed was that, for the most part, the CT let the C go on in the description, even though there were various moments when they could have inserted questions, for example, or other interventions into the C's telling. In our first example, the CT offers one receipt token ('yeah') during the C's initial description and, in the second, refrains from speaking until the caller has produced a lengthy turn at talk (note, for example, in Extract 2, the several pauses in the caller's turn (4, 6 and 9) where the call taker could have interjected). Two of the guidelines CTs are trained to observe are 'listen to the customer' and 'don't interrupt'; so this could be a local enactment of these guidelines. However, regardless of guidelines, this practice provides for the important element of having the C describe the problem in their own terms. This has the benefit for the CT of hearing how the C verbalizes the matter and, from that, the CT can gain a sense of how much computer- and software-based expertise the C has, information that is usable in designing their subsequent interaction with the caller. Maynard (1991) has termed this listening sequence 'perspective display', a method that professionals such as clinicians use to listen for a particular client's or patient's perspective, so as to determine how then to fit their information or advice to this particular person with these particular attitudes, history or relevances.[1] This fitting of talk to the relevances and so forth of a particular hearer is known as 'recipient design' (Schegloff and Sacks, 1973).

We also noticed that callers used a form of recipient design in the construction of their description of the problem. They used this in the manner in which they 'located' the problem for the call taker somewhere within the very extensive range of products and problems that could be encountered with software. This involved a two- or three-step procedure. Callers very often (a) focused by naming the software product they were working with and then (b) narrowed the focus, identifying where in the product the problem was, and then (c) named the concern. In the case of Extracts 1 and 2 (simplified) this works as follows:

Extract 1
(a) I've recently installed Microsoft office pro
(b) and in the access part of the thing
(c) I've got those Americanized dates

Extract 2
(a) I've installed office ninety-seven
(c) and my negative figures are different
(b) in excel

Note that, in Extract 2, the order of the last two components is reversed.

We further identified a 'turning point', where the parties to the talk turned from C's description to CT's initial substantive move, as in the following two cases:

(1) C phone numbers an' erm there's some form of ma:sking on
them?
CT yes there's an input mask on them?
C yeah I wanna- how do I get that bin to an Australian sta:ndard?
CT you need to edit the ma:sk

(2) C somewhere in the setup that I haven't- (0.8)
selected something
(0.5)
CT the- when you have negative numbers in your cells? (.)
er[m how are they displayed

We found these 'next things' working not just in one call, but in several. As we found a phenomenon in one call, we then looked for its equivalent in others, thus bringing in more and more examples as we proceeded. We did the analytic work together, re-listening to the tapes while reading (and revising and refining) the transcripts, making observations on what we saw to be happening in the talk, challenging each other with counter-examples, investigating the counter-examples, and building a cumulative sketch, on paper, of the shape of the calls and their components. All of this was done in constant reference to our knowledge of the CA research literature. These activities produced a stronger sense of confidence in our analyses and also generated some small epiphanies when the detective work on tiny details of counter-examples resulted in confirmations of our initial observations. There were equally significant moments when we conceded that some initially exciting idea was not going anywhere.

REFINING THE ANALYSIS: COMPONENTS OF THE OPENINGS

We now present two further call openings that we studied in concert with Extracts 1 and 2 above to confirm that there was indeed a 'structure' or 'form' to the openings of the calls, and to refine our description of the structure. Reading this next extract for structural parallels to the extracts presented above is aided by attending, as the extract does, to pauses within and between turns at talk:

Extract 3

CT how can I help you, Danny
C .hh okay I've got a problem with er word ninety
seven=a couple o' weeks ago we bought er the value
pack upgrade?
(0.4)
CT okay
C and er installed
(0.5)
the lot .hh a:nd since then I haven't been al- haven't
been able to print from within word (.) .hh erm I can
open up a document I can m:- make changes I can save
the changes .hh but while the document is open I
can't print (.) erm if I try an' print it just locks
up an' freezes? .hh in order to print I've got to:
select the document from outside of word, right
click, an' go down to print
(0.8)
CT what type of printer are you using?
(0.8)
C sorry what type of
CT printer (.) are you [using
C [printer? using a: erm (.) new
gen design express a:nd a: cyclone
(0.6)

er driver for a: canon laser printer
(0.8)
CT canon driver is it?
C e::rm that's a cyclone driver I think but it's a- the
same problem for both printers

We can see in this extract: the open character of the CT's invitation to the C to design their first turn (1); the caller's provision of pauses or spaces for the CT to enter the talk (3–17); the call taker's non-intervention during this initial description (3–16); the caller's three-part problem location ('word ninety seven' → 'value pack upgrade' → 'can't print in word' (2–10)); and a possible turning point where the CT asks a question (18). Similarly, the fourth and final extract shows this shape:

Extract 4
CT how can I help you?
C er problem with a (.) system running er power point
in actual fact uhm the customer's trying to do a pack
an' go
(1.0)
a:nd
(2.0)
it's coming up with a message towards the end of it
saying insufficient space
(1.5)
regardless whether we send it to the hard drive or the
floppy disk, y'know it does not even check the floppy
drive when it comes up with this error message
(1.0)
.hh also we cannot install office ninety-seven again
over the top .hh
(1.0)
CT you can't install it over the top?
C no it comes up with an el zed ((LZ)) thirty two dee
el oh ((32DLO)) file is corrupt or damaged or missing
(0.5)
CT el zed? ((LZ))
C el zed thirty two? (.) dot dee el el
((LZ32.DLL)) now this file resides in the
windows system directory? I have removed it renamed
it also (.) taken it back off of the see dee ((CD))
.hh a:nd put it back in the original location (.) it
refuses to accept it
(1.0)
CT okay I'm just having a look on the on the database
here to see exactly what that file i:s

COMPONENTS OF THE CALL

Reading through the four extracts above, we found further regularities. We worked towards a more elaborated and refined analysis of call openings by identifying the following ten components, some of which have already been introduced and some of which are additional. These components have been separated out but are clearly interrelated, part of a sequential order of things.

1. The 'open' opening by the call taker

The call taker opens with 'how can I help you?' or, in other calls, some other open question such as 'and what can we do for you this morning?' or 'and what seems to be the problem?'.

2. The prelude to first talk by the caller

The caller often begins with an in-breath (.hh) or other lead-in to the problem description such as 'erm' or 'okay'. This seems a very fine point but is part of the pattern we observed. It is related to the discussion above concerning the caller's composition of the call (and, not least, the indication of an awareness on the caller's part that he or she is about to produce an extended turn at talk) at the point of being connected to the call taker.

3. The narrative beginning of initial caller descriptions

The caller often begins with 'I'm working with . . .' or 'I've just bought . . .', or 'I've been installing . . .'. This turn design sets the scene for a narrative about what happened, when it happened, and shows the caller to be an 'active' user of the software. That is, the caller has been using something and has tried unsuccessfully – on more than one occasion – to do something about the problem, prior to calling the helpline.

4. The two- or three-step procedure within the narrative

As mentioned above, callers typically use a two- or three-step description: after mention of product, there is further specification of (narrowing to) *what aspect* of the program is causing difficulty, and then what is wrong there. We have treated these as indicative of callers' appreciation of the wide purview of products and matters that call takers could be asked about, and as a form of considerateness in their call for support. In this sense, we can say that the caller sees that, in order to get help, he or she must first help the call taker. This caller-based help is given in the way that 'problems' are described such that the caller has experienced them, as a user of the software. The C verbally recreates these experiences for the CT. Such descriptions are most often described as a narrative; that is, as an interrelated series of actions, the end-point of the series being the perceived 'problem'.

5. Callers give a narrative account of the reason for the call

Callers, then, routinely present a narrative about how they came to make the call to the helpline. Rather than directly issuing a question (such as: 'how do I change my date format to Australian standard?'), following the CT's 'how may I help you?', callers go back in time, so to speak, as the way of describing their problem. They describe how they came to notice a problem. This narrative often includes some description of what the caller has attempted to do to diagnose or to correct the problem on their own, without technical assistance. That is, they present themselves as calling technical support *after* making independent investigations, or at least after observing the repetition of the problem often enough to be sure it is recurrent. These are all included in their accounting for the call – in answer, as it were, to an unasked question, 'why are you calling technical support?'. This is a matter of presenting themselves as a competent user of the technical support line – you call, and thus make claims on an expert's time and attention, when there is warrant for doing so. A parallel might be found in making one's way to a doctor's office. If one woke in the morning with a mild pain in the arm, one would normally wait to see what happens during the morning, or during the day, and make an appointment only when one was sure the pain was persistent. Two items from Extracts 3 and 4 (respectively) display this feature:

(1) C .hh okay I've got a problem with er word ninety
seven=a couple o' weeks ago we bought er the value
pack upgrade?
(0.4)
CT okay
C and er installed
(0.5)
C the lot .hh a:nd since then I haven't been al- haven't
been able to print from within word (.)

(2) C uhm the customer's trying to do a pack an' go
(1.0)
C a:nd
(2.0)
C it's coming up with a message towards the end of it
saying insufficient space
(1.5)
C regardless whether we send it to the hard drive or the
floppy disk, y'know it does not even check the floppy
drive when it comes up with this error message

6. (x) and (y) and/but (z)

There is a common format in the narrative description that includes: scene setting – the customer has been doing or trying to do something in relation to product (x) or a specific domain within the product (y) – followed by '*and/but*', followed by what is happening or not happening (z), usually what the computer is doing or not doing. For example we see elements '(x), (y) and/but (z)' in the following:

C er problem with a (.) system running er power point in
actual fact uhm the customer's trying to do a pack an' go
(1.0)
C a:nd
(2.0)
C it's coming up with a message . . .

The component following the 'and/but' component is hearable as the statement of the problem that the call is about. Callers do not typically name it as a problem; more typically they describe what is happening, implicitly conveying that this is something anomalous and should not therefore be happening. They clearly assume that call takers, as experts, can recognize anomalous occurrences in the functioning of the software programs. This 'anomaly' is usually attributed to a problem in the computer/software. Here are '(x), (y) and/but (z)' in our other three extracts:

(1) C and in the access part of the thing I've- I wanna use
the membership (.) but I've got those Americanised
dates an' phone numbers an' erm there's some form of
ma:sking on them?

(2) C erm I've installed (.) office ninety seven?
(0.8)
.hh and (.) erm my negative figures are different
(0.8)
in excel (.) from this time=an' I think it's
somewhere in the setup that I haven't-
(0.8)
selected something

(3) C .hh okay I've got a problem with er word ninety seven=a
couple o' weeks ago we bought er the value pack upgrade?
(0.4)
CT okay
C and er installed
(0.5)
the lot .hh a:nd since then I haven't been al-
haven't been able to print from within word (.) .hh
erm I can open up a document I can . . .

7. *Turn-constructional units and pauses in the caller's description*

The narrative account is thus produced in successive turn-constructional units, delivered so as to provide possible transition places for CT to produce receipt tokens (for example, 'okay') or even to begin speaking.

8. *Minimal uptake*

The call taker often offers minimal uptake during this initial problem-description.

9. *Talk in relation to minimal uptake*

Where there is no uptake at possible points of entry by the CT, the caller offers more talk. Sometimes *a diagnosis is suggested*, as in Extract 2:

C erm I've installed (.) office ninety seven?
(0.8)
.hh and (.) erm my negative figures are different
(0.8)
in excel (.) from this time=an' I think it's
somewhere in the setup that I haven't-
(0.8)
selected something
(0.5)

Sometimes an *elaboration of the problem* is offered, as in Extract 3:

C and er installed
(0.5)
C the lot .hh a:nd since then I haven't been al-
haven't been able to print from within word (.)
.hh erm I can open up a document I can m:- make
changes I can save the changes .hh but while the
document is o̲pen I can't p̲r̲i̲n̲t̲ (.) erm if I try
an' print it just locks up an' freezes? .hh in
order to print I've got to: select the document
from outside of word, right click, an' go down to
print
(0.8)

Sometimes *further evidence of the detective work* that the caller has already done is offered, as in Extract 4:

(2.0)
C it's coming up with a message towards the end of
it saying insufficient space
(1.5)

C regardless whether we send it to the hard drive
or the floppy disk, y'know it does not even check
the floppy drive when it comes up with this error
message
(1.0)

These elaborations – in one form or another – are descriptions where not only is the 'problem' described, but also the competence of the caller is displayed. Just as we can read in these elaborations a glimmer of the caller's sophistication or expertise with computer software, so too can the call taker hear such a glimmer. What the call taker hears later might lead to a revision of this initial description. Hearing the caller's self-description at this very early point in the call is a valuable resource for them in the design of their next turns and actions.

10. First substantive insertion

The call taker makes a first substantive insertion into the talk that often serves as a turning point from problem-description to problem-diagnosis, as in:

(1) CT yes there's an input mask on them?

(2) CT the- when you have negative numbers in your
cells? (.) erm how are they displayed?

(3) CT what type of printer are you using?

(4) CT you can't install it over the top?

A SCHEMATIC SUMMARY OF THE ORGANIZATION OF CALL OPENINGS

In this list of components, it can be seen that some components are contingent on others. Not every component appears in every call, or appears in the same way. But there does seem to be a sequential structure that looks like this:

CT [how can I help you]
C [.hh erm]
C [I've been installing product x]
CT [+/– yeah, okay]
C [and + the specific domain of y]
CT [+/– yeah, okay]
C [and/but]
C [something is happening that should not happen]
[something is not happening that should happen]
CT [+/– substantive comment or question]

If there is no CT uptake at this point (no substantive comment or question), then:

C [elaboration: diagnosis, restatement, and so forth]
CT [issuing of first substantive comment or question]

These calls are, then, surprisingly regular in their structure. This is all the more remarkable because some of the callers might be calling the helpline for the first time. We therefore witness in these openings to calls the participants' patterned deployment and competent use of conversational resources in order to get a particular task done. CA is concerned with the discovery of conversational phenomena and their situated and locally designed use in the production of sequences – in this case, a problem-elicitation and description sequence done over the phone about a computer software matter in the situation where the call taker cannot see the caller or their computer screen. Conversational resources, then, carry this work entirely, and bring the parties to the talk to the point where the call taker can proceed with diagnosis and solution activities. Clearly the conversational load here falls on the *caller*, who has less technical expertise than the call taker. The expertise of the call taker to work with a description of a problem on a computer that she or he cannot see is found in what follows the opening sequences we have examined, but that is the subject of another analysis.

TRACKING BACK

Let us return for a moment to the call with which we began, and see how it develops over the next few turns.

Extract 1 – extended
CT how can I help you?
C I've recently installed Microsoft office pro:
(0.4)
CT yeah
C and in the access part of the thing I've- I wanna use
the membership (.) but I've got those Americanised
dates an' phone numbers an' erm there's some form of
ma:sking on them?
CT yes there's an input mask on them
C yeah I wanna- how do I get that bin to an Australian
sta:ndard
CT you need to edit the ma:sk
C e[dit the-
CT [edit the input mask=you just change it to:
(0.8)
what er whatever format you want (.) if you need me to
step you through the procedure Benny I'll need to set
up a support contract for it
(0.5)
C o:h dear me (0.4) an' what's that gonna cost me,

Leena?
(1.0)
CT it will cost you thirty five dollars for the issue
(0.4)
C o:h
(2.0)

The opening sequences that we have just described are in fact part of an organizational chain of telephone- and text-based work. Prior to reaching the technician who will handle the call, the customer first reaches a 'gatekeeping' section of the organization where a check is made as to whether the caller has paid in advance for the presentation of problems to the technician. When this matter is cleared, the caller is placed in a telephone queue depending on the character of the software problem, and the call is taken by the first available technician working in that queue. Waits of an hour are not unusual during busy periods. The customer pays a flat rate 'by the problem' rather than by the call – that is, if it takes seven calls to resolve the problem, then that's what it takes.

We see in the continuation of our first call, shown above, that Benny, the caller, has somehow got through to the call taker without having first set up a contract; that is, he has not pre-paid for technical assistance. The issue of payment raised in this call is a reference to the earlier 'gatekeeping' call which is the first point of contact between caller and the organization. Here, the call taker, Leena, in lines 12 to 16 begins to give advice to the caller. At the end of line 14, she hesitates in the giving of this advice. After the pause (0.8) in line 15, she stumbles a little – 'what er whatever format you want' – thus directly avoiding referring to Benny's interest in Australian specifications for dates. We next see that she stops in mid-turn (16) and introduces another matter: the payment for the call. Benny's reaction to this information – that Leena, the CT, will first have to 'set up a support contract' – is 'o:h dear me (0.4) an' what's that gonna cost me, Leena?' (20). As we can see from his response, the need for payment comes as news to Benny (or, more accurately, he gives the impression that this is news to him).

In our research, we have since traced 'backwards' to study the calls that preceded connection to the problem-solving technicians. This is another set of calls altogether, which have their own sequence and analytical specificities. What we were trying to do, therefore, was to understand the character of both of these call types as part of a complex of work practices that are serially interrelated within the organization.

Other parts of the organizational chain relating to solving callers' software problems include one technician 'escalating' the problem to another more specialized technician. Some call takers put callers on hold momentarily to consult a colleague, or to look up the information on the computer database where common problems and solutions are listed. Call takers also consult the software program in which the problem is located by calling it up on their own computer screen and watching what happens. If the call is about a computer game, they may run the game. If problems appear to warrant it, call takers may call the customer back a day or so later, to check on progress. In addition, call takers always make notations about the call on the customer's computer file, so that if the caller calls back on the same (unresolved) problem, any next technician can pick up the problem-solving process from that point.

The call-taking work detailed in this chapter thus represents only a small fraction of all the work that could occur in relation to a single problem that a customer may present to the organization. This work includes talking, writing and reading in a variety of formats. We see intimations of parts of this complex of practices in some of the calls that we have examined in this chapter. We have focused here on openings to the calls to show one way of *beginning* to appreciate how intricately and delicately talk is designed and interactionally managed in a telephone helpline.

Note

1. *Editors' note.* For a more detailed discussion of the 'perspective display series', see Chapter 9 by John Lobley. And, for criticisms, see Chapter 17 by Stephen Hester and David Francis.

5 Understanding who's who in the airline cockpit: pilots' pronominal choices and cockpit roles[1]

Maurice Nevile

EDITORIAL

As Paul ten Have has noted, applied CA sets out 'to study the local rationality *of members' practices'. In this chapter, Maurice Nevile uses this study policy to examine what pronouns* actually accomplish *in talk between pilots in an aeroplane cockpit and in the talk from the cockpit to other significant participants (such as the control tower). What he finds is, in many ways, extraordinary – in terms of both talk itself and how human lives are managed in potentially extreme situations through talk itself. We can summarize the significance of this in a few points.*

First, pronouns ('he', 'we', 'they', and so on) look as if they're relatively insignificant. They're phonetically simple and seem merely to substitute for nouns or noun phrases. In this respect, they should give us no cause for excitement. But what Nevile shows is that, in actual situations, where we go and record actual speakers and inspect their local rationalities, pronouns can do significant work over and above their supposed linguistic function. In fact, in actual circumstances, they turn out to be critical to the matter of deciding 'who's who' in the cockpit.

Second, where the 'play' of pronouns is concerned, members have a deal of discretion as to their use. So how pilots actually manage *that discretion (thereby marking, as we have seen, who is who) turns out to be critical for the success or failure of, for example, takeoffs and landings. And, in fact, Nevile suggests how wrong pronoun-attributions could have disastrous consequences for large populations flying in aeroplanes.*

Third, we have to draw the conclusion that the local-rational management of talk in such situations is no mere 'analytic' curiosity. Handling pronouns well is, in the end, life preserving. Bad pronoun management can mean real, material disasters. And the ordinary, everyday management of pronouns means that aeroplanes can take off and land without incident. Or not. So, if there were ever a good reason to do applied CA, then this study provides one – beyond reasonable doubt.[2]

INTRODUCTION

Immediately after an airline crash or serious incident, the airline industry, various government bodies, the media, and not least the general flying public, develop a keen interest in what happened and why. This includes finding out what the pilots did and said, a task made possible by 'black box' flight data recorders and cockpit voice recorders. Over time, evidence from these recorders (Faith, 1998; Helmreich, 1994; MacPherson, 1998) has suggested that human performance is a contributing factor in at least two-thirds of all accidents (Cushing, 1994; Pope, 1995). The modern airline cockpit may be the epitome of the high-technology workplace, with its array of computers, displays, buttons, switches, dials, levers and lights, but it is also very much a human setting. While every single flight is a mechanical and technological achievement and, some would say, miracle, it is also the outcome of human talk-in-interaction.

The data in this chapter is drawn from a wider research project on ordinary or routine talk in the airline cockpit, rather than crisis talk, not least because I was keen to collect the data myself. Ordinary cockpit talk is the talk that occurs when nothing wrong happens, the talk that is automatically wiped by the continuous recording loop of the cockpit voice recorder, the talk that gets the job done. Part of the work of such talk is to establish and maintain relevant cockpit roles as the pilots perform the tasks and develop the shared understandings necessary to fly their plane. I will suggest that one way this work is done is through pilots' choices of personal pronouns. Personal pronouns appear in spontaneous cockpit talk, as part of officially prescribed talk, and as impromptu embellishments of officially prescribed talk.

ROLES IN THE AIRLINE COCKPIT

In the airline cockpit the two pilots work together as a team, a 'flight crew', to successfully perform the numerous tasks required to conduct their flight.[3] Each pilot has individual duties and responsibilities although, to coordinate their work, each pilot must be familiar with both his or her own and those of the other pilot. This familiarity allows each pilot to better understand what the other is doing, is attending to, or knows about the flight at any one time, and allows expectations about what the other pilot might do at some future time in the flight. The pilots can therefore have expectations of each other, and be accountable to one another, in terms of the tasks they perform and the understandings of the progress of the flight which they have and demonstrate.

Pilots' duties and responsibilities are aligned to the particular official roles they have on each flight. Each pilot will always have two formal roles. One role derives from an official rank or status, as either Captain (C) or First Officer (FO). An individual's rank is typically commensurate with a certain level of training, qualification and experience, and this rank does not vary from flight to flight. The second role is as either 'pilot-flying' (PF) or 'pilot-not-flying' (PNF).[4] The PF and PNF roles are assigned and held for each individual flight, so an individual pilot might act as the PF and the PNF on different flights made over the course of a single day. The PF is the pilot in control of the plane. They make the more immediate inputs to affect the performance of the plane, especially during takeoff, climb and approach, and landing. The PF is also the pilot responsible for routine planning and decisions (for example, when to begin the descent, when to engage and disengage the autopilot). The roles of PF and PNF are not connected to the ranks of the pilots. On any one flight, the Captain could be the pilot-flying and the First Officer could be the pilot-not-flying, or vice versa. Ordinarily these roles are held throughout a flight, but the Captain has the authority to take control, and assume the role of PF, if he or she decides that the circumstances warrant it; for example if there is an emergency or the flight becomes problematic for some reason. Although the pilots share professional responsibility for the appropriate and safe management of the flight, as the senior ranking pilot the Captain is always the pilot with ultimate command, regardless of which pilot is the PF, and the Captain has primary responsibility for the conduct and welfare of the flight.

In the airline cockpit, we can identify five roles and, on any flight, each pilot will occupy simultaneously three of these. Each pilot is either the Captain or the First Officer, *and* the pilot-flying or the pilot-not-flying, *and* has a shared role as 'crew member'. These roles determine the pilots' expectations about who does what and when.

One way in which pilots can be seen to adopt and ascribe these relevant roles – make them visible and accountable to each other – is through the choice of personal pronouns in their talk. The respective roles of 'Captain' and 'First Officer', 'pilot-flying' and 'pilot-not-flying', and the shared role of 'crew member', are in part interactionally constructed and assigned through pilots' choices of personal pronouns. Personal pronouns indicate which role participants are playing in a context where more than one role may be available.

Variation in airline pilots' choice of personal pronouns contributes to their continuously evolving understanding of the distribution of roles and responsibilities in the cockpit as the flight progresses from the engine start-up and takeoff to the landing and engine shut-down. Pronominal choices are an important aspect of pilots' habitual communicative practice to achieve an awareness of who is doing what and what is going on as they control their plane.[5] Yet the work of personal pronouns is not limited to anaphora or simple social deixis.[6] For, as we shall see, in the setting of the modern airline cockpit, personal pronouns are a socially deployable resource for pilots to invoke relevant roles as they work together to perform the professional tasks required to fly a plane. The chapter, then, shows how – through pilots' pronominal choices – professional roles are accomplished *in situ*.

PERSONAL PRONOUNS COME OUT OF HIDING

Traditional accounts of English grammar tell us that pronouns substitute for noun phrases (Bernard, 1975: 35; Crystal, 1985: 248; Eagleson *et al.*, 1983: 81; Quirk and Greenbaum, 1973: 103). Typically, such accounts display the various personal pronouns in a table in which they may be arranged according to person, number, gender and case. Even proponents of functional grammar, who claim to study language as a social phenomenon, discuss personal pronouns primarily in terms of textual reference (Halliday, 1985; Halliday and Hasan, 1976). An emerging interest in personal pronouns in interactional rather than grammatical terms is often traced back to writings by Jakobson (1971/1957), Brown and Gilman (1960), Benveniste (1971) and Silverstein (1976). For example, Silverstein claimed that personal pronouns perform a 'creative function in bounding off the personae of the speech event itself . . . [and] make the social parameters of speaker and hearer explicit' (1976: 34). Brown and Gilman (1960), and later others including Friedrich (1972), Elias (1978) and Errington (1988) within sociology, began to link the use of pronominal forms to wider social categories and structures.

In naturally occurring talk, pronouns do not behave just as the grammar books tell them to, and they are not merely 'substitutes for nouns' (Sacks, 1992a: 333). Sacks noted that pronouns 'have an extraordinary transiency of reference' and told his students to 'at least be cautious in the use of what you've been taught about grammar' (1992a: 333–4). Sacks included pronouns in his discussions of 'tying rules/techniques' which 'comprise an ordering technique which is at least as important as are the sequencing pairs for ordering the parts of a conversation' (1992a: 716). This shows how much weight Sacks gave them, at one stage at least. The need to tie one's talk to another's preceding talk is a motivation to listen: tying properly shows that one has understood (Sacks, 1992a: 717). So personal pronouns do more than hold 'language' together.

Throughout his lectures, Sacks frequently comments on personal pronouns. For example, pronouns combine with relational terms in 'recipient design', as in the choice of 'our mother' and not 'my mother' when a sibling is present (1992b: 446), whereas 'we' may be used to represent organizational status or capacity; that is, when the speaker talks as an 'agent of an organization' (1992b: 391). A speaker may use 'we' for 'category-bound activities' (1992a: 333), as an indicator of a speaker's category membership:

> if A did something that B is talking about, and if A and B are relevantly co-members of something or other . . . then B may say 'we did' that thing that A did i.e., he may treat A's action as having been 'on behalf of' A and B. . . . [T]hat's often done with intentions of turning A's action into a categorical action, i.e., such a thing as 'we do'. (Sacks, 1992a: 573)

Making pronominal choices is one of the ways by which participants are able, in Goffman's (1981) terms, to establish, maintain and vary 'footings' in interaction. Pronominal choices allow participants to establish how they are related to one another, in the broad sense, within the interaction, and their choices are inseparable from the selves, identities, group memberships and roles which the participants adopt for themselves and ascribe to others (Hanks, 1990; Malone, 1997; Muhlhausler and Harré, 1990; Watson, 1987). So in this chapter, I will explore the *interactional* work that personal pronouns do; that is, look at how participants' ongoing choices of this or that personal pronoun play a part in holding interaction together. We will see how pronominal choices enable participants to establish who they are talking and listening 'as', with respect to one another (Watson, 1987: 271).

DATA COLLECTION

The data presented here was collected by arrangement with Qantas and Skywest Airlines. These airlines allowed me to sit in the cockpit to video the flight crews on scheduled domestic flights. I made eighteen flights, of which six were made on a Boeing 737, a twin-engine jet airliner seating approximately 130–140 passengers, and twelve were made on a Fokker 50, a 40–50 seat twin-propeller regional airliner. On these flights, I sat in the cockpit observer's seat, or 'jumpseat', which is positioned in between and immediately behind the seats of the two pilots. From the jumpseat I could easily video both the pilots and almost all the cockpit controls and instrument panels. I used an ordinary handheld video camera and I had access to a cockpit headset, assigned to the jumpseat, which enabled me to hear and record everything the pilots could hear. I was able to record the pilots' talk to each other, their talk to others outside the cockpit (for example, to air traffic controllers, and passengers), as well as the noise of the engines and the many cockpit alert sounds and automated voice warnings.

The extracts presented in this chapter are taken from the takeoff phase of just one flight. They are presented in order of occurrence to give a sense of how pronominal choices allow pilots to move in and out of the relevant roles according to the distribution of duties and responsibilities for particular activities and understandings about the conduct and progress of the flight. The extracts are taken from a period of approximately five minutes, beginning as the plane taxis to the runway and the pilots make necessary preparations, and ending as the plane makes its climb away from the runway. For this flight, the Captain is the 'pilot-flying' (C/PF) and the First Officer is the 'pilot-not-flying' (FO/PNF). In footnotes to each extract I give a brief translation of the specialist terms and phrasings used.

EXTRACTS

The first extract occurs as the plane taxis towards the runway. The Captain's turn is part of his ongoing talk which briefs the First Officer with details about the takeoff.[7]

Extract 1

1		(6.6)
→2	C/PF	and it's ah my go: wi:th (.) go-around ASE:L left (0.2) autopilot
3		command=
4	*Tower*	*=car six nine remain off runway two four*
5	C/PF	engine failure as discussed
6		(0.7)
7	*Car 69*	*ca::r six nine*
8		(0.5)
9	FO/PNF	check
10		(3.2)

The Captain uses the singular form 'my', in 'my go', to invoke and make salient his individual role as the pilot-flying. This 'my go' is a spontaneous variant of 'my departure' and is an explicit claim to the control of the takeoff and the role of pilot-flying. Saying 'my go' (or a variant) at this point in the flight is something the pilot is required to say as part of the briefing for the takeoff. So, this use of the pronoun is officially prescribed or scripted. Much of what pilots say to one another is given in operations manuals, standard procedures and so on, which specify, for many aspects of the flight, exactly what the pilots must say as professionals employed by that airline. Such materials are legally approved by an official aviation authority: the wordings are included in texts which official regulatory bodies use to approve and license an airline. Airline pilots are required, as a condition of their professional employment, to follow the 'scripts' provided for them in these texts. In the event of an incident or accident, pilots may be held accountable for their failure to, for example, follow the wording of emergency procedures (Flight Safety Foundation, 1996) or correctly complete a checklist (Flight Safety Foundation, 1997).

Although the wording is scripted and predictable, we can still consider its interactional work. The effect of 'my go' is to make salient the occupation of the respective roles of PF and PNF for this takeoff and ongoing flight. It is understood by the pilots to signal the distribution of responsibilities and rights to make certain inputs for the control of the flight. The Captain's 'my go' is therefore immediately a warrant for the rest of his talk in which he specifies certain instrument settings. That is, it is because the Captain is the pilot-flying that he is entitled to say, indeed is responsible for saying, the 'ASEL' setting and so on. The First Officer's response, 'check' (9), is not only a claim to have heard and understood these details for the takeoff, but is also an acceptance of the

Captain's right to say them. Saying 'check' is the First Officer's acceptance of the role of PNF for the flight. The effect of 'my go' and the First Officer's 'check' is that the pilots become publicly accountable to one another for their understanding of who is in control of the flight, and most immediately the impending takeoff.

A little later, and as the plane taxis and nears the runway, the Captain uses both singular forms to invoke his individual roles as Captain and PF, and also plural forms to invoke the shared role of crew member and category membership of this flight:[8]

Extract 2

		(0.2)
→	C/PF	okay and I'll ah wait until we get the lineup (.) before I take the
		locks off
	FO/PNF	yep (.) transponder's on (.) check's to flight controls
→	C/PF	and you can tell him we're ready (yeah)
		(0.2)
	FO/PNF	yep
		(1.4)
	FO/PNF	*>alpha novem<ber:: (.) romeo ready*
		(1.6)
	FO/PNF	[((coughs))
	Tower	[*alpha november romeo*
		(1.2)

The Captain says 'I'll wait' and 'before I take the locks off'. The 'locks' prevent movement of the control yokes, and the lever for the locks is on the Captain's side of the cockpit. It is the Captain's responsibility to disengage the locks soon before takeoff and to re-engage them soon after landing. His use of 'I' makes salient his individual role as Captain. So 'waiting' and 'taking off the locks' are activities relevant to him and for which he is individually responsible. They are what he does as Captain on this flight. He distinguishes these activities from what 'you' will do ('you can tell him'). That is, his use of 'you' invokes the First Officer's role as PNF, because it is the PNF who is responsible for speaking to air traffic control. The Captain's talk is interpretable as not just a request, but as a request he makes of a 'pilot-not-flying'. The Captain's talk makes salient the distribution, rather than sharing, of particular duties and responsibilities.

By saying 'we're ready' the Captain, in the same turn, also invokes the shared role of crew member: readiness is something that applies to both pilots as category members of the flight. As Captain and pilot-flying he might be entitled to say 'I'm ready'. After all, he is the pilot-flying, the pilot primarily and officially in control of the takeoff, and as Captain he has the authority to decide whether or not a takeoff will continue once begun. However, his choice of pronoun does not invoke an individual role. His use of 'we' presents the takeoff as something he does not conduct alone, but together with the First Officer and pilot-not-flying. During any takeoff, the pilot-not-flying is responsible for monitoring critical cockpit instruments and making specific standard 'callouts', for example with respect to engine performance and the plane's speed as it accelerates down the runway. The Captain's use of 'we' presents the performance of the takeoff as inclusive of the pilot-not-flying. This may be an example of what Spiegelberg (1973: 132) refers to as the 'we of co-presence', where 'we' reflects a moral right to speak for another. To use 'we' is to make 'a claim to unanimity': 'whenever they hear or sing the same song together as "we" . . . each partner in his experience is conscious of the other's experiencing, co-experiences it, and identifies with it' (1973: 142–3).

There are other and perhaps more compelling senses in which the plural form 'we' is relevant. The Captain's talk is a claim of 'readiness' which can be seen to be made not only on behalf of both crew members, but also for all those on board the flight. On any flight, a Captain can decide, and then claim, that a plane is ready for takeoff only after a member of the cabin crew has informed the flight crew that the passenger cabin is prepared and 'ready' for takeoff (passengers are seated, hand luggage is stowed, and so forth). So it is not just the pilots who must be ready, but all those on board. It is the flight itself which is 'ready'. The Captain's claim of readiness occurs as a request to the pilot-not-flying to contact the controller ('you can tell him . . .') and relay this information. It is only the PNF who will speak to the controller, and so he will speak as the representative of that flight, on behalf of all those on board. The work of the controller depends upon this. The controller is concerned with the location and movement of a particular plane, identified as a flight with a particular callsign. For the controller, the relevant participant 'identity' is 'alpha november romeo', and it is not relevant or helpful for the controller to distinguish between the individual persons who happen to be flying that plane. All talk to and from the controller is identified as to or from Flight X; for example, it is X that the controller will clear for takeoff. The Captain's choice of 'we' might therefore be seen to anticipate the pilot-not-flying's subsequent talk to the controller as spokesperson for the flight.

With the plane now positioned on the runway, the pilots complete final preparations before beginning the acceleration of the takeoff. Here the talk of interest is the Captain's response to the First Officer's call of the checklist item 'takeoff clearance', and the Captain's call of 'let's go' as he moves the engine power levers to begin the takeoff:[9]

Extract 3

		(1.0)
	C/PF	>rest of the check thanks< Robbie,=
	FO/PNF	=okay: flight controls,
	C/PF	checked,
	FO/PNF	checked, and takeoff clearance
		(0.4)
→	C/PF	we have that
		(0.4)

9	FO/PNF	taxi pre-takeoff's complete
10		(0.2)
→11	C/PF	let's go::
12		(0.3)
13	FO/PNF	okay
14		(1.0)

The Captain's response is to say 'we have that'. Recalling the discussion above, the Captain's use of 'we' may be thought to invoke the shared role of crew member, or to invoke the identity of the flight as 'alpha november romeo'. First, the crew-member role is relevant because it is not enough for an *individual* pilot to receive a takeoff clearance. The pilots establish, as a crew, a *shared* understanding that takeoff clearance has been given. It is worth noting here that the world's worst airline accident, in terms of loss of life, was a 1977 runway collision of two Boeing 747 jumbo jets where there was confusion in one cockpit over whether or not takeoff clearance had been received (Cushing, 1994). Taking off without a clearance is very dangerous, and a serious professional lapse. Each pilot must know, and know that the other pilot knows, that takeoff clearance has been received. The Captain's use of 'we' makes salient that receiving the clearance is part of the pilots' joint conduct of the takeoff. The clearance is relevant to both pilots as crew members: it is not something 'I have' or 'you have', but something 'we have' as a crew. The use of 'we' reflects an orientation to a professional responsibility and accountability to share an understanding of the conditions in which the flight is jointly conducted. Similarly, the plural form in 'let's go' presents the takeoff as something both pilots do, and for which both pilots are jointly responsible, not just the particular pilot-flying.

Elsewhere in the data for this research, pilots use 'we' not just in talk to each other, but when talking *to* air traffic controllers and other external participants. For example, in addition to providing the flight's callsign, a pilot might say 'we are climbing to ten thousand feet', 'we are ready for takeoff', or 'we request a heading of 210 degrees'. The use of first person 'we' makes an unambiguous distinction between 'those of us on board Flight X' and those to whom we are sending messages, or from whom we are receiving messages. In Sacks' terms, 'we' refers to members of the category 'alpha november romeo', and it is this category membership which is most salient when talking to non-members of the category (such as controllers), or discussing what they have said.

As the plane accelerates down the runway, the pilots make standard, that is required and prescribed, callouts and responses to ensure that the plane is performing appropriately and that the takeoff is proceeding acceptably:[10]

Extract 4

1		(1.7)
2	FO/PNF	that's sixty knots, (.) a::nd powers are normal
3		(1.1)
→4	C/PF	( ) my yo::k:e,
5		(0.5)

FO/PNF check
(8.0)

Like 'my go' discussed earlier, the Captain's saying of 'my yoke' is officially required; that is, it is wording that is scripted for him in manuals which he is professionally obliged to follow. There is a control yoke on each side of the cockpit, one directly in front of each of the pilots to allow for the fact that either pilot may take the role of pilot-flying. Each yoke is able to control external moving surfaces of the plane and so control the plane's flight, for example by raising and lowering the wings or the nose of the plane to turn, climb or descend. In this sense, the control yoke can be thought of as roughly equivalent to the steering wheel of a car. According to formal procedures, only the pilot in the role of pilot-flying is to manipulate the yoke to control the plane. The pilots must therefore come to a shared understanding of who is responsible for manipulating a control yoke, that is, which pilot's yoke will be the active one. The handling of the yoke is critical for flight, especially during a takeoff, and so it is important for the rights of 'ownership' of control of the yoke to be clearly established.

By saying 'my yoke' the Captain claims the right to manipulate the yoke as the pilot-flying on this flight. Only seconds before the plane leaves the runway, this talk is an explicit reminder of the distribution of individual roles on this flight and the associated distribution of rights and responsibilities to perform particular activities to conduct the flight. As before, the First Officer's response, 'check', is meant to signal, and is heard by the Captain to signal, that he has understood and accepted the Captain's claim, as the pilot-flying, to control of the yoke. The First Officer's 'check' is followed by eight seconds of silence with no further talk about control of the yoke. The use of a personal pronoun assigns the roles of pilot-flying and pilot-not-flying and so contributes to the pilots' understandings of who is doing what during the takeoff. The pronoun makes salient that control of the yoke is not shared. The pilots' understanding of this, and specifically of who is in control this time around, is demonstrated through turns at talk in a scripted sequence during the takeoff.

The next extract occurs as the plane climbs away from the runway:[11]

Extract 5

(7.5)
C/PF gea:r up,
(7.4)
FO/PNF a:nd the gear's up,
(2.8)
C/PF flaps up,
(1.4)
WZG *Big City tower ( ) whiskey zulu golf*
(3.4)
FO/PNF flaps up,

11	*Tower*	*whiskey zulu golf* ([ ) *make your approach* (
→12	C/PF	[yeah what I was about to say was I'll leave=
13	*Tower*	)]
14	C/PF	=takeoff power on for] a whi:le.
15		(0.5)
16	FO/PNF	okay ( )

The talk of interest here is the Captain's 'I'll leave takeoff power on for a while'. The Captain uses the singular form to invoke his role as pilot-flying on this flight. The typical sequence of events for the initial climb after takeoff is for the landing gear to be raised, the wing flaps to be retracted, and then the engine power setting to be reduced from 'takeoff' to 'climb'. The reduction to 'climb power' is achieved by the pilot-not-flying pushing a button, and this activity is initiated by the pilot-flying saying 'climb power'. So while the pilot-flying decides when 'climb power' is to be selected, and initiates the task through talk, it is actually the pilot-not-flying who pushes the button to make it happen. The Captain's use of the singular form makes salient his individual role as pilot-flying to make decisions with respect to the timing of this activity. Maintaining 'takeoff power' is not just a setting, a condition in which the plane is being flown, but is the outcome of the Captain's decision as the pilot-flying.

Pushing the 'climb power' button is something the pilot-not-flying would be expecting to be called to do soon after takeoff, an activity which he would perform in his role as pilot-not-flying as part of the typical sequence of events after takeoff. The Captain's talk can be seen to be orienting to this expectation, and his own accountability as the pilot-flying for not calling for 'climb power' to be selected. Not calling for 'climb power' at the expected and appropriate time could be interpreted as an omission, as a failing in his role as the pilot-flying. The Captain's talk makes public to the pilot-not-flying that not calling for 'climb power' is not a failing, but something of which he is aware. He is acting as the pilot-flying to postpone the activity of setting 'climb power'.

As the plane becomes established in its climb the Captain engages (turns on) the autopilot, and calls for 'climb power' to be selected:[12]

Extract 6

1		(3.2)
→ 2	C/PF	I'll ta::k:::e <autopilot's in::>. (0.9) heading (.) indicated airspeed
3		A S EL one three zero >it's in the window<.
4		(0.6)
5	FO/PNF:	checked.
6		(3.0)
→ 7	C/PF	a::nd I'll take climb power.
8		(1.0)
9	*Tower*	>*alpha*< *november romeo fly heading zero six five.*
10		(2.4)
11	FO/PNF	*heading zero six five* (.) >*alpha november romeo*<.
12		(0.8)
13	C/PF	zero six fi:ve.

		(1.2)
→	FO/PNF	okay (.) and you've got climb power set.
		(0.9)
	C/PF	thank you::.
		(27.7)

In this extract the Captain twice uses singular forms and so invokes and makes salient his individual role as pilot-flying. The First Officer uses the second person form and so also invokes that role for the Captain ('you've got climb power') and makes salient his own role as pilot-not-flying. The segment begins with Captain's talk associated with the task of engaging the autopilot and the various 'modes' which will be active, that is, by which the autopilot will control the plane. The Captain's talk accompanies his physical activity of pushing some buttons, and pointing to others, to perform this task. The Captain's use of the singular form ('I'll take') presents the performance of this task as something he does as the pilot-flying. The new autopilot setting is something of particular relevance to him as the pilot-flying.

In the same way, he calls for 'climb power' to be set by saying 'I'll take climb power'. Recall from the discussion above that it is actually the pilot-not-flying who will push the appropriate button. The Captain's use of the first person singular here therefore does not make salient the physical activity of the pilot-not-flying, but his own decision as the pilot-flying to select and use 'climb power' at this time. The pilot-not-flying may well push the button, but the Captain's use of 'I' presents selecting 'climb power' as something he does as the individual in the role of pilot-flying.

IMPROMPTU PRONOUNS

In Extracts 1 and 4 ('my go', 'my yoke'), I described the use of a personal pronoun as officially prescribed, or scripted, in that it was a part of a standard wording the pilot was required to say. That is, the specific wording was included in documents such as operations manuals which tell the pilots how they must perform certain tasks. However, what is interesting to note from some of the examples above is that pilots' talk may include personal pronouns where there are none in the officially prescribed wording. The personal pronouns are not in the script, but are impromptu. For example, the standard call to initiate the task of selecting climb power is simply for the pilot-flying to say 'climb power', and the standard response for the pilot-not-flying, after pushing the appropriate button, is simply to say 'climb power set'. During this particular takeoff, however, the pilot-flying actually says 'and I'll take climb power', and the pilot-not-flying actually says 'and you've got climb power set'. Similarly, in Extract 3, as the pilots complete the taxi pre-takeoff checklist, the pilot-not-flying calls the item 'takeoff clearance' to which the pilot-flying responds 'we have that', when the prescribed response is simply to say 'received'. Even in the highly scripted and economical wording of a checklist, a personal pronoun may be chosen. Such uses of personal pronouns are modifications, or embellishments, of prescribed wordings. What might the interactional effect of these pronouns be?

It may be that impromptu pronouns are an important part of pilots continually creating their work, in this high-technology setting, as human work, and creating themselves as more than just the facilitators of technological events, as participants in an interaction and not mere adjuncts to cockpit technology. It must be said that, without using a personal pronoun, a pilot can make a claim to a particular role, and be heard to be speaking in that role. That is, the Captain can, merely by virtue of saying particular talk, claim the role of pilot-flying. For example it is only the pilot-flying who can initiate the setting of climb power by first saying 'climb power'. To say 'climb power' first, before any activity to push a button, is to make a claim to be entitled to say it, and be heard to be talking in (claiming) the role of pilot-flying. However, the additional use of a personal pronoun serves to explicitly reinforce that 'this is who I am now', for example that 'I'm the one requesting climb power and that setting is for me because I am the pilot-flying'.

A number of the pilots I flew with were somewhat puzzled by my interest in recording their talk. They assured me that everything they said was 'in the manual'. From the examples above, it is clear that pilots produce talk which is not prescribed, and indeed often their talk modifies prescribed and legally enforceable wordings. Personal pronouns appear in pilots' talk as prescribed wordings are produced by actual pilots faced with the real-time demands of interacting with one another as they perform the tasks required to fly the plane. That is, personal pronouns occur as prescribed wordings move from the printed page to become naturally-occurring talk in the airline cockpit. The effect of the pronouns is that pilots' talk continues to present the participants involved, and their relevant roles, where the prescribed wordings may leave these implicit. It may be that retaining scope to improvise in this and other ways is an important resource for pilots in unusual or crisis situations where prescribed wording is inadequate, inappropriate, or simply unavailable.[13]

CONCLUSION

In this chapter, I have explored the interactional significance of personal pronouns in the talk of airline pilots. Personal pronouns come out of grammatical hiding and into the socio-technical setting of the airline cockpit. I have suggested that personal pronouns allow pilots to invoke, and make salient, relevant individual or shared cockpit roles. That is, personal pronouns make salient who a pilot is 'speaking as' moment-to-moment during a flight: pronominal choices contribute to the pilots' understanding of who's who in the cockpit. I have shown that while some pronouns are scripted in officially prescribed wording, others occur as embellishments of such wordings. If we agree with Wortham (1994) that there is value in looking at pronominal choices not in isolation but over stretches of talk, then it might be that exploring pilots' pronominal choices can reveal how cockpit leadership, crew harmony, and a sense of who is in control of the plane, for example, are built through talk. The industry has become increasingly concerned with such issues. For example, a pilot-flying who regularly invokes a shared crew (flight) role where the prescribed wording leaves this implicit (for example, 'we have that' rather than 'received'), or where it may be legitimate to invoke the individual pilot-flying role, may be perceived as more inclusive, as fostering a sense of partnership or teamwork between the pilots.

Notes

1. I am very grateful to Qantas Airways and Skywest Airlines for allowing me to film their pilots on scheduled flights. My research has been supported by an Australian Postgraduate Award, grants from the Faculty Grants Committee of the Australian National University and the International Graduate School in Language and Communication at Odense University in Denmark, and an M. A. K. Halliday Scholarship from the Applied Linguistics Association of Australia. For helpful comments on a draft of this chapter I am grateful to Alec McHoul, and for their general advice and support for my research I thank Tony Liddicoat at the Australian National University and Johannes Wagner at Odense University.
2. *Editors' note*: Any reader still in doubt about this matter should consult: <http://www.flightsafety.org/ap_2000.html>.
3. Both aircraft types on which I collected data had two crew members.
4. Other terms for this distinction are 'manipulating pilot' vs. 'support pilot', or 'P1' vs. 'P2'.
5. See discussions of 'situation awareness' in the aviation literature in, for example, the journal *Human Factors* 37(1), 1995.
6. These traditional treatments of pronouns are explained below in the section 'Personal pronouns come out of hiding'.
7. 'My go' is a version of the more typical 'my departure', referring to the control of this takeoff; 'go-around' is an engine power setting; 'ASEL' is an abbreviation of 'altitude select', which is a mode used by the autopilot; 'left autopilot command' means that the autopilot is under command of the pilot on the left of the cockpit (the Captain); 'engine failure as discussed' means that the pilots have previously discussed action to be taken in the event of an engine failure.
8. 'Get the lineup' is to receive permission from air traffic control to enter the runway and line up ready for takeoff; the 'locks' prevent the control yokes from moving (see discussion below); the 'transponder' allows them to be identified by air traffic control radar; 'check's to flight controls' means that the crew have worked through the relevant checklist up to the item 'flight controls'; 'you can tell him we're ready' – 'him' is the air traffic controller monitoring them; 'ready' means prepared and able to enter the runway; 'alpha november romeo ready' – the FO/PNF contacts by radio the controller in the tower; 'alpha november romeo' – the controller in the tower replies to the FO/PNF's call. Saying the flight's callsign in this way is common practice to indicate the message has been heard and understood.

9. 'Rest of the check thanks' is a call for the pilot-not-flying to resume calling items from an incomplete checklist; 'flight controls' is the next item on the checklist and refers to the control yokes; 'takeoff clearance' is the last item on the checklist and refers to permission from air traffic control to take off; 'we have that' means that 'clearance' to take off has been received; 'taxi pre-takeoff's complete' claims that the 'taxi pre-takeoff' checklist has been completed; 'let's go' announces intention to begin the takeoff.
10. 'That's sixty knots' refers to the plane's speed; 'powers are normal' means the engines are performing appropriately; 'yoke' refers to the 'control yoke' (discussed below).
11. 'Gear up' is a request to the PNF to raise the landing gear (wheels and assemblies), achieved by moving a lever in the cockpit; 'and the gear's up' informs the PF that the landing gear has been raised; 'Big City tower whiskey zulu golf' is an overheard radio transmission from a plane with callsign 'whiskey zulu golf' to the control tower controller; 'flaps up' is a request to the PNF to retract the wing flaps, achieved by moving a lever in the cockpit; 'flaps up' informs the PF that the PNF has retracted the wing flaps; 'whiskey zulu golf make your approach . . .' is an overheard radio transmission from the tower controller to a plane with the callsign 'whiskey zulu golf'; 'leave takeoff power on' means to maintain the engine power used for the takeoff.
12. 'Autopilot's in . . .', autopilot is engaged (turned on); 'heading' is a mode for the autopilot – the autopilot will maintain a specific directional heading for the plane; 'indicated airspeed' is a mode for the autopilot – the autopilot will maintain a specific speed for the plane; 'ASEL' is short for 'altitude select' and is a mode for the autopilot – the plane will climb to and then maintain a selected altitude; 'one three zero' is the selected altitude (thirteen thousand feet); 'it's in the window' – the altitude '130' has been selected in the relevant display; 'climb power' is an engine power setting.
13. See, for example, the cockpit voice recorder transcripts in accident reports in MacPherson (1998).

6 Reporting a service request

Ann Kelly

EDITORIAL

When members of the public use the telephone to request services of city council staff, the recipient of the call is required to make a judgement as to whether the problem falls within the ambit of council responsibilities and, if this is the case, engage in a negotiating process to ensure that the request is framed appropriately as a customer service request. In this chapter, four texts, all relating to the one request, are analysed to show:

- *how a problem is described by the caller in the course of the interaction;*
- *the particular ways it becomes formulated by the call taker and, in one instance, re-formulated by the caller during the course of the interaction;*
- *the match between these formulations and, initially, the handwritten notes recorded by the call taker and, subsequently, the text of a telephone conversation with an engineer who has responsibility to address the request;*
- *how the service request form acts as a critical resource in structuring all stages of the process of summarizing and detailing the problem to meet the organizational conventions of recording and acting on it.*

By minutely examining the details of how this complaint is dealt with by a council employee, Ann Kelly is able to track the various transformations that occur between the caller's initial account, the call taker's uptake of it, the relaying of the complaint to an engineer and, in between all of these things, the written record or documentation of the complaint. Accordingly we see how a fairly strong allegation of council neglect becomes progressively downgraded as the account is bureaucratized – so that fault and fault-attribution become potentially diminished as an official account is constructed.

Each transformation may, in its own right, appear relatively minor. For example, initial reference to a 'man with a bobcat' (a description readily connectable to council workers) is progressively downgraded to 'someone' (a description with no such connectivity). But, as all of the transformations are traced and considered, the very nature of the account alters in subtle ways. And, as Kelly notes, this may have to do with the council's own involvement in the nature of the problem.

So, is what we are seeing here, via Kelly's fine-grained analysis, the actual means whereby a bureaucratic organization protects its interests by deflecting 'allegations' into apparently minor 'problems'? Kelly quite rightly does not jump to this conclusion – or, at least, not quite. But the analysis does clearly provide a template for how applied CA can be used to track important bureaucratic transformations of how callers account for everyday troubles – in this case, a mound of sand blocking their passage to a beach. And further, for Kelly, this genre of CA may have significant implications for the curricula of vocational training, in so far as its fine tracking can be applied to developing trainees' report-handling skills.

INTRODUCTION

It is conventional that requests for services, enacted via the medium of the telephone within the city council authority that is the focus of this study, must be rendered into specific categories, syntactic forms and registers that align with the specifications of the customer service request form developed for recording such communications (Figure 6.1). However, these requirements are not necessarily known to the requester of the service and are not made explicit by the call taker. Thus, this rendering is never a straightforward process and may be heard as involving a number of different strategies that are adopted by both the caller and call taker to ensure that there is agreement about the information that is recorded.[1]

In this chapter, I show how the form used to record the caller's service request might be perceived as providing an organizational structure in two initial stages in the documentation of requests for services: first, during the management of the call by the trainee and her simultaneous recording of notes of the call; and secondly, in a reporting telephone call to a council engineer. This work has relevance to at least three fields of study. Within CA, it extends earlier findings derived from telephone interactions between citizens and police/ fire departments (Gilsinan, 1989; Sharrock and Turner, 1978; Whalen and Zimmerman, 1987, 1990; Zimmerman, 1992a, 1992b). Within the broader sociological field, it demonstrates how texts are implicated in enacting social practices and our understanding of them (Hak, 1998; Smith, 1984, 1990a, 1990b). Lastly, within the vocational education field, it builds on studies by researchers such as Billett (1992, 1994), Darrah (1997), Hull (1992), Kusterer (1978), Mulcahy (1995) and Searle (1996) who have been focusing on developing understandings of workplace practices in order to design training programs that are relevant to learners.

NEGOTIATING THE PROBLEM

In the transcript of the request call, the process of describing and negotiating the nature of the call occurred over three distinct sequences. These are reproduced below. In some cases, fragments of other work that is being done prior to or following the descriptions have been included. The symbol 'C' denotes the complainant and 'T' is the level-three city council administrative trainee who is

Records File No:

Customer Service Request | 12301

Provider Services

Works

Foreshores

Property No

Requestor

Name: Jane Smith Address: Telephone: 5492 4076	Recorded on: 10-Sep-1998 by: Brown, Deborah Allocated to: Goodwin, Dave on: 10-Sep-1998

Location

Detail: James, Sunshine Beach
Extra Detail: 6 Princess Street

Summary	
Bobcat pushed mound of sand from fence – now in middle of driveway.	

Details	
Apparently the bobcat has pushed the mound of sand from the fence and it is now sitting in the middle of the walkway. She said that she has trouble getting up the walkway and the mound of dirt makes the walkway inaccessible as it is too steep. Please investigate and arrange appropriate action. Thankyou	

Figure 6.1 Completed service request form

responsible for accepting or rejecting the request and, in instances of acceptance (the majority), of recording a summary and specified details of the problem as well as other details not addressed in this chapter. In addition, she typically assures the caller that action will ensue. In Extract 1, the complaint is made:

Extract 1[2]

1	C	an older pe:rson [(.) and I I can not get up other than craw:l up no:w (.)
2	T	[okay
3	T	okay what have they done ma'm [(.) (what's the problem . . .)
4	C	[they've lowered the bobcat and and
5		ah got the sand from the the footpath side and pushed it over onto
6		the beach (.) and they've made the pathway
7		down on to the beach in a corner of James Street (.)
8		just not not possible for anyone to walk up and do:wn it (.)
9	T	okay so it's too steep
		.
		.
		.
17	T	okay so the bobcat's pushed this sand on to the beach
18	T	[and it's made it
19	C	[and it's pushed it over the pathway down on to the beach (.)
		.
		.
		.
59	T	just to get this clear they've actually pushed the (.) pushed the dirt
60		from [the footpath
61	C	[the sand
62	T	yeh (.) sand from the footpath
63	C	yeh
64	T	the (.) is this the footpath
65	C	well [it's not actually a footpath (.) you know the fence that goes alon:g (.)
66	T	[to the beach or is the foot the walkway
67		(1.0)
68	C	they have pushed the sand over that but they've also pushed it over
69		the walkway (.)
70	T	o:kay
71		(3.0)
72	T	so what what what's actually blocking the walkway
73	C	sand=
74	T	that makes it [un
75	C	[a mou:nd of sa:nd=
76	T	=mound of sand=
77	C	=mound where he has tipped it off this morning
78		(2.0)
79	T	and he's just left it there (.)
80	C	yeh [that's right
81	T	[in the middle of the walkway
82		exactly (.)
83	T	o:kay

Bobcat – sand pushed onto beach
over the patway onto
too steep the beach
Opp. James St – Sunshine Beach
walkway to beach not accessible
mand of sand – left in the middle of walkway
Jane Smith – Holidaying
5492 4076

Figure 6.2 Trainee's notes of call

In contrast to other request calls in my corpus where the nature of the problem is foregrounded by the caller in the sequence of the talk immediately following the greeting, in this example the caller moves directly to an expression of warrant for making the request.[3] While the response of 'okay' by the trainee at the first pause in the caller's turn might be interpreted, on first glance at the extract, as a continuer, her intention becomes clear when 'okay' is repeated as the first word of her turn in line 3. It is evident that listening to a detailed reasoning for the call is not the initial item on the trainee's agenda which, I argue, derives from the customer service request form. Rather, she can be heard to be interested in focusing on the nature of the request. Thus, in line 3, at the first opportunity to talk that is allowed her, she asks directly: 'what have they done ma'm'. Her use of the third person 'they' is noticeable in the query. Because the early part of the call is missing, it is impossible to know whether there has been a previous reference to council workers as being the agents of the caller's problem. In addition, it is also noticeable that the call taker addresses the caller as 'Ma'm', a culturally respectful, though unusual form that indicates she is aware at this stage of the caller's self-reference as an 'older person' in line 1 but, as yet, has not been furnished with a more personal form of address.

In her response (4–7), the caller begins by narrating a three-stage sequence that she appears to have observed being enacted (Riessman, 1993). First, 'they' 'lowered the bobcat'; secondly, 'they' 'got the sand from the footpath side'; and finally, 'they' 'pushed it over onto the beach'. This final process is recorded as the essence of the problem by the trainee: 'Bobcat – sand pushed onto beach'. (See first line of text in Figure 6.2.) The use of the term 'bobcat' is significant because bobcats are part of council equipment and are likely to be used for the purpose of pushing sand on the foreshore, the maintenance of which is a council responsibility.

The detailing of the problem resumes with a formulation (Heritage and Watson, 1979) by the trainee (17). She again uses the marker 'okay' to indicate to the caller that she is changing the topic and introduces her formulation with the disjunct marker 'so': 'so, the bobcat's pushed this sand on to the beach'. The linguistic form that she chooses for this summation (17) closely resembles the first line of the summation on the notes that she has taken during the earlier detailing sequence: 'Bobcat – sand pushed onto the beach' (see Figure 6.2). However, she is interrupted from continuing with her detailing by an elaboration of the problem by the caller: 'it's pushed it over the pathway on to the beach'. This additional information is recorded by the trainee and can be seen on lines 2–3 of her notes: 'over the patway [*sic*] onto the beach' (see Figure 6.2).

The final detailing of the problem can be observed between lines 59 and 83 of the transcript. Again, the trainee uses a summary marker, 'just to get this clear', to make explicit to the caller that she is returning to this topic. She then begins a formulation: 'They've actually pushed the dirt from the footpath', which is noticeable for two aspects. First, we can note her use of 'actually'. In other data (Kelly, 1999), I have found that the use of this modifier in request-making stresses the *facticity* of the action that has been perpetrated.[4] This would appear to be the purpose for its use here as well. The second aspect that is noticeable to the caller is the trainee's substitution of 'dirt' for 'sand'. This is immediately corrected by the caller and accepted by the trainee in two ways in her next turn (62). First, she affirms the correction by the use of 'yeh' and then repeats it in her reformulation: 'the sand from the footpath'.

At this point (64, 66), the trainee diverts from formulating a summary and seeks clarification as to whether the 'footpath' or the 'walkway' is the major site of the problem. In response, the caller digresses in an attempt to correct the trainee's use of the notion of 'footpath' and situates the phenomenon relative to 'the fence that goes along'. This is followed by a pause which might be interpreted by an analyst as indicating that the caller recognizes that her meaning remains unclear. Whalen comments that such pauses may reflect a desire on the part of the caller to produce a 'story that will "work"' (1995: 228), that is, be perceived as a reportable matter. The caller in this case then returns to the strategy of narrating the events leading up to the problem: 'They have pushed the sand over that [the fence] but they've also pushed it over the walkway'. The trainee responds with an acceptance token of 'okay', spoken in an elongated way.

The trainee isn't quite satisfied, though, and after a three-second silence, seeks further clarification in her question (72): 'so what what's actually blocking the walkway?'. Again, we see the use of the modifier, 'actually', and again it appears to be used to determine facticity. The trainee's choice of the present participle, 'blocking', is also notable. It encompasses an appreciation of inaccessibility to the beach via the walkway. The content of the question, however, seems illogical when the substance of the problem has consistently been stated by the caller as 'sand'. The recognition of this illogicality can be heard in the

Table 6.1 Comparison of formulations in the talk and the text in the written notes

Formulations			Notes
Line	Speaker	Words	Words
17	T	so the bobcat's pushed this sand on to the beach	Bobcat – sand pushed onto beach
19	C	over the pathway down to the beach	over the patway [*sic*] onto the beach
30 35	T T	a walkway to the beach it's not accessible	walkway to beach not accessible
76 79 81	T T T	mound of sand and he's just left it there in the middle of the walkway	mand [*sic*] of sand – left in the middle of walkway

stress that is placed by the caller on her confirmation that it is *sand* that is the source of the problem. Yet, while sand is a major item throughout the talk, it is only at this point that it appears to become clear to the trainee that it is *sand* that is obstructing the walkway, indeed, 'a mound of sand' (75–77) which was deposited and 'just left' (79) in 'the middle of the walkway' (81). This clarification is also recorded by the trainee in the notes that she is taking (see Figure 6.2: 'mand [*sic*] of sand – left in the middle of walkway').

In examining these notes, it can be seen that there is a close match between the oral formulations by the trainee and the words that are recorded. In only one instance are the caller's words transferred to the notes (19) when she appropriates the formulating task (Table 6.1).

Through this tracking of the interweaving of the different textual forms used in this interaction, it might be argued that the categories comprising the customer service request form – two of which are relevant here (the Summary and the Details) – along with the use of particular syntactic structures and register that have become normative practice within this city council, are critical factors in orienting the trainee to participate in bureaucratic request-making.

In the next section, I show how the notes that were developed during the call with the holiday-maker also serve to orient the conversational work that is accomplished by the trainee in reporting, via the telephone, the nature of the problem to the engineer (E) responsible for foreshore maintenance (Extract 2). The engineer does not have a copy of the trainee's notes. At this point, the customer service request form has not been completed.

CALLING THE ENGINEER

Extract 2

7	T	. . . umm have you been doing any works out at (.) um (1.0) Sunshine
8		Beach this morning (.) on the beach (.) on the foreshore area
9	E	yes I have
10	T	you ha:ve (.) [umm (1.0) I've just had a resident call in (.)
11	E	[yes
12	E	yes
13	T	and she said (.) apparently (.) did (.) did you push a (.) she said someone
14		pushed some sand (.) like (.) with a bobcat they (.) [have
15	E	[yes (.) off the fence
16	T	ye:h
17	E	yeh (.) that was early this morning (.)
18	T	ye:h
19	E:	yeh
20	T	apparently she said (.) she's not happy because there's a mound
21		of sand left in the middle of the walkway and it makes the walkway
22		(.) um unaccessible
23	E	w-
24		(1.0)
25		nah what's she talking about (.) which walkway
26	T	opposite James Street (.) at Sunshine Beach
27		(1.0)
28	E	opposite James Street
29	T	yeh
30		(1.0)
31	E	a::::h
32		(2.0)
33	E	I'll slip down and have a look (.) I've had the (.) ah (.) she actually
34		definitely said it was the bobcat
35		(1.0)
36	T	yes she said it was a bobcat
37		(1.0)
38	T	it's probably about six inches high Deb (.) she's got to step over it (.)
39	T	o::::h o:kay (.)

In opening the interactive sequence focusing on the details of the problem, the trainee initially uses a circumlocutionary strategy. This is evidenced by first, her adoption of a very tentative and general question about the department's activities in the area of Sunshine Beach, namely: 'Umm have you been doing any works out at Sunshine Beach this morning?' (7–8). It is noticeable that the engineer fails to take up the opportunity to respond during the two pauses in this turn, the second of which is quite lengthy. In response to this silence, the trainee specifies the location of the 'works' in a little more detail.

There are parallels between this introduction to the topic and one that is presented by Heritage (1984b) in discussing the *pre-sequence* strategies people use to ensure that 'forms of accounting' do not threaten the 'face' (Goffman, 1955) of either party or the relationship between them:

((S's wife has just slipped a disc.))
H And we were wondering if there's anything
we can do to help
S [Well 'at's]
H [I mean] can we do any shopping for her
or something like tha:t?
(0.7)
S Well that's most ki:nd Heatherton .hhh At the moment
→ no:. because we've still got two bo:ys at home
(Heritage, 1984b: 271)

While, in Heritage's example, the questioner becomes more specific in her second turn, there are five turns subsequent to the opening one taken by the trainee in my example before the walkway problem is articulated in any complete sense. The particular forms that the turns take have the effect of gaining a continuing affirmative response until the final turn describing the problem (20–23) brings some transparency to its nature. The formulation of the problem by the trainee at this point elicits a denial from the engineer and subsequent questions about the specific location of the problem. Table 6.2 shows the patterning of this sequence of turns by both the trainee and the engineer in accomplishing the oral reporting of the problem.

These turns take both question and statement forms, the latter appearing to serve slightly more strongly as accusatory utterances. For example, in forming up the pre-sequence to the report, the trainee adopts a questioning form (7–8, 10). Similarly, she intersperses her statement fragments (10 and 13) with a question which is also affirmed by the engineer. As noted above, another feature of the trainee's talk is its tentativeness. As well as using pauses and hesitation markers such as 'umm', she chooses three other forms of tentativeness. First, the modal 'apparently' (in the sense of 'ostensibly') is displayed twice (13, 20) in the interaction and serves to mitigate the gravity of the problem. Secondly, the trainee does not direct culpability for the problem to the engineer. This is evidenced by her substitution of the pronoun 'someone' for the explicit term 'man' used by the caller. Further, contrary to the caller's specificity of a man '*with* a bobcat', the trainee lessens the force of this assertion by the inclusion of the *approximate* term, 'like'. It is only when the problem is formulated specifically (20–22) that there is a display of negation by the engineer. This encapsulation of the problem matches very closely the description of the problem on the latter section of her notes (see Table 6.3).

Thus, in the process of engagement in the task of redesigning the nature of the problem so that action can ensue, the notes generated from the formulating work, undertaken primarily by the trainee, become an *active* text (Smith, 1984). The specific details that are displayed on these notes also resemble those

Table 6.2 Pattern of turns in negotiating responsibility for the walkway problem

Trainee			Engineer		
Line	**Text**	**Type of turn**	**Line**	**Text**	**Type of turn**
7–8	. . . umm have you been doing any works out at (.) um (1.0) Sunshine Beach this morning (.) on the beach (.) on the foreshore area	Question	9	yes I have	Affirmative statement
10	you ha:ve (.) umm (1.0)	Question +	11	yes	Affirmative statement
10	I've just had a resident call in (.)	Declarative statement	12	yes	Affirmative statement
13	and she said (.) apparently (.)	Declarative statement +			
13	did(.) did you push a (.)	Question			
13–14	she said someone pushed some sand (.) like (.) with a bobcat they (.) have	Declarative statement	15	yes +	Affirmative statment
			15	off the fence	Declarative statement
16	ye:h	Affirmative statement	17	yeh (.) +	Affirmative statement
			17	that was early this morning (.)	Affirmative statement
18	ye:h	Affirmative statement	19	yeh	Affirmative statement
20–22	apparently she said (.) she's not happy because there's a mound of sand left in the middle of the walkway and it makes the walkway (.) um unaccessible	Declarative statement	23–25	w- (1.0) nah	Negative statement
			25	what's she talking about (.) which walkway	Question

Table 6.3 Comparison of oral text 'reported' by the trainee to the engineer with that recorded on her notes

Telephone report	Notes
There's a mound of sand left in the middle of the walkway and it makes the walkway (.) um unaccessible [*sic*].	Walkway to beach not accessible. Mand [*sic*] of sand – left in the middle of walkway

written on the customer service request form. On the one hand, I believe they are heavily influenced by features of the form, but in turn, also influence the content, syntactic structures and register of the text that is placed on the form. That is, they play a constitutive role in the bureaucratization of a request. In the next section, I examine the form that relates to this request to show how elements of the other texts that comprise this interaction are manifested in this document.

RENDERING THE REQUEST

The notes detailing the request that were taken during the call with the holiday-maker appear to have assumed a second life by their incorporation into the customer service request form. With the exception of the introduction of the fence as the original location of the sand, and the substitution of 'left' for 'now', the *summary* statement ('Bobcat pushed mound of sand from fence – now in middle of walkway') appears to comprise elements of a refrain that have been assembled slightly differently for each reporting occasion by the trainee. That is, these elements can be heard in both calls.

The first sentence within the *Details* section is an extension of the summary; except that there is a significant change of register in its rendering. The allegational nature of the reporting of the problem that was evident in the trainee's call to the engineer has been retained through her use of 'apparently'. This strategy is not typical of the detailing of the problems recorded by the trainee in my corpus. One reason for such an aberration might be the central role played by the council in this particular situation. In contrast to the other examples in my collection, there is a covert allegation by this caller of council negligence and this may serve as a stimulus for an immediate follow-up call to the person responsible for this transgression and in turn, for the assumption of scepticism that is adopted informally during the call by the engineer, but formally by the trainee in documenting the problem.

In tracking the roles that the two written texts play in this interaction, I have tried to show how pivotal and recursive their influence is in transforming a request by someone outside their bureaucracy into an official form that can be acted upon. Below, I discuss the pervasiveness and power of institutional texts in more detail.

INSTITUTIONAL TEXTS AND WORK PRACTICES

Dorothy Smith (1974) presents a case for 'the social construction of documented reality'. Like other ethnomethodologists (Cicourel, 1968; Wieder, 1974a) she claims that texts are not neutral but *actively* directed and organized social practices. The following passage from a later paper exemplifies this position:

> Texts are seen as active constituents of the social relations of public textual discourse. Texts organise relations within textual discourse in *active* ways, both with respect to how local happenings are entered into its interpretive practices and how its social relations are organised. (Smith, 1990b: 123)

In this chapter, I have shown how a form that has been developed for the purpose of recording the service requests of a city council can be used to *organize* the orientation of the description of a problem between a caller and call taker, specifically through the latter's use of formulations. I have also demonstrated the direct links between these formulations, the notes that were handwritten by the trainee and the oral text that was chosen by the trainee to report the problem to the engineer responsible for its rectification. Finally, in coming full circle, it can be observed that the content of the completed customer service request form is strongly influenced by the trainee's notes and the interpretive stances taken by both the trainee and the council engineer.

Yet, despite the integral part that texts play in bureaucratizing customers' requests for services in this council office, it is noticeable that the only reference to texts that is evident in the 'unit of competency' that has been endorsed as representing the skills and knowledge that competent level-three clerical trainees should demonstrate – that is, the ability to 'process client complaints (requests) to ensure the goals of the enterprise are met' (*National Clerical-Administrative Competency Standards: Private Sector*, 1997: 67; see the Appendix) – is that '*necessary documentation* [*sic*] is finalised' (emphasis in original). There is no mention of the role that this 'documentation' inevitably *must* play in organizing the way the complaint (problem, in this case) is structured and recorded.

Although studies such as this one can add to knowledge about work practices within both CA and mainstream sociology, it is even more important that this work is taken up by other researchers within the vocational education field. CA approaches have particular relevance at this time when syllabuses and curricula have been removed from the training framework and assessors are expected to interpret the separate elements of competency and their related performance criteria to meet local requirements. If specific texts are critical in this process, as I have shown them to be in this particular case, then to ignore their organizing potential would result in a failure to understand the institutional practice of service request reporting *per se*.

Notes

1. A similar conclusion relating to telephone complaint-making has been noted by Eglin and Wideman (1986) and Whalen *et al.* (1988).
2. Omitted lines (indicated by ellipses) have the following character. The talk between lines 9 and 17 comprises warrants proffered by the caller to legitimize her right to report the problem (Eglin and Wideman, 1986). Although the constitution of warranting the complaint is not a focus of this chapter, other authors (Meehan, 1986; Sharrock and Turner, 1978; Whalen and Zimmerman, 1987) have shown how this process is integral to determining the *seriousness* of a problem. The remainder of line 19 and continuing to line 23, lines 39 to 40, and lines 51 to 54 are characterized by further warrants by the requester that are met with single continuers by the trainee. In line 24, using the disjunction marker (Maynard, 1991), 'okay', the trainee changes the topic to a determination of the location of the problem (24–38) and the elicitation of relevant information about the caller (43–49):

43	T	okay what was your name ma'm
44	C	I'm Jane Smith
45		(1.0)
46	T	Jane Smith=
47	C	=yes and I'm staying (.) if you want my phone number
48	T	uh huh (.)
49	C	five four nine two (.) four oh seven six

3. Zimmerman (1984) and Whalen and Zimmerman (1987) have noted that this positioning of the provision of the reason for the call was also usual in their data.
4. My use of *facticity* differs somewhat from that of Meehan (1986) and Smith (1990b).

APPENDIX

Unit of competency: Process client complaints to ensure the goals of the enterprise are met

Element of competency	*Performance criteria*
Clarify the nature of the complaint (problem)	Details of the complaint (problem) are established Summary of inconvenience to the client is recorded accurately Any inconvenience to the client is acknowledged and any apology is made if appropriate
Identify options for complaint (problem) resolution	Appropriate options for resolving the complaint (problem) are identified Complaint (problem) referred to *designated officer* if resolution not possible
Act to resolve complaint (problem)	Optimal solution is negotiated with the client Chosen solution is implemented within agreed *time frame* *Necessary documentation* is finalised Effectiveness of solution and related outcomes is evaluated Any necessary changes to *enterprise procedures* are identified and passed on to *relevant person* for action

Source: *National Clerical-Administrative Competency Standards: Private Sector*, 1997: 67

7 Applying membership categorization analysis to chat-room talk

Rhyll Vallis

EDITORIAL

As we have seen already from Maurice Nevile's chapter, to be able to talk to, and about, the many persons we come into contact with every day, we have to be able, somehow, to grasp and deploy appropriate ways of referring to them. This may not seem to be much of an issue; but it becomes one when we consider that any given person can be referred to in an indefinite number of ways. Someone could be, correctly, referred to as 'Henry's mother', 'a great pool player', 'the bank manager', and so forth. The list is, as noted, indefinite. So the 'truth' of the matter is rarely relevant when it comes to describing people. What is *relevant is that our descriptions – whether through the use of 'categories' (roughly, ways of naming people) or through 'predicates' (equally roughly, ways of saying what they do) should be seen as both situationally relevant and culturally coherent. The study of these matters is called 'membership categorization analysis' (MCA).*

In this chapter, Rhyll Vallis shows how such categories and predicates get to be clustered (collected into 'membership categorization devices' or MCDs) so that, in effect, people can know (through mutual and/or conflicting descriptions of themselves and others) that they are 'talking' about the same (or different) things. In her collection of 'talk', she shows how 'who does what' and 'who is who' are distinctly related, if (and the 'if' is important) contestable.

The analysis in this chapter centres around an internet chat room. And what is remarkable about Vallis's analysis is that – even though the 'actual persons' are anonymized, and even though the 'talk' is actually a form of keyboard typing (such that the sequencing of the talk is radically different from live face-to-face conversation because of the electronically mediated timing of each participant's turn) – the 'speakers' still achieve identities for themselves, for each other, and even for absent parties through membership categorization.

In any form of membership categorization, as is now well known in MCA, to use a particular category from a device (or else to use one of its related predicates) is to get moral *work done (Jayyusi, 1984). In selecting such ways of referring to people, any selection is rarely neutral in the moral sense. And, given that predicates imply categories and vice versa, talk can turn out to be very subtle indeed.*

One might think that computer-based forms of communication – like chat rooms, e-mail or discussion groups – would be so 'wooden' or 'robotic' as to delete such 'lived' conversational subtleties. But Vallis shows that, even in this extremely 'controlled' environment, the complexities of MCD use prevail. Indeed, they (along with their critical implications for moral positioning) seem to be essential to the accomplishment of this variety of communication – so much so, perhaps, that the very idea that these environments are 'controlled' is one of the matters that participants can and do 'discuss' inside the chat rooms themselves. This makes internet relay chats (IRCs) ultra-rich in their visible dependence on MCDs. At the end of the day, the amazing possibilities of talk do not depend, even today, on computing – if anything, vice versa.

INTRODUCTION

This chapter seeks to provide an illustration of how MCA might be used in order to investigate how the orderliness of a recognizable phenomenon was achieved. The phenomenon is that of 'Users complaining about ops in a chat room'. The data (Extract 1) consists of a software file (log) of an extended segment of 'chat' within a chat room. The main focus is on how participants accomplish moral identities in their talk despite the seeming 'anonymity' provided by their communicative medium. Below, then, is a brief explanation of internet relay chat (IRC). The following sections consist of data analysis that applies Sacks' concepts of category and predicate (activity descriptor) for the purpose of explicating how members accomplish moral identities.

WHAT IS IRC?

IRC is a distinct form of computer-mediated communication generally less well known than other forms such as e-mail and discussion lists. IRC users type messages that are relayed, often within the space of a second, by a server to multiple users who are present within the same channel. Private messages may also be communicated using certain commands. Unlike MUDs (multi-user dungeons), the purpose of most chat rooms is just that: chatting rather than gaming or role play; although aspects of role play and MUD conventions and terminology can also be found in chat rooms. Channel participants treat the typed messages that accumulate on the channel screen space as 'conversation' (see Appendix 1).

GUIDE TO THE DATA

Computer-recorded log files of 'chat' occurring in a chat room are used as data. The extract used here is part of a much larger recorded conversation that begins with the researcher joining the channel and ends with her quitting. The topic of 'ops' (channel operators) has been used here to delimit the beginning and end of the extract. The extract was chosen because it was categorization-dense and could be used to exemplify the application of a spectrum of MCA concepts. A glossary (Appendix 2) is provided for those unfamiliar with chat-room terminology. A print-out of the chat-room screen as it appears to users is also provided in the appendices to facilitate understanding of the talk and activity. Lines have been numbered by the researcher for the purposes of this analysis only and do not appear on the chat-room screen.

As a guide to reading the log of chat below, readers should keep in mind the following points:

- '[16:35]' is the time the turn appeared on the researcher's screen given in hours and minutes.
- An alias (e.g. '<Elle_Elle>') prefixes each speaker's turn, as in script dialogue.
- Messages do not appear in the channel as they are being constructed, only when entered by users. This means that users cannot anticipate one another's turns.
- A phenomenon known as 'lag' means that some users are slower to receive messages than others and thus may appear to produce irrelevant turns but these are actually related to much earlier turns. This leads to the next point.
- Turns related to one another and pair parts may not be strictly adjacent. To make sense of what has inspired a turn (and whether it is a second pair part or not) look for lexical repetition, recipient address and read back in order to find turns that may have made a response conditionally relevant. Usually a turn-taking system between two or three speakers will emerge and you can follow their conversational 'thread'.
- ***, as in line 15, signifies auto-text such as a join message (see Appendix 2).
- # indicates a channel name. Thus '#Brisbane' means the channel called 'Brisbane'.

DATA

1 [16:35] <Elle_Elle> what does @ before ur names mean???
2 [16:35] <Vetman> i think it means neo nazi
3 [16:35] <Vetman> jokes
4 [16:35] <SideshowB'AtWork> Elle_Elle: it means we have power over
5 everyone else – we can kick and ban people, etc
11 [16:36] <Elle_Elle> how do u get it??
12 [16:36] <|ColdFusion|> U don't get it in this channel
13 [16:37] <SideshowB'AtWork> you get it from being here for quite
14 a long time, and getting along very well with other ops
15 [16:37] *** MigraineBoy (dialup11) has joined #brisbane
16 [16:37] <Elle_Elle> oh ok
17 [16:37] <MigraineBoy> well howdy again folks
18 [16:37] <Vetman> i think sideshow summed it up pretty good,
19 when he said you have to get on very well with other ops
20 [16:37] <|ColdFusion|> That's not true, I have been here for

21 two years and I get along with the op's yet I'm not an op yet
22 [16:37] <Vetman> sssssllllllluuuuuuuuurrrrrrrrrpppppp
48 [16:39] <|ColdFusion|> I've met them all in real life
49 [16:39] <|ColdFusion|> They're good ppl
50 [16:39] <|ColdFusion|> Yet I'm not an op
51 [16:39] <|ColdFusion|> They like me
52 [16:40] <Vetman> it is true that if you dont agree with them
53 100% and laugh at their jokes all the time you will never be
54 an op
55 [16:40] <Edac> i am good dude 2
56 [16:40] <|ColdFusion|> Yes!!!
57 [16:40] <Vetman> its the way it works, there a very click group
58 [16:40] *** Forsaken' (~ Dar.49) has joined #Brisbane
59 [16:40] <SideshowB'AtWork> it IS true that we are a very click
60 group . . .
61 [16:41] <Elle_Elle> lol
62 [16:41] <Vetman> i dont mean that in a nasty way sideshow, it
63 is just my opinion
64 [16:41] <Elle_Elle> So u basically tell them what they want to
65 hear
66 [16:41] <Elle_Elle> and do the things they want us to do?
67 [16:41] <SideshowB'AtWork> i don't take it in a nasty way
68 [16:41] *** Montery (dbox.m01–04.ktb.net) has joined #Brisbane
69 [16:42] <SideshowB'AtWork> no, you actually have to get
70 recommended by another op, and the final decision comes down to
71 the founder
72 [16:42] <MigraineBoy> lol, a group of under-educated, over-
73 pampered geeks is what you're REALLY trying to say, aren't you
74 Vetman?
86 [16:43] <Vetman> the only thing that worries me a bit, is that
87 i chat on mirc to relax and have fun, but in some channels and
88 some ops seem to take the job with a sence of power and really
89 do lose the fact that it is only mirc and not real life
93 [16:44] <SideshowB'AtWork> Vetman: some people have irc as
94 their main form of inter-personal communication
95 [16:44] <MigraineBoy> lol, Vetman . . . I've got just two words
96 for you . . . these are geeks with no life, power in chat rooms
97 is all they have
100 [16:44] <Vetman> is that the thing migraineboy, its just i
101 enter some chat rooms, and i believe they actually bate you to
102 stuff up so they can kick you

ANALYSIS

Extract 1 includes accounts about what having an '@' next to your name means and how you get it. In the process of explaining what the '@' symbol 'means', members accomplish their present setting while commenting on it. That is, members organize their accounts about channel operators (ops) within a framework that simultaneously orients to, thus accomplishing, the setting as being that of 'IRC Users in a chat room criticising "ops" in the presence of an op'. The way in which members organize their accounts accomplishes the setting as 'Users talking about ops in an IRC channel' while also treating it as a fact existing prior to and outside their talk.

The approach taken here, following Jayyusi (1984), is that there are at least three methods by which devices can be legitimately located. The device may be:

1. Provided for by the fit between the semantic-taxonomic sense of the category-concepts used and the talk's relevances (e.g. task).
2. Explicitly provided for in the talk, i.e. named.
3. Available through conventional or pragmatic implication. (Jayyusi, 1984: 82)

Importantly, then, as Jayyusi points out, analysis should not involve:

> a mechanical application of the consistency rule where one decides what device these two categorizations (or any co-selected categories) are drawn from, but rather to see what device-category they could, strictly or conventionally, imply for the task or relevance at hand displayed in the talk within which this category list is embedded. (*ibid.*: 83–4)

LOCATING CATEGORY DEVICES

One method by which participants in the talk invoke relevant categories and predicates is by naming them. Within Extract 1 the following category names are used: 'this channel', 'on MIRC', 'chat rooms', 'ops', 'not an op' and 'founder'. Readers may already have discerned a possible pattern to the talk from the naming of persons and locations: that is, that the topic of the talk is chat rooms (specific and general) and the people who use them. There is reference to 'getting opped' (11–13), and the activity of 'kicking' (5 and 102). The activity of 'chatting' or 'being on IRC' (including specifically in #Brisbane) is referred to, as is 'getting on' with ops.

One example of predicates implicating a certain category is that of the use of the terms 'kick' and 'ban' (5). The pro-term 'we' as the subject of the predicate is hearable as an incumbent of the category 'op' since these predicates are category-bound to ops. Warrant for this assertion is found when Coldfusion (7) proposes the use of this category, and this selection is confirmed by other members' use of the category throughout the rest of the sequence. Frequently named activities reinforce a provisional characterization of the talk as organized by the 'chat room' membership categorization device (MCD). Participants categorize themselves as incumbents of the categories that are the topic of their talk through their use of pronouns. This alignment of speakers' category incumbency with the categories under discussion is meaningful in terms of how statements are to be interpreted.

CATEGORY DEVICES AND SENSE-MAKING

The category device of ops/user makes sense of 'indexical' terms throughout the talk. Thus, the sense of participles such as 'getting along' and 'sucking up' is provided with contextual meaning through members' knowledge of the topic at hand and their knowledge that 'awarding op status' is an activity done by 'ops' (and 'founders'). Thus, the conventional relationship between categories in regard to the activity of 'getting opped' provides interpretive resources. That is, the relationship provides for a coherent interpretation of talk being about Users who may or may not behave inappropriately in order to be appointed operator status.

An example of category-generated features within the talk can be seen in the category-predicate tie formulated between the category 'op' and the predicates 'being (in the channel) a long time' and 'getting along with other ops'. Thus, while 'having power' and 'kicking and banning' are treated as predicates conventionally constituting and accompanying the category 'op', category-generated features of being an op are situatedly produced according to the task at hand: explaining how you get to be an op. Thus, category-generated features of 'ops' are that they 'have been in the channel a long time' and 'get along well with the other ops'. Another example is the category-generated feature of the motives of 'abusive types' of op. That is, that they are geeks 'without lives', a social type motivated by the need for power in MIRC to compensate for their lack of power and success in 'real life'. The category device of 'user-op' once again provides a resource for making sense of items of the talk in that predicates such as 'getting along' can be seen as sensibly invoked via their relation to device incumbency.

In the talk, members can also be seen to attach clusters of related category predicates to constitutive category predicates. Reasonable warrant for ascribing non-category-constitutive predicates may be found in the logico-grammatical relationship of category concepts that share predicate concepts (clustering) (Jayyusi, 1984). That is, further predicates of subjects may be generated through consideration of constitutive predicates and their possible trajectories. Hence, the constitutive predicate of 'ops' (channel power) may be clustered with category-related attributes shared by 'neo-nazis' (oppression) because one's use of power may become oppressive. That is, power and oppression as concepts can be seen to be related. Concepts of being 'under-educated' and 'over-pampered' may be clustered with the concept 'geek' in the language game of describing ops' deficiencies. One can thus see how these predicates may be clustered due to their conceptual links.

By further applying the 'chat room' device established earlier in the talk, members might have no trouble unpacking the expression 'taking the job with a sense of power'. Hence, using the categorization device 'a chat room', one could find that 'taking the job with a sense of power' (orienting to rights and not obligations) referred to ops being oppressive by kicking Users at every opportunity and also engineering such opportunities (line 101).

THE IMPLICATIVE LOGIC OF DEVICES AND BLAME ALLOCATION

The talk constitutes the categories of 'op' and 'User' as a locus for a set of mutual rights and obligations related to enforcing and abiding by channel rules. The categorization of persons using this 'standard relational pair' (SRP) logically provides for the relevance of moral evaluation of paired individuals' performance of their category-bound obligations and rights. For example, the description of 'some ops' as 'taking the job with a sense of power' may be seen as a negative moral evaluation of ops. That is, this predicate is treated as violating ops' obligation to use their power to protect Users (from harassment) rather than oppress them, and provides for the hearing of a complainable violation. Alternatively, Sideshowbob's turn describing chat rooms as rule-abiding societies invokes and emphasizes ops' right to enforce rules and Users' obligations to obey them. Furthermore, it provides for possible negative moral evaluation of Vetman and Coldfusion as Users who may have violated their obligation (to ops) to obey the ops and their channel rules.

Non-incumbency of one of the pair positions 'op/User' is observable in lines 73 and 96. That is, here, the category of 'geeks' is substituted for 'ops' in a turn explicitly addressed to Vetman and recognizably responding to his comments about 'ops' (57 and 88). A search for 'ops' in this turn finds them absent and the inference that can be made from that 'fact' is that redescription was required of the persons being referred to because they did not engage in the programmatically relevant activities of 'avoiding abusing their power' and 'treating Users fairly'. As Jayyusi (1984: 149) notes, explanation for the absence of a feature or redescription may be required upon finding the absence of a feature made programmatically relevant by some categorization. The absence of the programmatically relevant features of ops ('fairness' and 'a proper perspective of their power') is explained by Migraineboy in terms of their social type's ('geek') attributes ('power in chat rooms is all they have'). Thus, the 'op/User' SRP is programmatically relevant on this occasion where mutual rights and obligations 'in a chat room' are implicated as part of members' work of producing descriptions of 'ops'.

The use of the SRP categories 'ops' and 'Users' is essential for doing the moral judgement (of a set of unnamed individuals) that Vetman and Migraineboy accomplish through their descriptive work. That is, without first categorizing a bunch of people (as ops) and thus establishing their moral obligations to another bunch of people (Users), Vetman and Migraineboy could not sensibly produce criticism (or perform other activities expressing negative moral evaluations) about the bunch of people they talk about. In other words, members orient to the provision of warrant in the organization of accusations, complaints, criticism and blame about 'misconduct'. That is, reporting 'transgressions' requires establishing warrant for the expectations of specific rights, obligations and duties and, hence, warrant for their absence to be construed as a 'breach'. Members produce the warrant for their expectations of conduct through invoking the use of what Sacks (1992a,b) calls 'collection K' category sets (SRPs) tied to the task of giving help. By using their knowledge of which categories the absence of certain predicates (giving help) is programmatically relevant for, members can select categories for the purpose at hand. In this case, the purpose at hand is criticizing ops and complaining about them; and so the complainants describe the activities of 'ops' in a way that makes observable the absence of ops' category-bound obligations to 'help' Users. Furthermore, in claiming incumbency of the category (Users) to which some obligation was rightfully owed by the 'violating' party (ops), Vetman, Migraineboy and Coldfusion can accomplish themselves as 'victims' or 'wronged parties'.

The specific category obligation of 'ops' attended to in the initial part of the extract is that of 'giving ops fairly'. 'Opping' refers to the practice whereby 'Users' may be 'appointed' channel operator status by existing ops, who have access to the 'opping' command within a chat room. The 'snide remark' in line 12 and the comment in line 20 provide for the inference that, in this particular channel, ops are 'withholding' operator status from those 'Users' entitled to it. Thus Coldfusion performs 'hinting' (12) with his formulation of the particular location category (this channel as opposed to all other channels) being relevantly attached to 'you' not getting 'it' (ops). Note, as discussed earlier, the use of 'you' provides for inclusion of Coldfusion and the recipient (Elle_Elle) and others (anyone) within the category of 'people not getting ops'. In performing a search procedure, then, for reasons why 'you' (anyone) might not get ops, Coldfusion's inclusion of a category location in the organization of his turn provides a 'hint'. That is, by supplying a category (locational) members may refine their search to focus on items that constitutively distinguish that particular channel from others (as reasons for 'not getting ops'). One constitutive predicate differentiating channels is the incumbents of the 'op' category in each channel. Thus, competent IRC members may easily see that the criterion distinguishing this channel from others (in regards to 'opping') is the population with op status. The hint thus provides for the inference that it is the particular ops in #Brisbane who are the reason that 'anyone' may not get opped there. Furthermore, participants' talk generates 'the right to ops' as a feature of particular types of user (those who have been in the channel a long time and get along well with the established ops). Therefore, the reason 'anyone' fulfilling these criteria may remain un-opped is that #Brisbane ops are withholding op status from those 'Users' entitled to it.

CATEGORY, PREDICATE AND TASK

The activities of accusing, complaining, pre-emptively defending against inferences, blaming, and contesting blame can be seen to be performed in regulars' accounts of ops' behaviour. The participants' wider task at hand is that of chatting in a chat room. A more specific task at hand for participants is explaining the social order of the channel to a 'newbie' and (for some parties) using the request for explanations as an opportunity to produce criticism and complaints. Participants, then, may orient to the attribution of blame and responsibility in accounts in the implications of criteria selected, just as hearers of a 'dirty' joke listen for the obscenity and punch-line, or readers of a headline read in a way attentive to finding a tell-able story or 'news'. Hence, the activity involved in the task at hand requires participants to monitor, assign and contest category responsibility and/or blame used to account for the accountable matter (why some have ops and others do not). Because the wider task at hand is multi-party 'chat' in a chat room between incumbents of different task-relevant incumbencies, participants may also orient to soliciting and offering corroboration for complaints and affiliation with account versions.

Participants' category selections in their accounts allocate and reallocate blame for regulars' failure to get opped. Thus, the category predicates of a 'clique group' may be invoked to reallocate blame for regulars not having been made ops. That is, in a search for reasons for not 'getting along with ops' (a criterion for getting opped), a number of conventional reasons can be located that attribute blame to the individual 'User'. Conventional reasons for not getting along with others may attribute blame or be blame-free. That is, a blame-free version might be that both parties were simply too different to get along. Versions attributing blame for the state of not 'getting along' might point to deficient character or conduct on one party's part. Hence if un-opped Users have been in the channel a long time and are thus logically ascribed the property of not getting along with ops well by Sideshowbob's account, they may seek to pre-empt inferences that they are the parties at fault for that state. Describing 'ops' as 'a clique group' reallocates the blame for 'not getting along very well' from individual 'Users' to 'ops'. Vetman's description and Sideshowbob's agreement that the ops are a 'clique' provides for a possible hearing of Users' failure to 'get along with ops' as the fault of ops' exclusivist attitudes and activities. Disjunctive categories (and their inferable predicates) used here, then, include that of 'people who get along well with ops/suck ups' and 'people who get along/clique group'. Another disjunctive category set found was that of 'ops/geeks'. Again, the purposefulness in 'Users' describing 'ops' as 'suck-ups', 'a clique group' and 'geeks' may be to defend against the possible inference that they are not themselves 'ops' because they are somehow deficient 'types'.

To focus on the 'op/geek' disjunctive category set, 'some ops' are re-categorized and attributed the features (motives, social competence) of 'geeks', features treatable as deficient in comparison to those of 'non-geeky', 'ordinary' channel users. That is, since category-constitutive features of the category 'geeks' is a social life and competence limited to computing, 'geeks' can be treated as a category that is socially deficient in comparison to, and potentially exclusive of, 'ordinary' people. Ascribing to ops co-incumbency in the category 'geeks' then, is a deft way to tie the (topic-relevant) category requirements (motives and personality) for 'getting opped' to a routinely disavowable category, 'geeks'. Thus, Migraineboy's tying of the categories 'geek' and 'clique group' – through his formulation of Vetman's prior turn (57) – works defensively against inferences that Migraineboy, Vetman and Coldfusion are not ops because they are deficient in avowable features. Rather, their lack of disavowable features – those of 'geeks' and 'suck-ups' – is provided as reason for their exclusion from the clique formed by ops. It is possible to see, then, how disjunctive category sets in the sequence reapportion blame for 'failing to get ops' and also provide for the understanding of their lack of op status as a complainable matter. That is, Vetman, Migraineboy and Coldfusion formulate ops' behaviour in the channel in relation to opping as unfair, a violation of their category-bound obligations to their SRP partners – Users. The specific violation dealt with is ops' failure to carry out their obligation to distribute op status 'fairly'.

A resource that readers may use to decide between disjunctive accounts is the notion of 'category transformation'. Schegloff (1972) developed the use of the concept 'category transformation', and Jayyusi (1984: 114) similarly refers to the phenomenon as 'category accretion'. This is a resource whereby: 'the recipient of some utterance which includes some such categories (such as 'young man') has to categorise the categoriser to know how they would categorise the one who had been categorised in the utterance' (Schegloff, 1989: 206). The fact that the description of 'ops' as 'geeks' and 'suck-ups' is recognizably performed by 'Users' provides for the interpretation of their criticism as motivated by 'sour grapes' or 'jealousy'. That is, readers may resolve the difference in competing accounts in the extended sequence by attributing it to a difference in motives inferable on the part of different categories. In this case, the disjunctive accounts produced are hearable as products of the alternative motives of 'sour grapes' (on the part of un-opped Users) and 'self-interest' or 'professionalism' (on the part of 'ops'). That is, by seeing that the disjunctive accounts are produced by incumbents of asymmetric category sets, readers can attribute account differences to the different motives and features clustered around asymmetric categories. Note that Vetman (62) appears to orient to his comments being treatable as 'nasty' and, hence, motivated by nastiness or antipathy (inferably due to his 'sour grapes' attitude).

Another device in the talk made relevant for categorization purposes is that of 'social types'. The important feature of the geek 'type' is that it (or they) cannot see that IRC is just a fun activity and not real and that their power in IRC is therefore not to be taken too seriously. A tie between the criticism of ops as 'cliquey' and as 'geeks' may be found by seeing that the category concepts are mutually elaborative. That is, 'geeks' may be used to find what 'types' make up the clique, while 'clique-ishness' as a possible feature of the 'geek' type provides for that trait. For instance, the predicates constitutive of the type category 'geeks' – including taking computing seriously – may carry a cluster of motives for 'geek' behaviour; for instance, 'attempting to compensate for lack of "real life" social inclusion and accomplishment by taking on-line activities seriously'. The category-generated motive of 'geeks' (a desire for power), then, can be elaborated by, while also elaborating, the concepts of a 'clique group' and 'having a sense of power'. That is, ops are redescribed from a possibly élite clique into a 'geek-clique'. Redescription of the population as 'geeks' permits the inference that the population described shares in common the trait of taking IRC too seriously because of their obsession with computing. Thus, the implicative work done by Vetman and Migraineboy's categorization is that some ops' sense of their own power and superiority to Users is out of perspective with 'reality', and that this lack of perspective is due to their social type's attributes. That is, some ops are power-tripping because they have the attribute of the 'geek' type of taking computing too seriously.

In contrast, Sideshowbob treats the 'chat room' device as relevant over the 'social type' device. He invokes the relevance of chatting on IRC as a task (93) in order to give chat-room task categorizations (ops, Users, and so on) precedence over social-type categorizations (such as 'geek'). Participants, then, can be seen to appeal to which device categories have greater relevance in the task of describing persons and, consequently, judging them. While Vetman and Migraineboy appeal to the relevance of 'social types' in accounting for their treatment in chat rooms, Sideshowbob appeals to the relevance of the task and its particulars (that is, the need for rules) in interpreting their experiences.

There is a disjunction, then, between reasons ascribed for ops having a sense of power. One version ascribes these predicates to the faulty (blameworthy) perspective of a social type (geeks) while another competing version confirms ops' attitudes as legitimate in terms of the task being 'serious business' for the IRC society.

CONCLUSION

Instances of categorizations being procedurally relevant for the talk were found in Extract 1. Thus, subsequent affiliation in the form of agreement and disagreement with complaints about ops' category violations (20, 100) are somewhat predictably organized according to members' claimed incumbencies. Also, use of disjunctive categories provided for disjunctive accounts in the extract and provided for recognizable 'complaints' and 'disagreement'.

Categorizations of participants as 'Users' and 'ops', then, are consequential in terms of sensibly interpreting what is said (and project possible future actions within the talk). Thus, category transformation may occur where the description of 'ops' as 'geeks' and 'suck-ups' (performed by persons categorized as 'Users without ops'), provides for the possible interpretation of their 'opinion' as 'biased', motivated by disgruntlement at lack of promotion. Likewise, categorizations provide for the interpretation of pro-terms and other indexical items. Hence the gloss 'taking the job with a sense of power' (88) is further unpacked (Jefferson, 1985) by participants using categorization of participants as 'ops' and 'Users' to find that it possibly refers to (or consists of) too strict an enforcement of rules (through kicks). Thus Migraineboy (96) hints at ops' eagerness to exercise their only form of power in life and Vetman (101) further unpacks his own gloss by providing the elements of it: 'kicks' and over-eagerness to kick. Participants thus interactionally achieve the unpackaging of the gloss through further category work.

Analysis of the talk, then, reveals a number of ways in which parties organize their talk sensibly via the use of categorization devices. That is, the sense of the sequence as 'criticism/complaint about ops by Users in a chat room' is accomplished through parties' meaningful selection and arrangement of items from category resources. Thus, particular resources provide for a reading of subjects being discussed as incumbents of the categories 'op/User' belonging to the 'chat room' device. These resources include the implicative logic accomplished through the invocation of category, predicate and task (Hester and Eglin, 1997).

The invoked device categories provide for hearing the talk as complaint and/or criticism due to particular category member actions being treated as a warrant for negative inferences and recategorization. This suggests an existing orientation by parties to category violations having been committed. The use of disjunctive categories (and production of disjunctive accounts) provides for the reading of the talk as a 'disagreement' between parties as to who is to blame for the IRC-specific phenomena of 'not getting ops' and 'being kicked'.

The analysis shows, then, how the 'ops' and 'Users' category memberships are central to the organization of the talk. For example, we can point to how parties provided for the hearing of particular 'activities' being done through tying categories, predicates and task through co-selection. What parties talked about and how, were achieved as relevant and sensible according to categorization work. Categorization work was also shown to accomplish parties' moral adequacy (or inadequacy) within their settings.

APPENDIX 1: PRINT-OUT OF SCREEN INTERFACE SEEN BY MIRC USERS

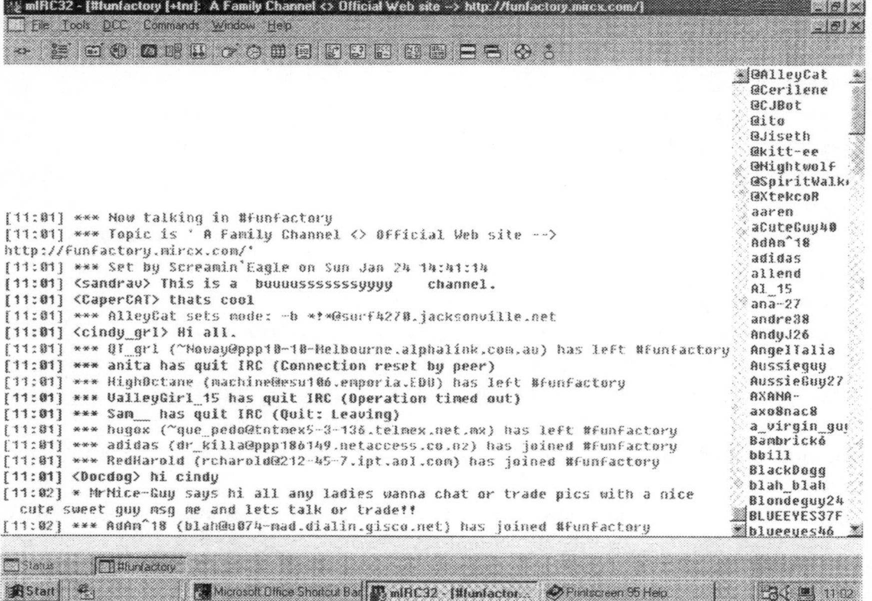

APPENDIX 2: GLOSSARY

g* and *s grin and smile

Alias Channel nickname. So that users may 'recognize' whom they are speaking to, servers do not allow nicknames to be shared, and nicknames may be registered to prevent others from using them.

Auto-text Text automatically generated on the screen by IRC programs written to respond to cues/commands (i.e. not typed by users).

Ban Command available to channel operators that prevents kicked users from returning to a channel for a specified amount of time.

Channel A channel is a 'place' on IRC where group conversations occur. People can join the same channel and see each other's typed messages and names on the user list. The number of users in a channel may vary.

Chat room Synonymous with channel.

Founder The individual who created the channel.

IRC Internet Relay Chat.

Join message Auto-text displayed in the channel upon a user joining that channel. See line 15 for an example. Notifies other users that a new user has joined the channel.

Kick A command that removes a user from a channel. Available only to ops.

Log files The logging command in MIRC allows any user to save all text in windows as files.

Lol Lots of laughter or laughing out loud.

Mirc Microsoft Internet Relay Chat, one of the most popular types of chat programs.

Newbie A person new to using IRC or (sometimes) a channel.

On-line Using the internet.

Opped/Opping (verb) To bestow or receive channel operator status from another.

Ops Channel operator status within a chat room.

Ppl Abbreviation for 'people'.

Regular Used to describe a person who has visited the channel regularly for a period of time and is recognized and known by others.

Screen interface The visual organization of the screen display into tool bars, message boxes, icons and buttons within windows that users point and click on with a mouse in order to perform commands.

Time stamp Prefixes each user's turn in the channel with the time in hours and minutes. Appears only on the user's screen and log files, not all users' screens.

Un-opped A person without operator status in a channel, a (capital-U) 'User'.

User The status of one in a channel who does not have founder or operator status. 'User' appears with a capital 'U' to distinguish it from *channel* users, *all* the persons within a channel.

User list See the right-hand side of picture in Appendix 1 where the names of all the users in a channel and their status is listed.

User status The status of a channel user in relation to what commands are available to them within that channel. Thus founders have access to commands not available to ops and ops have access to commands not available to Users.

8 Investigating the 'cast of characters' in a cultural world

Kathy Roulston

EDITORIAL

Rhyll Vallis's chapter shows that membership categorization analysis (MCA) is an important sub-branch of applied CA. Here Kathy Roulston offers some extensions of its fundamental insights in her examination of how itinerant workers operate in the institutions they encounter. In the education sector, with music a rare part of the full-time curriculum, music teachers often work in marginalized positions across a number of different schools. In this respect, they work *in institutional settings but hardly* identify *with them. So how do they account for this problematic positioning?*

Kathy Roulston, who has investigated diverse aspects of the lives of today's music teachers, looks at how they cope with those around them in the various schools they encounter in their everyday lives. What she finds is that they use a particular kind of membership categorization device (MCD), which Roulston calls a 'cast of characters'. That is, each school scenario opens up contacts with local personalities, particular and actual people. But, as a matter of fact, the music teachers in Roulston's data collect these 'others' together into such 'characters' as principals (head teachers), groundsmen, full-time teachers, and so on. They become 'possible' instances as much as actual individuals.

True to Sacks's original idea of MCDs, each of these 'cast members' carries with it a particular known predicate or category-bound activity. Thereby, groundsmen and some other ancillary staff can be taken as aiding, helping and assisting in such things as arranging concerts. And, by contrast, full-time teachers can be equally taken (at best) as unconcerned about such things and (at worst) as actively constituting obstacles to them.

In this way, Roulston gives us an insight into the culture of itinerant teachers and shows us how they carry with them, from institution to institution, a picture of typical persons and their expectable actions. And she shows how this picture makes sense of an otherwise contingent and insecure existence. The analysis she offers, then, could be usefully extended to any job or profession where there is institutional instability but where, nevertheless, members must *make sense of their remarkably mobile and unstable circumstances.*

INTRODUCTION

In this chapter, I demonstrate the application of CA methods to the analysis of transcripts from research interviews and conversations. Through the application of tools made available by conversation analysis (CA) – and, in particular, by its membership categorization (MCA) arm – I show how it is possible to access a distinct order of data which Silverman (1993: 108) describes as a 'cultural universe and its content of moral assumptions'. In particular, I outline a number of 'scenic practices' used by speakers to portray the 'cast of characters' in one cultural universe. In this chapter, I show how the examination of such scenic practices in interview talk provides a means of investigating institutional talk. In this case, the institutional talk is that of accounts and descriptions of work practices produced by primary-school music teachers in research interviews.

I begin by describing the three theoretical assumptions upon which this type of analysis is based. First, the interview is viewed as a socially situated occasion in which the interviewer and respondent interactively produce descriptions and accounts which will be 'locally comprehensible' in the setting at hand (Holstein and Gubrium, 1997: 117). Second, the categories, moral order and practical reasoning attached to school worlds that are produced in these descriptions and accounts (Baker, 1997: 139) are themselves topics for analysis. These descriptions and accounts provide cultural particulars concerning the social organization of a given world (Silverman, 1993: 105). Third, accounts and descriptions assembled by speakers may be viewed as invoking 'possible worlds'. Speakers produce different versions of 'what could be' and how the social order 'might be arranged' (Baker, 1997: 143).

I use an applied CA approach to data analysis (Heap, 1997), drawing on procedures outlined and demonstrated by Baker (1983). Baker argues that when interview data is viewed as 'talk-in-interaction', the process of data 'collection' may be better described as data 'making' or data 'generation' (Baker, 1997: 131). In this view, the interviewer and respondent are 'ordinary competent members of the culture and the analyst, [the] *post-hoc* ethnomethodologist, looking for the social-organizational work being done by interviewer and respondent' (Baker, 1997: 131). This type of reading relies on locating members' own devices for membership categorization (Sacks, 1992a,b; Silverman, 1998). Baker (1997: 131) outlines a procedure which the analyst might follow: 'Look for the use of membership categorization devices by the interviewer and respondent, and show how both are involved in the generation of versions of social reality built around categories and activities.'

The focus of my analysis here is 'how *participants in the interview* make use of the resources of membership categorization' (Baker, 1997: 142). By identifying the 'cast of characters' used by speakers in interview talk, and the activities with which these characters are associated, the cultural knowledge of the participants is made audible. As noted by Silverman (1998: 86), although we may be tempted to use MCA 'in order to understand things *better* than members', the 'MCD apparatus is entirely a member's apparatus. This means that it exists not as another social science concept but only in and through the way in which it is demonstrably used by lay members' (Silverman, 1998: 86).

This approach to analysis leads to a distinct order of research question. For example, how do speakers characterize their work through their talk? How is this talk expressive of cultural knowledge? What moral portrayals of members are achieved in talk? The findings from this type of analysis reveal a vast fund of knowledge of cultural particulars used in 'story-making' in response to a particular interviewer in a particular social setting.

DATA GENERATION

Transcript extracts included in this chapter are derived from the third phase of a three-year study investigating the work of itinerant music teachers in Queensland, Australia (Roulston, 1998a, 1998b, 1998c, 1999). This phase consisted of a one-year multiple-case study with six primary music teachers working in a variety of teaching contexts. All were itinerant and had varying lengths of teaching experience and different pre-service training. Data were generated in a variety of ways: (a) audio and/or video recording of naturally occurring events during the school day (for example, music lessons and/or rehearsals); (b) audio recording of conversations between participants and the researcher; (c) journal writing; (d) official documents; and (e) notes of observations made during field work. In this chapter, I use data derived from the second of these data sources, transcriptions of audio-recorded interview talk.

IDENTIFYING THE 'CAST OF CHARACTERS'

By using the phrase 'cast of characters', I wish to invoke the notion of 'character' as a role in a drama or play. The 'characters' appearing in speakers' accounts presented here should be thought of not in terms associated with personal, intrinsic or moral qualities of actual persons. Rather, they emerge as would roles from a script interpreted by actors as speakers' co-productions within conversational settings. While actors create their roles through visual, kinaesthetic and oral means, the characters appearing in these accounts are cooperatively produced in talk between the researcher and respondent. Each speaker uses their knowledge of the cultural particulars and social order of a world known and experienced in common to produce and recognize such characters within the scenes described.

I now introduce a number of 'scenic practices' employed by speakers in accounts of their work, after which I provide examples of each. I then show how these scenic practices might be identified in a single section of talk. First, direct and indirect reported speech may be used in the production of 'scenes' in descriptions. The use of direct reported speech serves to underscore to the recipient how the purported event should be heard, adding a moral dimension to the account. Second, characters depicted in scenes are morally laden through their assigned attributes and may be read reflexively as indicative of the speaker's place in the moral universe portrayed. Third, the researcher's co-categorial incumbency as a music teacher is particularly important in the generation of these scenes, and her receptivity to the implications of scenes described is apparent in the talk. Fourth, category descriptions are unstable across talk and may be read as indicating that any particular character might appear with different sets of attributes on multiple occasions. Fifth, teachers provide unique descriptions of a range of actual scenes, many of which could be easily recognizable by other music teachers. Each scene is 'local' in that it is related to a particular setting and to recent and prospective events within that setting. Each 'actual' scene is selected from an array of 'possible' scenes recognizable as ways in which the world could (or should) be ordered. I now turn to examples illustrating how each of these scenic practices appears in interview talk.

Use of direct reported speech

The following extract includes a reported scene which employs direct reported speech. The prosody employed by the speaker points to the moral implications of the scene and *how* it should be heard. In this example, Shannon, a teacher for ten years, describes the reaction of classroom teachers at a staff meeting at one of her two schools to her announcement that there will be a Carols Night.

Extract 1

S actually some teachers are sort of saying (.) o::h ((groaning)) (.) when we said (.)
no we are going to have a Carols Night like last year and (they) were going oh::
and I actually said at the staff meeting I said 'I don't understand peoples'
objection because (.) I teach them the carol=
R =mm=
S =I I look after the (.) the ↑whole lot and um (.) your only expectation is to (.) maybe
be there on the night [and to help get them on the stage and off the stage'=
R [and just make sure yeah
R =which is not that hard=
S =yeah heh heh [so u::m u::m
R [what did anyone say anything after that?
S no one heh heh no one said BOO after that but you know there were sort of
groans and 'O:::h o::h' and like I think there's=

In her retelling of what occurred at the staff meeting, Shannon has boldly countered opposition from some classroom teachers by publicly noting that they have no legitimate grounds for complaint concerning the organization of the Carols Night. First, Shannon has taken responsibility for the teaching of carols to classes (4), and second, the only expectation of classroom teachers is that they 'maybe' attend the Carols Night and assist her by helping her to get classes on and off stage (6–7). Shannon's use of extreme case formulations (Pomerantz, 1986) at line 6 ('I look after the whole lot', 'your only expectation is to maybe') serves to maximize her own involvement in the event and minimize the classroom teachers' responsibilities. Shannon uses direct reported speech in her account. According to Holt (2000), 'when a speaker claims to reproduce words said on a previous occasion, prosody can be used to suggest that he or she is not only reproducing *what* was said but also *the way it was said*'. Here, Shannon's use of groans to portray the classroom teachers' resistance to the idea of having a Carols Night depicts them as being selfish and unprofessional in their lack of support for her work. In this extract we see an example of the 'peculiar blending between the reconstructed moral activity from the past and the in situ moralization enacted in the present', a feature of reported utterances described by Bergmann (1998: 289).

The assignment of morally laden attributes to characters

In the following example, first-year teacher Tony describes organizing one of his end-of-year performances, a Carols Night at his second school, Durham Heights. Rather than respond to the researcher's question 'did you do special stuff for that?' (12), Tony provides information on how the principal (head teacher) had asked him what he was doing for the Carols Night. From lines 14 to 16, Tony describes the principal's relation to himself ('he called me in and goes . . .'), perhaps suggesting a surprise or surplus demand from the principal.

Extract 2

12	R	did you do special stuff for that? or did [you just did you did you
13	T	[↑yeah well see I finished
14	T	the concert on Tuesday night I got here on the Wednesday and it was
15		like yeah Gerry called me in and goes 'Oh we got a Carols Night on
16		Sunday night' he says 'What have you got for that?'
17		(0.5)

At line 18 below, the researcher restates her question from line 12, achieving a topic switch from the 'principal' to the 'music teacher'. Implicit in the restatement of her question is an assumption that one way for music teachers to manage Carols Nights as a performance genre is to have classes or performance groups present 'special' items. Again, Tony avoids directly answering the question, by noting what he has done – he has taught Christmas carols to the choir. However, in this account, choir members are not reliable ('half of them didn't turn up') and do not present items:

18	R	and and you and you had done special items for the classes?
19		or or they they just got up and sang
20	T	I taught the ↑choir different [Christmas carols but I just (.) um but=
21	R	[yeah

T =even then half of them didn't turn up last night so it was like
(2.0)

In the next section of talk, instrumental teachers appear fleetingly as fellow-members with Tony in a hastily formed band. These individuals are sketched as multi-skilled performers, with the string teacher playing piano, the woodwind teacher playing bass guitar, the percussion teacher playing drums and 'another guy' playing saxophone. In their participation in a performance organized at short notice, these teachers show their credentials not as instrumental instructors, but as performers in their own right:

T basically I organized all the instrumental teachers that teach (.) I got them to play
them with [me like the guy that does saxophone and that he actually played <u>bass</u>
R [mm
T [guitar for them I played guitar and sang=
R [oh OK
R =yeah
T percussion guy played drums and um (.) there was actually another guy that played
sax and then Sue was up playing the keyboard the strings teacher was playing piano

Thus far, the cast of characters assembled in Tony's account is arranged into 'unreliable' and 'versatile' types. Such selections of attributes are reflexively descriptive of the conditions of Tony's work and of his identity as a school music teacher. The notion of unreliability invokes this teacher's dependence on others (in this case, children as performers), as well as his responsibilities for ensuring events actually occur. The versatility of the music teachers depicted here points to the need for improvisation that may be required when reliability does not eventuate. Thus, in this extract, the cast of characters and attributes may be seen as a way of documenting the social organization of the environment in which Tony works.

The researcher's co-categorial incumbency

In Extract 3, the researcher's receptivity to the implications of scenes described is displayed in talk. At line 14, the researcher invites the continuation of Shannon's report concerning an upcoming Carols Night (mentioned in Extract 1) by noting that she (alone) will be 'doing the work'. In this section of talk, Shannon and the researcher cooperate in a portrayal of a music teacher who accomplishes 'the work' of teaching the carols with no assistance from classroom colleagues. This segment provides an indication of the important role played by the recipient of the account. The scene described is one that is possibly professionally humiliating, as other teachers are groaning at Shannon's proposal concerning the Carols Night. However, Shannon emerges from the scene having silenced her detractors. In the setting of this interview with a researcher who is also a music teacher, the design of Shannon's account is well crafted. Another music teacher who would know about the plausibility of colleagues actually showing such disrespect at a staff meeting may hear this as a victory. This is in fact how the researcher does hear Shannon's report:

Extract 3

R = ↑you're the one doing the work=
S =yeah ↑yeah and that's what I said 'I don't understand peoples' objection=
R =mm=
S =because I'm the one who prepares everything' and I said 'In fact I was um last year
I I spent times with a hundred kids trying to play keyboard and teach them the carol
and control behaviour of with a hundred kids with not one ↑teacher who came to the
↑lesson' so heh heh heh so sorta went POW [heh heh heh heh
R [heh heh heh heh
S like I wasn't I wasn't [rude I said it in a tactful way but
R [I know yeah yeah

At lines 17–20, Shannon lists the activities she undertook during preparation for Carols Night in the previous year in a replay of what she said to the teachers. While supervising 100 children single-handedly, she has played keyboard and taught the carols without the support of 'one teacher'. Since this has been her experience in the past year, Shannon undertakes to assign supervision responsibility to classroom teachers. In explicitly noting in her description that she 'wasn't rude', but 'tactful' (22), and including a precise example to support the validity of her claim, Shannon acknowledges that her initial description may be hearable as an unwarranted, if not rude, rebuke of classroom teachers.

Unstable category descriptions

Below, Paige's production of two dramatically different types of parent, in her prospective and retrospective accounts of a school concert, provides a vivid example of how moral portrayals of characters may be achieved as part of different scenes on different occasions. Such scenes, in their variety – 'imagined' or 'actual' – represent an infinitely wider array of possible scenes. Similarly teachers, principals and others are produced as figures in some scenes and accounts and not in others. Their appearances on some occasions and non-appearances on others indicate that the moral universe of music teachers is not a fixed array but an occasioned corpus. The work of calling forth characters as parts of imagined or reported scenes suggests that characters, and their selected attributes, are most usefully understood as resources for descriptions in accounts.

In describing the organization of an upcoming concert, Paige inserts a portrayal of what it is that audience members (in this case, parents) prefer at concerts. In Paige's view, parents' predilections do not include instrumental items and they would rather go home 'after three quarters of an hour' (40).

Extract 4.1

(2.0)
P a::nd (.) then I I think there's a couple of kids that are coming and going to do some

instrumental item type [thing which I don't want to I mean parents would rather go
R [yeah
P home at quarter past eight after three quarters of an hour=
R =yeah=
P =than wait 'til eight thirty and have a whole lot of instrumental stuff. . . .

The listing of concert items organizes and occasions the production of various kinds and categories of people, as is shown as the list continues:

(2.0)
P yeah and then I've got the year (.) six seven choir and I'm thinking of putting the four
fives and six sevens because ↑once you come to night see a lot of them don't ↑come=
R =mm

The next extract from a subsequent interview with Paige describes the aforementioned concert in retrospect. In the preliminary sequence below, Paige describes her pre-concert 'panic' that she did not have enough items for the concert:

Extract 4.2
R did you have anyone from the school come?
P well I started to (.) panic a little bit because heh heh heh
R it was in this room? oh it was over in the hall
P oh ↑no it was in the hall and the hall is it's a ↑really big I mean it just gets
absolutely crowded out and I (.) I always just panic that I haven't got enough=
R =mm=
P =that I hadn't taught the choir enough songs (it's supposed to be) an hour and a half
anyway but I talked to Year 1s I've got good friends in the Year 1 teachers=
R =mm=
P =so I said to Brenda 'Can you help me'=
R =and they came along=
P =and she thought the Grade 1s could sing two songs but the funny thing was she
was just gonna bring along a few grade ones but they invited them and stacks of
Grade 1s it just shows when there's teacher support there the parents support their
kids coming along so they the place was just (.) exploding there were people outside

This account not only locates 'Year 1 teachers' as a satisfactory answer to the researcher's initial question, but provides an account of how these teachers came to be involved, given that the concert had previously consisted of a showcase of instrumental and choral (rather than classroom) items. Here, in panic at not having enough items for the concert program, Paige enlists the support of the Year 1 teachers, with whom she is 'good friends'. Given their assistance and support, the concert is well attended to the point that the hall is 'exploding' with people. In this example, Paige both asks for and receives help from classroom teachers. The classroom teachers' assistance is made explicit through the example of Paige's friend, Brenda. Brenda's assistance is constructed over several utterances ('so I said to Brenda . . .', (10); 'and she thought . . .', (12); 'she was just gonna . . .', (13)). This support, however, is predicated on being 'good' friends with the classroom teachers concerned. Brenda, the starring player in the drama, is transformed into an exemplification of what it means to have 'teacher support' (14–15).

Parents appear in Extracts 4.1 and 4.2 as two different collections. In their first appearance in Paige's account prior to the concert, parents are uninterested audience members who would rather go home after three-quarters of an hour than sit through 'a whole lot of instrumental stuff'. In contrast, the parents in Extract 4.2 have come at the request of the Year 1 teachers and are so keen to attend the concert they cannot fit in the hall. The parents' keenness is attributed to Brenda's assistance. This enthusiastic parental support for the performance of young children in Year 1 stands in contrast to the lack of parental support for the performance of the choir, many of whom do not attend night-time concerts (45).

Actual and possible scenes

In interview talk, scenes reported as 'actual' stand for an array of other possible scenes. The 'actuals' may be understood as instances of 'possibles'. The descriptions of 'how things are' imply alternative scenarios, 'how things could be' or 'how things should be'. The scenes described by speakers may be potentially interchangeable; they are recognizable to other teachers either as actualities from personal experience, or at least as possibilities.

The following segment is drawn from the conversation previously cited in which Paige describes an upcoming end-of-year concert. This section of talk is initiated by the researcher's question (11) – 'will Graeme [the principal] come?' (to the concert). In this instance the character of the principal is cast into doubt through the questioning of his commitment to the music program. Paige notes that, while she expects the principal to attend (12), he did not attend the musical performances at the school fete (14, 18, 20).

Extract 5
R will Graeme come?
P we:ll (.) I would expect so=
R =yeah=
P =but he didn't come to the fete (.) he wasn't at the fete performance=
R =yeah he was at the fete but he didn't come to your performance=
P =no=
R =he didn't go to the ↑fete?
P yes (.) he came to the [fete but not to the performance
R [he was at the fete but he didn't go to any of the music things
P no
(3.0)
P and yet I could have done with the help that time=
R =yeah=
P =yes=

The principal's non-attendance at any of the music items at the fete is noted as an accountable lack by both the researcher and Paige, who notes that she 'could have done with the help' (22). Implicit in this jointly constructed sequence is the notion that the principal has some responsibility to attend (to provide 'assistance') at musical performances. In lines 14–20, Paige and the researcher jointly clarify the nature of the principal's (moral) failure – that is, he attended the fete, but did not attend or assist with the musical performances. The implication is clear: since the principal should have attended, his neglect is established through his absence. After a three-second silence, Paige then offers a reason for why the principal should have been there to help her, thus spelling out the implication (22–24).

In this extract, it is possible to see explicitly how *actual* events are described as options within a wider range of *possible* and preferable events. Here, the principal did *x*, but not *y*. The character of the principal is portrayed here as having made a choice *not* to come to the musical performance specifically. Whether in fact the principal was *able* to make a choice is irrelevant to this portrayal. Who comes to a performance and who does not is the moral question pursued here: who surrounds the music teacher and assists her with her work? This implies that such surrounding and, by implication, *assistance* is a significant condition of work for music teachers.

INVESTIGATING THE 'CAST OF CHARACTERS' THROUGH SCENIC PRACTICES

I conclude this chapter by showing the multi-layered way in which scenic practices may be employed by speakers to invoke a particular cast of characters. The final extract is derived from interview talk in which Olivia, a teacher with 19 years' experience, describes the staff members with whom she works at each of her schools. In this sequence of talk (extracts from which are cited here), Olivia both names and portrays the office staff at each of her schools, and the type of working relationship which she pursues in each setting. These are some new characters who are part of the moral universe of music teaching. In this account, Olivia artfully employs the scenic practices described earlier.

For purposes of brevity, I include and discuss pertinent extracts. At one school, Roseview, Olivia feels free to 'muck around' with one of the office staff:

58 O o:h yeah (.) the um (.) the office la(h)dy at Ro(h)se(h)view heh heh -hhh Lara
59 is as nice as pie=
60 R =yeah=
61 O =down to earth (.) and (.) you know (.) yes she's got a bit of a loud voice
62 and you know and she'll muck around and the other one
63 (2.0)
64 is a real bitch

At Varsity, Olivia takes care to avoid offence, since the administrative officer is sometimes 'a bit touchy' (89), and the list continues:

O =and you know at Varsity with Gina (.) sometimes it's a bit touchy so
you've got to be able to read the situation=
R =yeah=
O =sort of before you put your foot in it

It is evident from Olivia's account that the maintenance of these relationships is both desirable and, in some cases, tricky, sensitive work. Whereas, with one staff member, she is free to 'muck around', in another setting, Olivia must carefully 'read the situation' in order to avoid putting her 'foot in it'. Here again, attributes of characters co-produced by Olivia and the researcher are morally laden, unstable (that is, sometimes helpful, sometimes not), and imply a range of alternative types. Below, Olivia provides a summary list of people in schools with whom it is necessary to 'get on' – office people, cleaners and groundsmen:

O but o:::h it's (.) yeah the office people (.) if you can get on with the
office and the cleaners
R I'll tell you what [that counts for a lot doesn't it
O [and the groundsman

In the next section of talk (108–125) Olivia, in like manner to the previous assessment of office staff, details her working relationships with the groundsmen in each of her schools along with vignettes of her experiences in working with each of them. Olivia begins her description with a portrayal of the groundsman at Varsity – Frank. In this account, Olivia provides multiple examples of Frank's demonstrated helpfulness. Direct reported speech is again used to describe the interaction between Olivia and Frank. In these examples, Frank is depicted as carrying out Olivia's requests quickly and without complaint:

R =because they're the ones that you're working with really aren't they heh heh heh=
O =you know I can go to Frank at um Varsity and say 'Oh Frank (.) I've
got a little job for you' he'd say 'Oh OK what is it' and I'll tell him and he said (.)
you know one day I wanted a filing cabinet [moved from my block (.) two blocks over
R [yeah
O we're exchanging he said (1.0) 'OK when do you want it done' I said 'Whenever you
can' [you know 'I'll empty it' (1.0) and within five minutes he was there to do it
R [yeah
R wow
O you know 'Oh Frank I'd like the piano moved' heh heh ((mock annoyance)) 'I
don't ↑know these pe(h)ople that wa(h)nt' heh heh you know but he always (.) he's
always friendly about it (.) [the one at Roseview depends on what mood he's in=
R [yeah
R =yeah yeah=
O =Austin don't have one (2.0) and the one at (.) Eldergrove (.) he's pretty good=
R =yeah=
O =he's only part-time he works twenty hours a week but if I've asked him to do
something (.) he's he's done it he mightn't have been able to do it straight away (.)

Olivia then repeats her formulation of the previous section of talk (initially made at lines 104–107). From her perspective as an itinerant teacher, the key personnel within the school are cleaners, administrative staff and the groundsman. The moods and relative helpfulness of these staff are a crucial part of Olivia's depiction:

126 O but (.) he comes in and does things for me so (1.0) yeah but this is it get on
127 with the cleaners the secretary (.) and the groundsman and you're fine
128 (1.0)

Unlike the administrative and ancillary staff with whom Olivia must perform delicate emotional work in order to derive information or to get jobs done, classroom teachers are, in this account, largely peripheral to Olivia's work. In fact, Olivia notes that it is possible 'to cope' with poor relationships with classroom teachers (129), a matter she treats with some amusement. The researcher supports this assessment by providing an excuse: they simply 'drop their kids off' (134) and 'you can't remember their name' (136). Olivia and the researcher construct a portrayal of classroom teachers as 'unknown quantities', unfamiliar people who 'drop their kids off' at music lessons, people whose names music teachers do not recall nor need to know (134–137):

129 O you can cope with not getting on with the teachers [heh heh heh heh heh heh heh
130 R [well that's it because they're
131 O [heh heh heh heh heh heh heh heh heh -hhhh yea:::::::h heh heh heh=
132 R [they're the people that you need to ah the infrastructure won't work
133 O =isn't it ↑awful heh heh heh
134 R well teachers drop their kids off sometimes you don't know them do you=
135 O =no=
136 R =I mean you can't remember their name heh heh heh=
137 O =well I'm gonna have some when I go back it'll be Mrs a::::h heh heh heh heh
138 R yeah
139 O so:::

In this account, it is essential that Olivia form good working relationships with those whose work directly intersects with her own. These include office staff, groundsmen and cleaners. In the extracts presented in this chapter, Olivia is the only music teacher to talk at length about ancillary staff, while others refer to principals and teachers. Common to all the accounts, however, are issues of willingness to assist the music teacher, and specifications of the kinds of assistance required.

SUMMARY AND CONCLUSIONS

In this chapter, scenes described by teachers are hearable as moral tales (Baruch, 1981; Silverman, 1993). Through the presentation of transcript data I have examined a number of scenic practices employed by speakers in the development of these moral tales. To summarize, these include the following.

Direct and indirect reported speech is used in the production of 'scenes'. Direct reported speech is used with a high degree of frequency in teachers' descriptions. This serves to underscore to the recipient how the purported event should be heard, adding a moral dimension to the account.

Characters depicted in scenes are morally laden through their assigned attributes and may be read reflexively as indicative of the music teacher's place in the moral universe portrayed.

The researcher's co-categorial incumbency as music teacher is particularly important in the generation of these scenes, and her receptivity to the implications of scenes described is apparent in talk.

Category descriptions are unstable across talk and may be read as indicating that any particular character might appear with different sets of attributes (or in different guises) on multiple occasions. As Bergmann (1998: 287) has noted, categories are used *locally* as a 'major resource for the construction of moral actors and courses of moral action'.

Speakers provide unique descriptions of a range of actual scenes, many of which could be easily recognizable by other music teachers. Each scene is 'local' in that it is related to a particular setting and to recent and prospective events within that setting. Each 'actual' scene is selected from an array of 'possible' scenes recognizable as ways in which the world could (or should) be ordered.

By using procedures drawn from CA and MCA, it is possible to discover vital clues as to *how* portrayals and descriptions of institutional life occur in research settings. In doing so, it is possible to elucidate key features of the cultural universe in which particular speakers involve themselves in everyday life in institutions. These features include the following:

- an understanding and elucidation of the key role the researcher as a co-incumbent hearer occupied in the generation of data for analysis; and
- insight into the moral world of the 'actual' and 'everyday' as it concerns the cultural world of speakers; which will
- generate analyses of how those 'actuals' are artfully depicted against a backdrop of 'possibilities', 'how things might possibly be arranged' (Baker, 1997).

The ways in which 'actual' and 'local' scenes are portrayed in the talk presented in this chapter provide insight not only into 'unique' situations in which speakers might find themselves; they also imply a much wider array of 'possible' scenes, conditions or situations. These selections of 'actualities', along with the collections of other 'possibilities', are recognizable as ways in which the world of schools as one institutional setting could (or should) be ordered.

9 Whose personality is it anyway? The production of 'personality' in a diagnostic interview[1]

John Lobley

EDITORIAL

As a number of other contributions to this volume note, the notion of personality bulks large in standard psychological accounts of the human person. But, as Edwards and Potter have reminded us, 'both "reality" and "mind" are constructed by people conceptually, in language, in the course of their performance of practical tasks'. At the risk of conflating Edwards and Potter's important distinction, we might say that 'personality' is one of psychology's most central 'mental realities'. If so, then any discourse-centred approach would want to show how 'personality' is, in fact, in actual face-to-face encounters, talked into conceptual existence. If personality is neither a prior mental disposition of 'clients' nor a mere set of results, Lobley reasons, then how is it that persons come to be ranked and grouped as having particular personality traits – for example, as introverted or extroverted, prone to judging as against perceiving, and so forth? DP's answer to the question is that this must have something to do with the in situ *testing encounters themselves.*

Turning to some of the central concerns of applied CA (as outlined by Paul ten Have in Chapter 1) – including the organization of turn-taking and sequence organization – Lobley shows how these devices are strategically employed by psychological testers to co-implicate clients in resolving conflictual personality-based accounts of themselves (by themselves, and by others).

We have already seen how such matters as rights to the floor and obligations to respond are often asymmetrically distributed in institutional settings. Callers to helplines have different rights and obligations from call takers (Baker et al.*, Chapter 4; Kelly, Chapter 6), and the same can be said for politicians and their audiences (Herschell, Chapter 10). In this chapter, however, Lobley shows how these* rule-like possibilities *for participants (as opposed to firm and fixed* rules to be followed*) work on a turn-by-turn basis to accomplish what looks to be, after the fact, a 'factual' clinical statement about a particular person's 'personality'.*

A trained and practising psychologist and frequent administrator of personality assessments, Lobley has recently adopted a discursive-psychological (DP) approach to reflecting on his own work. Novices in the field will be able to see (and emulate) how he has critically mobilized many of the concepts already encountered in this book to that end. His chapter effectively provides an initial model (or, as he would say, 'a first run') for anyone considering the work that talk does in their own local professional settings.

INTRODUCTION

Constructionist scholarship is devoted to understanding the generation of what we take to be objective knowledge. It means 'exploring the literary and rhetorical devices by which meaning is achieved and rendered compelling' (Gergen, 1997: 723), and presents a fundamental challenge to traditional 'psychological' tools (for example, personality inventories). These measures, based on essentialist and realist assumptions, take 'personality' to be a property of individuals and a predictive or explanatory variable. The problem, from a constructionist perspective, is the elevation of these models to the status of a real inner world of causal mechanisms (Harré, 1998). Yet, mental processes are not necessarily the grounds for explaining human action and the 'psyche' does not necessarily serve as the locus of understanding (Gergen, 1997).

If the way individuals conceive of themselves will influence what they choose to do and what they expect from life (Gergen, 1970), then what are the consequences of self-knowledge defined from an epistemology that denies the importance of discourse as a fundamental sense-making process? The limitations of a rational psychological world are well described by Coulter (1989: 152–3): 'mystifying reifications in the domains of "personality characteristics"' provide causal explanations of conduct 'with reference to features of "personality" type'. However, he continues, 'if theoretical reifications of the mental and of the personality cannot serve as genuine explanatory "mechanisms", then many psychologistic explanation strategies fail'.

Wittgenstein's (1953) challenge to psychologistic explanations grounds 'phenomena' in everyday language. In the interactional setting of a diagnostic interview, the 'languaged' constructions of personality inventories may provide the 'resources through which individuals' subjectivities and experiences are shaped' (Widdicombe, 1998: 197). The focus of this analysis will be upon the practical nature of language, in an institutional interaction, and how it is used to do things – an example of fact-construction through talk-in-action (Potter, 1996a).

DATA

Our fragment of actual face-to-face interaction is drawn from a diagnostic interview between an occupational psychologist and a client. The client, as part of a process for planning personal development, has completed a Myers-Briggs Type Inventory (MBTI). This inventory is based on the theory that people have a 'preference' for one of two opposites on each of its four scales.

The purpose of the 'diagnostic' interview is to enable the client to 'self-assess' his or her preferences, to compare these with the inventory results, and to reach agreement on a 'best-fit' type. In the fraction of the interview to be analysed below, a discrepancy arises between the inventory results and the client's self-assessment of his preferred way of making decisions (thinking or feeling).

ANALYSIS

The analysis will identify the action performed by talk and the conversational resources used to resolve the above-mentioned discrepancy and reach agreement. The analytic interest is in social action achieved in language – or, as it has come to be called, 'talk-in-interaction' (Schegloff, 1991). This study attempts to discover how that social action works by using CA to ask the following questions:

1. To which mechanisms of talk-in-interaction can the participants be heard to orient?
2. How do these 'oriented-to' conversational structures influence the social activity?
3. How do these conversational organizations 'bring off' the personality construction?

The data were first approached without any pre-formed theory, adopting the analytic approach described by Psathas (1995: 45) as 'unmotivated looking'. In effect, this means: 'giving some consideration to whatever can be found in any particular conversation' (Sacks, 1984: 27). A 'bracketing' strategy was also incorporated, according to the suggestions of Heritage and Atkinson (1984: 1) who argue that

> analysis can be generated out of matters observable in the data of interaction. The analyst is thus not required to speculate upon what the interactants hypothetically or imaginably understood, or the procedures or constraints to which they could conceivably have been oriented.

Approaching the data without pre-specified analytic goals (Schegloff, 1996) exposed an action being accomplished. It was only from the transcribing process of repeated listening and close analysis of the transcription that the means by which this was happening were unveiled.

For the second stage of analysis an exploratory analytic strategy to dissect the fragment and reveal its contents was adopted. Described by Heritage (1997: 164) as places to probe the 'institutionality' of conversation, I used the following conversational features to conduct a 'first run' (Bergmann, 1992):

1. turn-taking organization
2. overall structural organization

3. sequence organization
4. turn-construction design
5. epistemological and other forms of asymmetry[2]

Accordingly, this chapter turns to this framework (Heritage, 1997) to reveal and analyse conversational features in our fragment of talk by means of one or two examples. Although considerably more could be revealed by further analysis, the following insights are, hopefully, sufficient for the analytic interests of this study.

TURN-TAKING ORGANIZATION

Conversation unfolds sequentially through participants taking turns at talk (Sacks *et al.*, 1974). This apparently trivial observation belies the fact that the turn, as a basic unit of social action, 'provides a simple and extraordinarily efficient way of allocating activities' (Boden, 1994: 66). Sacks *et al.* (1974) describe the 'rules' for the various ways in which 'turn taking' may take place. The 'rules' for talk-in-interaction formulated by Sacks and his colleagues are not causally determining. Rather: 'It is the parties to the conversation who determine the distribution of turns at talk amongst them' (Button *et al.*, 1995: 200); thereby the parties themselves manage the implementation of the rules. Rules are not followed but oriented to: they only ever exist as resources for local accomplishments.

All interactions use some sort of turn-taking organization that shapes the parties' opportunities for action. The asymmetrical distribution of questions and answers in this interaction is a product of the task the parties are engaged in rather than a formal pre-allocation. Nevertheless, the collaborative turn-taking does give the psychologist greater opportunity to pursue his interests. The action potential of the psychologist's turns is heard in the following questions:

26 P °How would ↑other people describe you do you think°
44 P So ↑which is, (.) as you put it, which box would other folks put you in?
60 P Right so you think that best fits you

The jointly managed question–answer turn-taking organization provides the psychologist with a leading role and opportunities to decide much of the content and direction of the conversation. As Sacks (1992a: 55) puts it, 'the one who is doing the questions has control of the conversation, [but only] *in part*' (see also McHoul, 1987).

OVERALL STRUCTURAL ORGANIZATION

To look at the overall structural organization of a conversation is to investigate institutional interactions so as to identify their task structures, their sub-goals, and whether the parties work together on the task and its parts. This is not a framework into which data must *fit* but rather – to the extent that parties orient to it in organizing their talk (Heritage, 1997) – is something to look for. We can then begin this section by speculating that the structure of the entire diagnostic feedback session follows a pattern that is mirrored in each of the sections of the assessment. The psychologist outlines the task, gains permission to ask questions, elicits information, confirms that information, and then finally provides an assessment or 'diagnosis'. In ordinary conversational terms, this has the following series of five phases:

- *Permission* – Can I ask you a question?
- *Probe* – Question
- *Account* – Answer
- *Verification* (and *challenge*) – Is this what you said?
- *Interpretation* – This is what you said

Permission This follows the format of 'Can I ask you a question?' (Schegloff, 1980). In the next extract, following an unsuccessful attempt at resolution, P begins to reframe the task and propose a revised inquiry process:

P Right (.) You don't have to be bowled over by them [its=
C [no
P =just which
which most accurately fits you
(0.9)
P No?
C No
P Right. (6.5) erm what about (0.9) some of these then (3.5) cos we don't
have to erm (0.5) conclude this today [its=
C [right
P =ok for you to go away
with a (0.7) a hypothesis or a theory or [a=
C [right
P =best fit that still has
some slack in it for you to (0.7) erm you know work out (5.2) What I'd
like to try and do is (.) you know figure out what the issues are=
=Right

P unsuccessfully attempts to circumvent a 'standstill' by moderating the extreme position expressed by C's earlier use of 'bowled over'. Then P tries a different 'tack' with 'cos we don't have to conclude this today' (15–16). His permission to continue is occasioned by C's agreement, 'right' (17, 20, 24). The psychologist's reframing is cautious and tenuous ('just', 'don't have to conclude', 'slack', and so forth). His artfully vague 'offer' (22–23) is accepted. Having taken the pressure off C to decide, P gets permission to continue the inquiry.

Probe P 'opens up' the conversation (26), steering away from the MBTI theoretical constructs, and moving towards C's own knowledge. He 'invites' C's perspective on information that might contribute to the diagnosis: 'How would other people describe you do you think?'

Account C provides an account of how, in his opinion, other people view him ('she'd say', 'they would say'), qualified by his own self-perception ('I'm', 'I would', 'I think'). C's account reveals an inconsistency between his own perspective and the views he ascribes to others.[3]

Verification (and *challenge*) P selects items from C's account to corroborate specific information, and uses it to 'expose' the conflict within C's account and between C's perspective and others' ascriptions (31, 38, 40 and 44, cited later). He then passes the 'problem' to C:

80 P So what's that <u>about</u> do you think?=
81 C =Dunno

We could say more about what C is 'doing' with his choice of utterance at line 81 but for now it serves to point to the transition to the next phase.

Interpretation P moves on to 'diagnose' (82–86, cited later), also using information gathered earlier in the interaction, and enlisting additional observational information about C (90), and both accept this as appropriate for this interactional context. The client agrees with the assessment via a series of minimal utterances ('right', 'yes' and so forth) and the psychologist concludes his tentative diagnosis.

It is unlikely that such a structure would be routine in ordinary conversation. Although it bears some of the same structural features as in everyday talk, in the present context its 'working' indicates a form of institutional interaction. The parties orient to an evolving structure that helps them complete the task: assessment, interpretation and diagnosis – and, as we shall see, construction of a personality.

SEQUENCE ORGANIZATION

Turns at talk are linked together in definite sequences. As Paul ten Have (1999: 114–15) has noticed: 'Sequences are *patterns* of subsequent actions, where the "subsequentiality" is not an arbitrary occurrence, but is rather the realisation of locally constituted projections, rights and obligations'. Further, from another source: 'It is by means of specific actions that are organized in sequences that the participants initiate, develop and conclude the business they have together, and generally manage their encounters' (Heritage, 1997: 169). In conversation, then, there are some very familiar utterance-pair sequences – question–answer, invitation–acceptance, greeting–return, and so forth. These are referred to in CA as adjacency pairs: 'two contiguous utterances from different speakers which are heard as connected such that the first part . . . makes the occurrence of the second . . . expected' (Buttny, 1993: 39). The question–answer sequence is one such powerfully routine conversational mechanism.

Ten Have (1999: 113) illuminates this conversational mechanism as follows: 'the idea of "*sequence*" refers to the common experience that "one thing can lead to another"'. The effect of sequencing on participants' rights and opportunities to speak can be seen in the following extracts. The psychologist uses a sequence-like structure of repetitive cycles of questioning to steer the conversation. Sacks (1992a) refers to this phenomenon as a 'chaining rule' – a person who gets to ask a question gets to talk again and can follow with another question and so on.

→26 P °How would ↑other people describe you do you think°
27 C You don't want to talk to my wife ha ha ha ha ha ha
28 P (   )
29 C Sh she'd say I'm er I'm a machine (0.5) unfeelin (1.9) she'd say (0.2)
30 she'd say log very logical
→31 P °Right,° (.) and (.) do you (.) disagree with that?

→38 P You're detached?
39 C Yeeah
→40 P So like this sort of stuff?
41 C Yea (0.2) that that she'd put me in that box definitely although I can see
42 meself with some characteristics in this feeling (1.5) but er (0.5) that is
43 is the one that tends to be the front
→44 P So ↑which is, (.) as you put it, which box would other folks put you in?

P gets to ask a series of questions (as indicated), each 'designed for its occasion' (ten Have, 1999: 121), often choosing words previously supplied by C. The chaining rule, then, allows P to pursue his goal and to elicit particular and selected information from C. Here we can see how sequence organization is a 'phenomenon through which the institutionality of talk is substantiated' (Drew and Heritage, 1992a: 37). That is, the psychologist gets to 'do' a series of similar questions to obtain information, to assemble it, and to draw conclusions.

TURN-CONSTRUCTION DESIGN

Utterances are built to fit specific recipients ('recipient design'), intended to perform an action, and designed to maximize the occurrence of the actions being performed. How a turn is designed for its occasion, and the means used to construct it, is a meaningful choice informed by speakers' knowledge of the situation. For example, P uses a 'judicious, cautious and "institutional" piece of question design' (Heritage, 1997: 173): 'How would other people describe you do you think?' (26). This conversational manoeuvre – somewhat like a perspective display series (PDS) (Maynard, 1991) – opens things up. P invites C to give an opinion and then, as Psathas (1995: 61) puts it, 'the matters elicited from the [client] can then be used by the clinician in the formulation of his report'. The PDS works as follows:

- clinician's opinion-query, or perspective display invitation
- recipient's reply or assessment
- clinician's report and assessment

This device is of particular interest here because it occurs at a significant point in the conversation and has implications for the subsequent interaction. The assessment has become 'stuck', providing limited (or even no) diagnostic possibilities: 'Initiating the series is an inherently cautious maneuver' (Maynard, 1992: 355). The opinion-query is followed by further questions that permit the recipient 'to talk at length' on the topic (Maynard, 1991: 168). An additional feature of the PDS is that, by way of this series, clinicians can deliver a diagnosis that confirms and co-implicates the recipient's perspective (Maynard, 1992: 351–2). In our case, C responds to this opinion-query without any noticeable hesitation: 'You don't want to talk to my wife ha ha ha ha ha ha' (27).

What does C want to do with this action? He works against the ascriptions of his wife and others using contrasting extreme case formulations. P designs his next audible utterance (31) to elicit more, relevant, information by challenging C to account for the contrast between his wife's assessment and the self-perspective he is maintaining in the interaction: 'Right, and do you disagree with that?'. P then continues to move the agenda forward by designing his utterances to fit the evolving situation, using previous expressions and compatible pronouns ('you're detached?', 'as you put it, which box . . . ?'). Working to be careful about what he says, P 'packages' his actions to develop the discussion, and the 'evidence' of others, until a point (80) where he uses his turn to challenge C about the discrepancies and hand the 'dilemma' over to C:

80 P So what's that about do you think?=
81 C =Dunno

C does not take up the chance to speak ('Dunno'), thereby handing the floor back to P who constructs his turn so as to tentatively proffer suggestions:

82 P ( ) its just a risk for me you know (.) putting ideas in your head its
83 about (.) maybe that you want to be (1.3) more like that, develop more

The psychologist is careful not to enter the 'dispute' (Buttny, 1996). Instead, he designs his turns to avoid contentious information and presents his case tentatively ('maybe', 'perhaps') so as to maximize the occurrence of the action being performed. In such ways, the psychologist can be heard to be designing his utterances to accomplish the agenda. His utterance designs may have been 'perfected' from what Heritage (1997: 173) refers to as 'wind tunnel' experiments. Repetition in a number of similar contexts – repeating similar actions (ten Have, 1999) – leads to the discovery or development of turn designs or constructions with least resistance. P should not be heard as 'Machiavellian' (Heritage, 1997: 173) but, having done it before, he has learned what works in this task. The interactional consequences, nevertheless, have a significant effect on the process and outcome of the conversation and the jointly constructed reality.

ASYMMETRIES

All social interaction must inevitably be asymmetric, for 'if there were no asymmetries at all between people, i.e. if communicatively relevant inequalities of knowledge were non-existing, there would be little or no need for most types of communication!' (Linell and Luckmann, 1991: 4). So, although institutional interactions are characteristically asymmetrical, it is important not to overstate the case. Four types of asymmetry are used by Heritage (1997) to examine institutional interaction: participation; 'know-how'; knowledge (and epistemological caution); and rights of access to knowledge. Let us deal with each in turn.

Participation Drew and Heritage (1992a: 49) write: 'Institutional representatives may strategically direct the talk through such means as their capacity to change topics and their selective formulations, in their "next questions" of the salient points in the prior answers.' Recall P asking 'You're detached?' (38). Here, the psychologist's question serves as but one example of the interactional consequences of asymmetrical participation. In two words, he uses salient points to make a selective formulation to choose and shape the next topic.

Know-how Unequal knowledge about the process-at-hand (know-how) arises from the fact that this is a routine experience (case) for the professional, whilst being unique and personal for the client. The client might not know what kind of protocol or agenda the psychologist is working from. For example, P uses the 'right' to observe C's behaviour (90) and to 'match' this with other information from the model as 'evidence' of his personality 'type':

90 P but a erm let me just give you some feedback from watching you do
91 that (.) erm (2.1) er before I heard that stuff about (.) yer wife is

The psychologist is doing some actions on the basis of 'know-how' which have an interactional relevance and noticeable effect on the outcome.

Epistemological caution and asymmetries of knowledge Professionals act cautiously when telling clients something about themselves. They tend to avoid taking a firm position on issues and avoid committing themselves. Clients may co-produce roles (expert and layperson) and ignore important aspects of their own experience. Tentativity and epistemological caution can be heard, for example, in the following lines:

82 P ( ) its just a risk for me you know (.) putting ideas in your head its
83 about (.) maybe that you want to be (1.3) [more like that, develop more
84 C [Yeah (.) I've yea
85 P of that erm this is your perhaps your (.) preference in terms of it
86 describin (0.5) your: (0.7) way of being and er how you've become (1.9)

Here, the psychologist tentatively proposes his assessment using 'maybe', 'more like' (83) 'perhaps' (85). This strategy works interactionally to avoid resistance. In a similar fashion, Drew and Heritage (1992a: 52) refer to 'the striking finding that, at the point in the consultation when doctors announce their diagnoses, patients typically withhold responding, neither commenting upon nor questioning the diagnosis'. A further important feature of this asymmetry is illustrated by the psychologist's utterance 'its just a risk for me . . . putting ideas in your head' (82) – paradoxically, he is doing exactly what he claims not to be doing (personal communication with Charles Antaki).

Rights of access to knowledge Asymmetries of knowledge arise when people have limited resources to answer, 'what do I know?' and 'how do I know it?' (Heritage, 1997: 178). Professionals are accordingly given the larger share of the 'right to know'. Clients might then be heard as hiding or suspending their rights to knowledge:

45 C They'd put me in this one as well I think ((tapping paper)). (3.0) But
46 you're askin me aren't you (1.2) where I would put myself and I would
47 put myself somewhere in between

The client, then, maintains his own perspective until lines 80–81 where, as we have seen, he gives the 'right to know' over to the psychologist ('So what's that about do you think?'/'Dunno'). The presence of this feature of talk-in-interaction has an impact on the 'reality' and 'personality' constructed in this institutional interaction.

HOW IS PERSONALITY 'CONSTRUCTED' IN THIS INTERACTION?

This necessarily brief analysis has served to demonstrate the illuminating power of a CA perspective. It has indicated the interactional consequences of the 'rules' of talk, their flexibilities, and the powerful influence these have on sense-making in context and on how 'reality' is constructed in talk. The study adopts the strategy of: 'noticing of the action being done and being pursued by specifying what about the talk or other conduct – in its context – serves as the practice for accomplishing that action' (Schegloff, 1996: 172). This EM/CA-based stance has not queried whether the diagnosis is 'true', or indeed whether it is useful, but has instead investigated how it happens in practice. We have asked how institutional reality is interactively constructed and illustrated this by a close examination of the talk itself.

Heritage's (1997) framework has revealed the following matters:

1. how turn-taking is jointly managed to enable the psychologist to ask questions and the client to provide answers;
2. how the parties orient to an overall structure that elicits client information that is interpreted against the MBTI framework;
3. how the sequence-like structure (repetitive cycles of questions) and the 'chaining rule' allow the psychologist to steer the conversation in the direction of the task;
4. how turns are designed to fit the parties in the ongoing interaction, and how the psychologist's use of 'practised' utterances maximizes progress towards (and co-implicates the client in) the diagnosis;
5. how the tentative diagnosis is achieved by the parties orienting to asymmetries of knowledge, know-how and participation; and finally,
6. how the tentativity of the diagnosis further serves to secure the client's acceptance of his 'personality' as credible, objective and relevant.

The action takes place at all levels of interactional organization, so it is difficult to say which is the most crucial feature as they are 'thoroughly interrelated' (Heritage, 1997: 179). The simple conclusion is that both parties construct a 'reality' for the client by orienting to and artfully using the 'rules' and sequential structures of talk-in-interaction. Rather than blindly *following* pre-given rules, that is, both parties *orient to* them in order to *jointly manage* the interaction at a local level. The client gives up certain rights and obligations in interaction and the psychologist uses his reciprocal rights and obligations to accomplish what counts as a legitimate outcome. The mechanics of conversation to which the parties are socially accountable work to jointly accomplish this construction. A locally contexted social reality of talk-in-interaction is oriented to and provides the means to create a psychological reality for the client. The psychologist then interprets the client's talk within the MBTI framework to provide the client with a new 'map' of his behaviour and experience: his 'personality'. C's 'personality' has been 'talked into being', or constructed in practice, through a socially accountable orientation to the 'rules' of conversation and its sequential implicativeness – one thing leads to another.

Notes

1. This study is part of a British NHS (NW) R&D Fellowship: RDO/33′25.
2. Heritage's list also includes 'lexical choice', a relatively unimportant parameter in the present instance.
3. Space precludes inclusion of all the relevant data here, but see 'Sequence organization' (pp. 119–20) for some of C's account.

10 Howard's way: naturalizing the new reciprocity between the citizen and the state

Karen Herschell

EDITORIAL

From the late 1990s, the Australian Liberal government under John Howard embarked on a campaign of 'mutual obligation'. On the surface, this appeared a commonsensical and perhaps, to some, even a reasonable policy since it only required that those who benefit from government assistance should be obliged to offer something concrete in return for it. What it ignored was the enormous social disparities between welfare and non-welfare recipients in terms of their capacities *to 'give back'. To reverse Marx's formulation, it meant, in effect: from each according to their needs to each according to their abilities.*

So how did the Prime Minister bring off the rhetorical task of making such a policy seem to be, as Karen Herschell puts it in this chapter, 'common sense'? Turning to the CA literature, Herschell locates a number of familiar discursive devices that politicians use in order to gain support from different audiences. She looks in particular at the use of three-part lists, pronominal devices and contrast pairs.

The first of these (the three-part list) works analogously to the speaking clock: 'On the third stroke . . .'. Logically, the minimal number of tones is three: one tone to get the list going, a second to establish a frequency of tones, and a third to mark a specific moment using the established frequency. As Herschell points out, politicians can mobilize the same sort of device to design their talk so that audiences will know just when to applaud – that is, to display concurrence.

The second device is also well known in both ordinary conversation and political speeches. That is, pronouns can be used, as Maurice Nevile shows in his chapter, not just to refer to other nouns but also to achieve moral connections and/or disconnections between speakers and listeners (or between them and absent parties). Hence, 'we' can be inclusive of the one who hears it ('We do such and such, don't we?') or else exclusive of them ('We do such and such, but you . . .'). Herschell shows how Howard carefully selects and deploys such pronominal choices in order to attach himself to, or detach himself from, policy positions.

Finally, contrast pairs work to show the 'naturalness' of one side of an argument in opposition to the apparent wrongness of what it stands against. These take the discursive form

'X would say Y, but I say Z'. Hence Howard uses phrases like 'Where some would scrap work-for-the-dole, I remain passionately committed to extending the principle of asking people to give back something to the community'.

In these and several related ways, Herschell shows us how Howard is able to build up a suite of rhetorics that 'naturalize' or 'make credible' what is, on some other readings, a radical and draconian cutback in government welfare assistance. We often ask how political leaders 'get away with' introducing such measures (whether we agree with them or not). Standard accounts of this have to do with 'power', 'railroading' and 'numbers'. But what Herschell shows is how such political effects are discursively constructed in the institutional environment of the political speech.

INTRODUCTION

In this chapter, I analyse how Australian Prime Minister, John Howard, accomplishes the task of making a new reciprocity between the citizen and the state appear commonsensical. In order to do this, I analyse the text of his Federation Address, 'The Australian Way', presented to the Queensland Chamber of Commerce and Industry in January 1999. In the current political climate, particular groups of welfare recipients are in the process of being rearticulated as 'undeserving' of public support because of their perceived failure to contribute to the 'broad national economic agendas' laid down by the Howard government. The Australian welfare state has historically been framed around notions of 'deserving' and 'non-deserving' citizenship. This attitude dates back to colonial Australia when debates about who ought to receive care emphasized the dominant 'virtues' of thrift, self-help and self-reliance in the practice of charity (Wearing and Berreen, 1994: 12). Governmental policy creates and reinforces, rewards and punishes, particular groups according to the moral categories to which they have been assigned. Economic contribution has become the moral yardstick by which the 'deserving' are measured and citizenship is (re)defined.

This represents a radical change in the operating principles of government and a redefinition of the notion of reciprocity between the Australian state and its citizens. Particular categories of welfare recipient are being reconstructed as *actively resisting* the goals of the Australian nation. I will demonstrate how Howard, in this speech, attempts both to de-politicize welfare and to attack welfare recipients on the basis of their perceived contribution, while simultaneously dismantling welfare.

Both the 'situational context' of a statement (the social situation in which it occurs) and its 'verbal context' (its position in relation to other statements which precede and follow it) affect what is said or written, how it is interpreted and how it varies from one discursive formation to another. Consequently, I will use a combination of CA and CDA techniques in order to demonstrate how Prime Minister Howard makes the new reciprocity appear commonsensical.

ANALYSING PRE-SCRIPTED SPEECHES

I have chosen a pre-scripted speech for analysis here for the following reasons. First, as the speech was retrieved from the official prime-ministerial webpage, it can be considered to represent official governmental policy. Secondly, in a pre-scripted speech, the politician – or the political speech writer – is consciously involved in the organization and selection of each lexical item and each syntactic construction in an effort to achieve the maximum required effect on the audience. Therefore the pre-scripted speech has been deliberated over, discussed and carefully worded. It is not 'off-the-cuff'. Finally, this text is interesting as it provides the context in which the Liberal Party chose to introduce a new 'mutual obligation policy'.

CONVERSATION ANALYSIS

CA has been accused of having little relevance to 'real world' issues and problems. However, Hutchby and Wooffitt (1998) maintain that CA's findings and analytic orientation can be a valuable tool for the investigation of social activity in a number of areas, including political rhetoric. Political rhetoric has become so familiar to us that it can easily be taken for granted. We hear politicians' speeches on television, on the radio, and at public addresses. We may read extracts of speeches in newspapers and articles and they are often reproduced on the internet. The internet also allows public access to any political speech by a political party, provided they have supplied the information on a website. Posting a speech on a webpage is, then, in itself, a political act. Below, I will examine the linguistic devices used by Howard in the Federation Address in order to make his policy linking literacy skills to 'the dole' appear to be commonsensical. First, however, I will define the way 'common sense' is used in this chapter.

COMMON SENSE

When trying to identify features which demonstrate 'common sense', particular qualities come to mind – good sense, level-headedness and practicality. A perusal of the thesaurus adds 'gumption', 'horse-sense', 'prudence', 'reasonable-ness', 'sound-judgement', 'soundness' and 'wit'. Even the words themselves have an 'aged' quality. But mostly, '(common) sense' assumes a shared sense or understanding. It is important for politicians to be considered to have 'common sense' and to be able to convince their voters that their ideas and beliefs extend beyond political rhetoric and into the practicalities of 'everyday' life. Politicians rely upon their supporters to show their approval, and consequently to convince others that their views meet with widespread support. Approval of the views espoused in politicians' speeches is most obviously and immediately demonstrated through applause. Consequently, in the following section, I will identify ways in which Howard attempts to generate applause through the use of common linguistic devices.

RHETORICAL DEVICES

Atkinson (1984) has identified a number of rhetorical devices used by politicians which successfully generate, or precede, enthusiastic audience applause, including the use of 'three-part lists' and 'contrast devices'. These tend to be prevalent in more extended texts written with a view to eliciting approval. Furthermore, they are popular as they tend to elicit responses which last for longer than the average eight seconds, and are thus more likely to be noticed and reported in the media (Atkinson, 1984: 151). According to Hutchby and Wooffitt (1998: 234–5), audience members feel uncomfortable about applauding in isolation and need to be 'under the impression that others will also applaud at the same time as they do'. Rhetorical devices such as lists and contrasts solve this problem because they project their own completion: as they are being built, they signal when they are going to end. The devices themselves provide the audience with a cue for when to clap and thus allow collective displays of affiliation. In this sense, we can say that devices like lists and contrasts are audience-management devices (Hutchby and Wooffitt, 1998: 235).

THREE-PART LISTS

Jefferson (1990) has demonstrated how people routinely produce three-part lists in conversation. The three-part list is 'simply some point made via the use of three specific components' (Hutchby and Wooffitt, 1998: 232). Jefferson maintains that, in ordinary conversation, when one speaker is producing a list, a co-participant can anticipate that when the third item is produced, then the list is likely to be complete (1990: 63). Accordingly, third items are treated as possible completion points in speeches. Furthermore, Hutchby and Wooffitt (1998: 236) claim not only that an audience can 'see' that a politician is making a list – and their tacit sensitivity to everyday conversation enables them to anticipate that it will be completed – but also that they will anticipate that it will be completed. This occurs 'not after two points, and not after four, but after three' (1998: 236).

In the following extracts from 'The Australian Way', Howard uses the rhetorical device of the three-part list. This may be read as an attempt to 'strengthen or affirm a broader overarching position or claim' (Hutchby and Wooffitt, 1998: 233). The lists are shown by added emphasis.[1]

> These have been years of remarkable *consolidation, strengthening and reform* of the Australian economy. (p. 2)
>
> And we've tackled the most fundamental challenges facing Australians today by drawing on their own strengths and values – *individualism, a willingness to take on responsibility, the desire for choice and opportunity*. (p. 2)
>
> And just as economic reforms of the past have delivered strength and prosperity now, so it is the reforms of today and tomorrow that will deliver the *higher economic growth, employment and living standards* of the future. (p. 3)
>
> And as we stand on the edge of the new millennium, Australia's fortune lies not so much with parliaments or business, or political parties or money markets but with individual Australians – *young and old, men and women, Australians by birth or choice*. (p. 1)

In these statements, Howard offers optimism and the prospect of prosperity for all, as all categories and groups are included in his final statement. The more attractively packaged politicians' statements and speeches are, the more likely they are to be followed up and reported in the media. In summary, as Atkinson (1984: 159) notes, three-part lists and contrast devices 'provide a snappy way of summarising and simplifying quite complicated arguments'.

PRONOMINAL CHOICE

Wilson (1990) shows how aspects of the pronominal system of English can be manipulated for political effect – arguing that pronouns do not form neat categorical divisions and as such are open to manipulation. The pronominal system can be employed both to 'distribute responsibility' and to 'distinguish the individual view' (1990: 63). Consequently, politicians are able to manipulate the pronominal system to good effect in order to:

> indicate, accept, deny or distance themselves from responsibility for political action; to reveal ideological bias; to encourage solidarity; to designate and identify those who are supporters (with us) as well as those who are enemies (against us) and to present specific idiosyncratic aspects of the individual politician's own personality. (1990: 76)

Chafe (1982), in a comparison of scripted and non-scripted speeches, found that there were more first-person singular pronouns in unscripted speeches. In a pre-scripted speech, we can expect that most attention will be given to the selection of pronouns (Wilson, 1990: 69), so demonstrating the power of pronominal choice. Below, I show how Howard manipulates the pronominal system in his Address, alternating between ownership of, and distancing himself from, his statements.

First, as we have seen, in his introductory remarks, Howard's employment of the exclusive 'we' immediately aligns him with 'all Australians': 'And as *we* stand on the edge of the new millennium'. Then, in the following extract, he outlines particular human qualities that he suggests are desirable and necessary for Australian citizens:

> A century ago, Sir Henry Parkes – that great hearted champion of federation declared Australia ready for unity, for the dazzling prize of nationhood because of, in his words, *the vigour, the industry, the enterprise, the foresight, and the creative skill of its people.* (p. 2, emphasis added here, and in subsequent quotations from same source)

He attempts this by first attributing the idea to 'Sir Henry Parkes – that great hearted champion of federation'. He later uses the inclusive 'I' to personalize the sentiments, making them the sentiments of John Howard 'the man', rather than as Prime Minister or as party leader. This also allows him to align himself with Australian 'tradition' and 'old-fashioned values'.

Howard reformulates this into a three-part list in his summation, when he declares that 'Australians remain the *enterprising, vigorous and creative* people of whom Parkes spoke so lovingly' (p. 7). The values this suggests are that the necessary 'characteristics of a nation' include 'vigour', 'industry', 'enterprise' and 'foresight and creative skill' – attributes which fit Howard's axiom of individualism. Considering his audience (the Chamber of Commerce and Industry), Howard has made a relatively safe choice of 'desirable qualities' if his aim is to achieve common agreement and audience approval and applause. The characteristics upon which the Australian character has been traditionally mythologized, such as 'mateship', 'camaraderie' and 'larrikinism', are notably absent from this speech. Interestingly, by contrast, in an address to a social services congress in Adelaide in 1998, Howard described the Australian character as 'democratic and fair-minded . . . with a sense of fair play and a strong egalitarian streak'.[2]

Howard's alignment with his Australian political forebear Sir Henry Parkes works to reinforce his image as conservative and traditional, thus appealing to his party's supporters. However, his references to the past also construct Howard the Prime Minister as one link in a long political chain, giving the impression of stability and steady progress. I argue that this allows him to introduce a radical, new policy to the public in a manner that makes it appear as effectively a 'natural progression'.

In the next extract, Howard shifts to an *inclusive* 'we' to refer to his political party. Shifting from the singular to the plural allows him to state the policy goals of the party, while at the same time distancing himself personally. Obviously, in democracies, a politician's personal survival relies upon votes. Consequently, this device is regularly employed in political speeches in order to protect individual politicians from potentially unpopular decisions made by the party they belong to. Howard's use of the inclusive 'we' is also evident in the statement:

> *We* have already extended the Seniors' Health Card and the Veterans' Gold Card and provided the farm families assets test concession just as *we* have recognised the

> desire of older Australians to be cared for in their own homes through our Staying at Home package. (p. 6)

The first-person singular pronoun can be used in order to establish rapport and, when attached to mental process verbs, to communicate sincerity (Wilson, 1990: 62). Wilson maintains that blocks of 'I' (three or more) are used to communicate sincerity and dignity (1990: 62). In the next extract, Howard makes use of the personalized voice encoded in 'I' to communicate his resolutions for the future:

> So it is that in this address I will *define the main domestic goals* of the government in 1999, *indicate a significant strengthening* of the application of the principle of mutual obligation and *announce Commonwealth assistance* for a major resource project here in Queensland – a tangible demonstration of our commitment to nation building as we move into the next century. (p. 2)

This section is very much in electioneering mode, with Howard combining the rhetorical devices of the three-part list (emphasized in the extract) and the personalized voice encoded in his 'I' statements. As he moves from the hypothetical (as he describes his intentions) to the practical (something that has actually been done), he shifts from using 'I' to 'we', thereby including his government and the relevant ministry: 'We are resolved to pursue policies that are likely to maintain our remarkable rate of economic growth and strength' (p. 2). He goes on with:

> We are absolutely committed . . .
>
> Thirdly, we will not tire . . .
>
> Fourthly, we will further expand . . .
>
> Finally, we will work to create . . .

CONTRASTIVE DEVICES

Another major rhetorical device used by politicians is the use of 'contrastive devices'. Hutchby and Wooffitt (1998: 233) maintain that, through their use, politicians can 'positively evaluate their own position in a much more explicit way while, at the same time, still criticizing another position or set of policies. One example of a contrast structure from Howard's speech is now illustrated: 'Where some would scrap work for the dole I remain passionately committed to extending the principle of asking people to give back something to the community in return for assistance in time of need' (p. 7). The views of the unnamed '*some* who would scrap work for the dole' sit in contrast to Howard's 'passionate commitment' to extending the program. His use of 'I' makes this a strongly personal statement of intention. The use of the term 'asking' is also interesting here. 'Asking' suggests choice. Few governmental policy decisions actually allow for choice, and so his use of 'asking' suggests that he is invoking voluntarism – a considerably softer and more crowd-pleasing option than terms such as 'expecting', 'demanding' or 'requiring'.

Furthermore, in this extract, there is a separation between the word 'people' and the phrase 'in time of need'. This serves to obscure the fact that those unemployed people who *are* seeking assistance are 'in need'. In this way, unemployment is depoliticized and the 'needy' are situated as persons who at present contribute nothing, or have previously contributed nothing, to the community. Additionally, Howard uses the term 'dole' throughout his speech, rather than the more strictly correct 'unemployment benefit'. 'Dole' carries significant stigma, being constantly associated in the common vernacular with the slang term 'bludger.'

CONSTRUCTING CREDIBILITY

Incumbent governments use opportunities to make what may be boastful claims and which have an 'election fighting' familiarity. Howard's following claims may be cases in point: 'In pursuing our goals for the coming year we build on the strong foundations of what has been achieved over the past three years. These have been years of remarkable consolidation, strengthening and reform of the Australian economy' (p. 2); then 'And just as the economic reforms of the past have delivered strength and prosperity now, so it is the reforms of today and tomorrow that will deliver the higher economic growth, employment and living standards of the future' (p. 3). Claims such as these can be seen as an attempt to showcase the 'credibility' of Howard and his government prior to his announcement of a new policy initiative. In the above extracts, Howard has laid the foundation for announcing his intention to link literacy to 'the dole' later in his speech. First, he draws the attention of his audience to the 'strong foundations' achieved through his past 'economic reforms'. Second, he reinforces the need for future reform in order for Australians to maintain their standard of living. He then follows with a warning: 'Let no-one sell Australia short by understating the impressive economic achievements of recent years.' By these means, Howard creates an environment in which any attack upon his economic policies (or regarding his claims about the 'economic achievements' of his government) should be viewed as an attack on Australia itself, and by association, all Australians. 'Let no-one sell Australia short' also suggests that someone *is* trying to sell Australia short and Howard is enlisting the support of Australians to prevent the implied slight.

(RE)DEFINING 'DESERVING'

Howard announces the extension of his party's 'mutual obligation' policies – the introduction of the concept of linking literacy and numeracy skills to unemployment benefits – by making the following commonsense, irrefutable statement: 'We know that a *school child* without basic reading and writing skills will not be able to realise his or her full potential' (p. 7). Following this, he shifts his argument from schoolchildren to 'young adults' and then to 'young unemployed':[3]

> That is why I commit my government to requiring unemployed *young people* who lack basic literacy and numeracy tests to undertake appropriate remedial courses if they are to receive their full dole. (p. 7)

> Previously, *young people on the dole* were able to satisfy their obligation by taking up one of a number of options. But I believe, and most Australians would agree, that reading and writing properly are the most fundamental prerequisites for getting a job. (p. 7)

> So to enhance our mutual obligation policies this government will require young people who lack basic literacy and numeracy skills to undertake training in those areas as a condition of receiving their full unemployment benefit. Refusing to learn how to read and write will deny *young unemployed* the full dole. (p. 7)

> Further work is being undertaken on improving compliance and extending the coverage of mutual obligation. (p. 7)

Through these discursive shifts, Howard accomplishes several things. First, in his statement that young children require literacy and numeracy skills, he is appealing to the 'common sense' of the audience. He then distances his audience's sympathy by shifting the reference to 'young unemployed' – a category viewed as a social and economic problem – as opposed to children as such. Finally, he further distances this group from the sympathies of his audience by referring to them as 'young unemployed' who are '*refusing to learn*', thus positioning this group as *actively resisting* their duty to become independent and potentially economically useful citizens.

Implied in the statement that there are young unemployed who are 'refusing to learn' is the idea that they have already wasted the educational resources provided to them. Furthermore, it assumes that all young people who do not pass 'basic literacy and numeracy tests' were in fact capable of learning if they had *not* refused – thereby dismissing any notions of social, physical or intellectual disadvantage impinging upon their ability to perform. It also firmly places the responsibility for young people's unemployment upon themselves, despite a large body of research that describes the myriad complex factors that combine to form the global problem of declining youth labour market opportunities. In this context, young unemployed people with literacy and numeracy problems are constructed as 'deliberately unemployable', such that the social issues surrounding employment are absent from the discourse.

In order to turn the new reciprocity into common sense, 'need' is redefined as 'resistance'. Those previously categorized as 'needy' or 'disadvantaged' are now targeted as persons requiring moral retraining. Punishment in the form of removal of the full rights to welfare from those who have failed to attain a certain level of educational success can then be viewed as a new technology of governance.

DOING WHAT COMES NATURALLY

In conception and practice, our policies have mirrored the Australian character, Australian priorities, in short – the Australian way. (p. 3)

This statement, delivered quite early in the speech, overtly states that this is how things are done in Australia. So Howard creates the foundations to naturalize the policy he announces toward the end of his speech; he creates the conditions under which any policy announced is not necessarily Liberal Party policy – but developed because it reflects something called 'the Australian character'. In 'The Australian Way', Howard turns around basic precepts that have provided the framework of the Australian welfare state since the 1970s. In a speech devoid of sympathy for the unemployed or the disadvantaged, he makes a plea for the government to receive 'help and understanding' from the community. 'Few Australians would deny the proposition that governments alone cannot solve immense social problems. They need the help and understanding of great community organisations, dedicated individuals and the corporate sector' (p. 6). Turning this sentence around we read: 'Most Australians agree that governments cannot solve immense social problems' – a much more difficult position to defend – and one that invites the question, 'What then *is* the role of government?'

CONCLUSION

In this chapter, I have identified a number of linguistic and discursive devices employed by the current Prime Minister in his Federation Address in which he announces his government's policy of linking entitlement to unemployment benefits to achievements in certain standards in literacy and numeracy. I have identified instances where he uses the proven 'applause-generating' device of the three-part list. Further, in 'The Australian Way', Howard uses contrastive pairs in order to positively evaluate his own position while, at the same time, criticizing the policies of those who oppose it. In addition, through a manipulation of the pronominal system, Howard is able to distance himself personally from the policies of his party when necessary, as well as to personalize his statements in order to convey sincerity and personal commitment. Howard then invokes the words of his political forebears, drawing upon a long tradition and thereby appealing to his conservative supporters. Over and above this, contribution to the economy becomes the moral yardstick by which the social 'deserving are measured'. Economic contribution is now articulated as the new morality of government and the moral guiding principle of its techniques.

The notion of 'cleansing oneself' is an important concept here as government has taken responsibility for identifying and creating a particular category of citizen. However, rather than seeing this group as requiring support at a systemic level, the state has identified it as one that is undeserving of full citizenship rights. Those who, for the past 30 years, have been recognized as having special needs and as being particularly disadvantaged, will henceforth be dealt with by having their full rights of citizenship suspended until they comply with the 'mutual obligation' policy and develop literacy and numeracy skills to an 'appropriate' level. Simply put: this group has been rearticulated not only as undeserving of welfare, but as a group to be *punished* for being unemployed, having been labelled illiterate and innumerate. In this speech, Howard attempts to de-politicize the concept of welfare and justify the dismantling of the welfare state through an attack on welfare recipients on the basis of their perceived lack of contribution.

Notes

1. References are to John Howard's Federation Address, 'The Australian Way', presented to the Queensland Chamber of Commerce. Brisbane, 19 February 1999. See <http://www.pm.gov.au/news/speeches/1999/federationaddress2801.htm>.
2. See Howard's keynote address to the ACOSS national congress, Adelaide, 5 November 1998.
3. It is perhaps ironic that, in the oral version of the third extract, Howard replaces 'literacy' with 'literary'.

11 History as a rhetorical resource: using historical narratives to argue and explain

Martha Augoustinos

EDITORIAL

There is now a growing and influential body of literature on racist discourse. Discourse analysts in several countries have identified common and recurring racist tropes that can be combined in flexible and contradictory ways to justify and legitimize social inequalities between groups. In this chapter, Martha Augoustinos focuses on a common discursive resource that members of two particular student groups draw upon in accounts of 'race relations' in Australia. This is identified here, and in other work by Augoustinos, Tuffin and Rapley – henceforth 'et al.' *– (1999), as 'the historical narrative' of Australia's colonial past. This narrative has also been identified as a common, pervasive and enduring resource in New Zealand (Nairn and McCreanor, 1990, 1991; Wetherell and Potter, 1992).*

After introducing a selection of the literature on these important socio-political topics, Augoustinos then turns to her data set: a collection of transcribed discussions between psychology students on current relations between Aboriginal and non-indigenous Australians. Here she locates a number of tropes. Among these are: historical generality and studied vagueness combined with snippets of historical fact; the negotiation of blame and responsibility; metaphors of evolution worked up in terms of developmental hierarchies; appeals to the irreversibility of past actions and a concomitant insistence on the present time's relation to a putatively better future.

In this way, while Augoustinos draws heavily on the DP literature, she also shows how thin the line is between its potential for social critique and that of CDA. Like Herschell and LeCouteur (Chapter 10 and Chapter 12 in this volume), then, Augoustinos shows how such previously 'speculative' (macro-theoretical) concepts as 'ideology', 'racism', 'colonialism', and even 'history' itself, can be anchored in empirical studies of talk-in-interaction.

INTRODUCTION

The aim of this chapter is to demonstrate how members draw upon well-known historical and consensual narratives to argue and explain the contemporary plight of Indigenous people in ways that present those narratives as factual, neutral and disinterested versions of the past. As Wetherell and Potter (1992) have demonstrated in their analysis of the discursive delicacy and ambivalence of Pakeha ('European') talk about Maori and Polynesian populations, the normative ideological parameters of this talk occur within an enduring and pervasive discourse of colonialism and imperialism. McCreanor (1993) has referred to this normative account of New Zealand 'race relations' as 'the standard story':

> The standard story of Maori/Pakeha relations . . . says that Maori/Pakeha relations are the best in the world, rooted as they are in the honourable adherence to the outcome of a fair fight (the 1860 wars) which has seen the Maori succeeded in their dominance of the country, just as they displaced earlier Indigenous inhabitants. The treaty of Waitangi is a document of historical interest only and is irrelevant to Maori/Pakeha relations in the modern context . . . Mutual respect for each other's strengths and tolerance of idiosyncrasies has integrated the Maori people into a harmonious, egalitarian relationship with the more recent arrivals, the whole working constructively for the common good. This narrative explains Maori failure as due to their inability to cope in the modern world because of inherent flaws in their character or culture. Maori dissent is the work of a minority of troublemakers who seek to arouse a wider Maori discontent to further their own political ends. (1993: 61)

While this is a relatively short narrative, it manages to traverse considerable ground: history, the nature of contemporary New Zealand society, Maori/Pakeha relations, and Maori failure and political dissent. This 'standard story' of contemporary New Zealand race relations is organized into a coherent and sequenced narrative. It begins with a general gloss on current Maori/Pakeha relations as the 'best in the world' which, in turn, is accounted for by moving back into the past and citing events such as the 1860s wars and the Treaty of Waitangi. These are cited as forerunners to the legitimate basis upon which Pakeha sovereignty was established. The narrative then moves forward again to 'the modern context' where New Zealand is represented as a harmonious and egalitarian society as a result of the mutual respect and integration of Maori and Pakeha. This inexorably leads to the conclusions that Maori 'failure' must be due to Maori themselves (since New Zealand is a fair and egalitarian society) and that Maori political grievances are the work of a noisy minority of political malcontents.

What is remarkable about the narrative is that it manages to say so much in so few words and with little recourse to specific details. While some specific historical events are mentioned, the narrative can only be described as a vague and global thumb-nail sketch of New Zealand society and its history of race relations. As Potter (1996a: 118) has argued, '[t]he use of vague or formulaic descriptions may provide just enough material to sustain some action without providing descriptive claims that can open it to undermining'. Such vague and schematic narratives, then, work well as credible and factual accounts precisely *because* they lack detail; rich detail can be subject to scrutiny, challenge and criticism.

This narrative then has just the right balance of vague description and detail to make it a familiar, robust and authoritative explanatory resource that members can deploy in everyday argument and debate on racial matters. Moreover, the account is treated as a realistic and accurate construction of the historical 'facts' as they occurred in time and place. These are woven into a seamless and coherent story of the significant people (in this case, cultural groups), events and deeds in New Zealand's past.

Yet history is shaped by competing theoretical perspectives regarding what and who counts as historically significant, important and worthy of detailed documentation, examination and explanation: what stories are worth telling, retelling and celebrating in the present and future; what stories remain untold, absent and forgotten. All historical accounts are narratives, subject to alternative constructions; all can be undermined and criticized as defective or lacking in some way. Every history is a version: it is not necessarily a veridical and unproblematic record of the 'great deeds of great men'. Referencing the work of Hayden White (1978), Potter reminds us that

> it is a mistake to see history making as a collection of facts about the past. Rather, history making is a combination of fact finding and producing narratives that give those facts sense. . . . [P]lausible, believable accounts of the past are produced by placing facts within a narrative. (1996a: 169)

And only when those 'facts' are embedded in a narrative that is recognized as culturally familiar and coherent can the history be made to appear factual and authoritative.

DATA AND RESOURCES

The data in the present analysis are drawn from two discussion groups conducted in 1995 on 'race relations in Australia'. Eight undergraduate psychology students took part: a group which might reasonably be expected to be particularly aware of, and sensitive to, issues of anti-racism and whose talk may offer some insights into the localized, contingent, working-up of issues of race within an Australian social context. Group discussions were selected in preference to individual interviews to facilitate a closer approximation to the kind of spontaneous talk, argument and debate likely to be found in everyday interaction.

Open-ended discussions were conducted for each of the two groups of four students. While both groups were asked to consider the same probe issues, there were slight variations in the order of presentation. The schedule of issues to be discussed included: the extent of racism in Australia; observed instances of racial discrimination; the appropriateness of racist jokes; definitions of racism; Native Title legislation; the Hindmarsh Island Bridge Royal Commission; affirmative action and equal opportunity. Additional questions were asked throughout the discussion for clarification as considered necessary by the facilitator. Each discussion ran for approximately 90 minutes.

The broader aims of this particular research were to identify how everyday talk about Aboriginal people and about Australian racism was organized, and to examine the ways in which participants constructed Aboriginal people during their discussions. Overall, the analysis identified four recurring discursive themes or topics within which discussions of Aboriginal people were framed. These were: a colonial historical narrative of Australia's past; the contemporary plight of Aboriginal people; a defensive discourse of 'even-handedness' which downplayed and denied racism in Australia; and a nationalist discourse emphasizing the moral necessity of all inhabitants of Australia identifying collectively as 'Australians' (see Augoustinos *et al.*, 1999). This chapter, however, focuses only on the first of these discursive resources: a very specific and particular account or version of colonial history that members of the groups drew upon to explain present-day inequalities and disadvantages experienced by Indigenous Australians.

THE HISTORICAL NARRATIVE: AUSTRALIA'S COLONIAL PAST

As with all nations' histories, Australia's has been subject to turbulent contestation and debate. 'Official' accounts construct Australia's colonial past as the 'white settlement' of a previously uninhabited land. The doctrine of *terra nullius* had (until overturned by the High Court's Mabo decision in 1993) embodied in nearly 200 years of Australian law the view that pre-European Australia was literally an empty continent. Alternative versions of the European settlement of Australia have referred to the same historical events as the 'invasion' of an already possessed land, inhabited and owned by the Aboriginal peoples living there for thousands of years. This version of history emphasizes the genocide and dispossession of the Indigenous population and their subjugation by European invaders.

The historical accounts presented by the students participating in these discussions were commonly organized around the notion that an understanding of (a version of) the past was critical in informing explanations of contemporary Aboriginal 'problems'. Featuring strongly in these narratives was a recognizably 'traditional' version of colonialist-imperialist discourse (Said, 1993) which, while acknowledging that the British 'imposed' their 'lifestyle' on Australia's Indigenous people – and that this lifestyle was in direct conflict with existing Aboriginal social practices – also deflected blame from the British by stressing the 'benefits' of European culture for its recipients. The lifestyle imposed by the British was invariably described as 'culturally advanced' and 'superior', while Aboriginal culture was commonly referred to as 'primitive'. This 'clash of cultures', it was argued, inevitably led to a mutual failure of 'understanding' between British settlers and existing Aboriginal communities. This explanatory account is clearly evident in Extract 1:

Extract 1

M I think it's very difficult because I mean there is so much past history and the fact that the British came over and a set up you know *this lifestyle* and almost imposed it on the Aboriginals, umm, even though money's been given to the Aboriginals to to build houses and whatever, but that just didn't fit into their lifestyle so there was a real, I think not an understanding of each other's lifestyles? And the way that they differed and it was like the British were trying to impose their type of lifestyle on the Aborigines and that just hasn't gelled, umm so umm it's caused a lot of problems, for like example alcoholism umm with Aboriginals etc.

Note how M begins his account: 'I think it's *very* difficult because I mean there is *so* much past history'. This cautious prefacing suggests that M is shaping his talk to locally contingent social goals, signalling that he may be entering into a sensitive subject matter. To stress the delicacy and problematic nature of the issue, M does not simply describe it as difficult, but as 'very difficult'; there is not just history to consider, but 'so much past history'. This vague formulation suggests that the issue is a complex one, requiring considerable historical analysis, but at the same time allows M to offer a very general gloss of this history as 'the fact that the British came over and a set up you know *this lifestyle*'. Moreover, M warrants this gloss by referring to it as a 'fact'.

Also of significance in this extract is the way in which British responsibility in the social dislocation and dispossession of Aboriginal people by their occupation of Australia is obscured by the use of specific lexical selections and nominalizations. M represents the British as active agents in this process but as agents who merely 'came over and . . . set up . . . this lifestyle'. As Sacks (1992a,b) points out, such innocuous pro-terms are routinely deployed in talk to avoid conflict between interlocutors.

References to the British 'almost' imposing their lifestyle on Aboriginal people, subtly alludes to the possibility of coercive British practices in forcing a way of life on the Indigenous population. But M argues that these practices resulted in '*mutual* misunderstanding' of each other's cultures. The imposition of a British 'lifestyle' is talked about contrastively in both vague and specific terms. M is very specific about the resultant problems. Alcoholism is specified as being prototypical of contemporary problems that collectively constitute the discursive resource referred to elsewhere as 'Aboriginal plight' (Augoustinos *et al.*, 1999). The *cause* of these problems, however, is dealt with less specifically, with the speaker providing an account that relies on such notions as 'not an understanding', the uncontentious-sounding differences in 'lifestyle' and the vague 'that just hasn't gelled'.

Again, as Potter (1996a) suggests, such carefully framed combinations of vagueness and detail perform delicate rhetorical work. While vague formulations are difficult to undermine, whatever small detail is provided also works to minimize criticisms that the account is lacking in specificity. M's vagueness can thus be read as doing important work in withholding an unambiguous attribution of responsibility, while still carrying the implicit suggestion that accountability for failures of understanding should be *jointly* shared by both British and Aboriginal people. Arguably, this non-specific account leaves open the inference that the contemporary plight of Aboriginal people is explicable in terms of British colonization *and/or* Aboriginal failure to adapt. Such a construction, of course, by including *Aboriginal* 'failure' to adapt, also serves to diminish British moral and political accountability for the contemporary plight of Indigenous people.

While M offers a gloss on Aboriginal 'problems' stemming from the British lifestyle ('houses and whatever') 'just' not 'fit[ting] into their lifestyle', the implicit contrasting constructions – of Aboriginal people and the British – are more explicitly exemplified by A in Extract 2. Drawing upon an imperialist discourse of European 'progress', 'modernity' and 'sophistication', A emphasizes Aboriginal people's lack thereof:

Extract 2

A I think too and also when you look at history you look back at the fact that the Aborigines were very very primitive (Mmm) and they confronted our culture that was superiorly more advanced, the wheel had been invented and whatnot but the Aborigines hadn't seemed to to advance past that very primitive stage and whatnot (Mmm). Umm, they had sort of had no modern technologies as such as the British had. Like the British had gunpowder and alcohol and these things, ahh, I think that was another big problem.

Here we see the very specific deployment of 'history' as a rhetorical warrant for A's account. A carefully employs both distanced footing and an implicit appeal to factuality ('when you look at history') to deflect personal accountability and to give the account the appearance of neutrality and objectivity. Hence it is not just A who says that 'Aboriginal people were very very primitive', it is 'history' itself; it is merely a factual and unproblematic description. Note the extreme case formulations (Pomerantz, 1986) used to describe Aboriginal people as '*very very* primitive', as a people who 'hadn't seemed to advance past that *very* primitive stage'. The construction of Aboriginal people as undeveloped and primitive is further instanced by reference to the 'facts' that they failed to develop the wheel and possessed 'no modern technologies'.

As with M in Extract 1, who talks of lifestyle differences resulting in mutual misunderstanding between Aboriginal people and the British, A locates such misunderstanding in the contrast set up between a 'primitive' and a 'superior' culture which was much more technologically advanced. Moreover, A claims identification with the 'superiorly more advanced' culture by the use of the indexical pronoun 'our'. Again, as with M in Extract 1, note the vagueness instanced by the use of non-specific list completers such as 'and whatnot', 'and these things'.

The next extract provides a further illustration of how participants delicately manage discussions about Aboriginal responses to colonization and, ultimately, to a dominant European lifestyle. Again, while most of the discursive work done in accounting for Aboriginal difficulties in coming to terms with the British is vague, the students participating in the research primarily constructed the issue in terms of Aboriginal 'failure'. The accountability of Aboriginal people is emphasized by setting up Aboriginal people as one part of a contrast pair, in opposition to other (more recently arrived) ethnic groups, whose differential success in 'fitting' into Australia is stressed. While the previous extracts imply that contemporary Aboriginal problems have resulted from a failure to adapt (usually glossed as a consequence of differing 'lifestyle' preferences), the following exchange makes this position explicit:

Extract 3

M Well I think it it gets back to the lifestyle situation though? The fact that those other ethnic communities can come in and tend to fit in and=

J =Yeah, that's right.

M They've sort of got the European type lifestyle which is not a lot different and ours particularly now we're becoming a lot more multi-cultural where I think the Aboriginal umm that was the problem is that they, we, wouldn't fit with, it wasn't a good fit.

M claims factual status for the adaptability of other ethnic communities arriving in Australia and goes on to provide an explanation for this degree of 'fit' in terms of similarity of lifestyle and the increasing multi-culturalism of mainstream Australian society (that 'we' are becoming). Note too how M receives consensual validation from J who offers independent agreement for this explanation ('Yeah, that's right'). The case of Aboriginal 'fit' is considered separately and described as '*the* problem'. M's talk floats responsibility for this problem across a self-correcting 'they/we' contrast pair, prior to settling with the vaguer 'it wasn't a good fit'. This vagueness again distances the speaker from a particular position, while keeping open the possibility that either or both sides of the pair ('they', Aboriginal people vs. 'we', non-Indigenous Australians) are accountable for the putative failure to fit. This delicate management of accountability mirrors that accomplished in the first extract where 'failure' was cast in similarly 'neutral' terms ('it just hasn't gelled').

Of particular interest in the extracts we have analysed thus far are the recurring and interrelated metaphors around which participants structure their talk of Aboriginal people. The first of these is the familiar imperialist metaphor of hierarchy (itself symbolizing progress) which relies on a set of spatial dichotomies: above vs. beneath, advanced vs. backward, and which serves to position Aboriginal culture as beneath British/European culture. We see this spatial metaphor in Extract 2 where Aboriginal culture is referred to as 'very very primitive' in comparison with European culture, which is described as superior and 'more advanced'. This hierarchy metaphor is also implicitly used in other parts of the data where the absence of Western examples of technology and civilization is used to confer inferior status upon Aboriginal culture. As Lakoff and Johnson (1980) argue, this up-down spatial or 'geographic' metaphor is both integral to Western notions of status and social hierarchy and also historically coincident in its development with European colonization.

Indeed cultural hierarchy was also evident in McCreanor's (1989) data in which speakers compared Maori culture unfavourably with the 'mainstream'. McCreanor notes that such hierarchical judgements were sustained by contrasting the material culture of European society with pre-European Maori society. Comparisons across a range of specific aspects of culture (language, history, art and music) promoted the more general conclusion that Maori culture was 'primitive'. In the extracts above, similar comparisons are invited by the way in which participants talk about technology and architecture.

Another prevalent and related metaphor was that of 'fit'. Aboriginal people are represented as having failed to fit with and adapt to the dominant culture. In Extract 1, M uses clichéd expressions like 'just didn't fit into their lifestyle' and 'that just hasn't gelled'. This is also evident in Extract 3 when M constructs Aboriginal 'problems' primarily as 'it wasn't a good fit' and contrasts Aboriginal failure to adapt with other ethnic communities who 'tend to fit in'.

HISTORY AS A CONSTRAINT: 'YOU CAN'T CHANGE THE PAST'

While the historical narrative is an important resource in explaining (away) and accounting for contemporary Aboriginal problems, it is also deployed paradoxically to argue that a focus on 'things that happened in the past' is 'not constructive' and that an orientation to the future would, in contrast, be more productive. In Extract 4, A deploys the aphoristic, 'commonsense', notion that 'you can't change the past' as an argument for leaving it behind in order to 'move on into the future'. This notion is akin to the pervasive and self-sufficient rhetorical argument, 'you can't turn the clock back', that Wetherell and Potter (1992) identified in their analysis of text and talk on 'race' by Pakeha New Zealanders. This self-sufficient or 'clinching' argument appeals to everyday, commonsense, familiar verities so that no more need be said; no further warrant is required.

Extract 4

A But I think arguing over things that happened in the past is just ridiculous, it doesn't get you anywhere umm they sort of say that umm they keep bringing up the point that umm they were here sort of in Australia before the British and whatnot and that it was the British background that did all this and they seem to be taking it out generation after generation. Until people sort of let go of the past and say, well we can't do anything about that, let's just try and get something done in the future umm it's just always going to be bickering=

J =it's not constructive.

This exchange illustrates how a single discursive resource – a recurring version of a historical narrative – can be used flexibly and rhetorically for differing (but complementary) ideological purposes. In previous extracts, both A and M invoke the historical narrative in talk as a way of accounting for and rationalizing current inequities. This time, A argues that *Aboriginal* insistence on talking about history is a 'ridiculous' constraint which prevents 'us' from 'get[ting] something done', and orienting ourselves to the future. Further, J's completion of A's turn with the complementary utterance ('it's not constructive'), not only offers consensus but also demonstrates a shared, intersubjective achievement of the argument that Aboriginal-directed discussion of history is not helpful. Note also the active agency attributed to Aboriginal people here in bringing up the past ('they keep bringing up', 'taking it out generation after generation'). This is in stark contrast to the dominant representation and construction of Aboriginal people throughout the previous extracts as passive. So, by the attribution of 'unhelpfulness' to Aboriginal agency, the deployment of vague pro-terms – '*things* that happened in the past', 'the British background that *did all this*' – and carefully chosen lexical selections which minimize the seriousness of Indigenous political grievances (ridiculous arguing, bickering), injustices perpetrated against Aboriginal people are downplayed and dismissed.

GENERAL DISCUSSION

Australia's colonial past is constructed paradoxically, as both contributing to and constraining of understandings of present-day Aboriginal 'problems'. The practical and ideological force of such narratives is to justify and rationalize the well-known and dominant imperialist narrative of British settlement and occupancy: a 'sanitized' version of history that rarely speaks of genocide and the dispossession of Indigenous people.

This culturally partial, grand narrative of British settlement, then, both forms a locally contingent historical background against which the student groups constructed accounts of current social problems and inequities experienced by Aboriginal people, and also serves to provide a detailed local backdrop to ongoing Indigenous accountability. Present-day problems such as racism and alcoholism are linked to events in the past, in particular to *Aboriginal people's* failure to 'fit' into an historically factual process of morally untroubled 'white settlement'. Indeed, while it is not possible to examine the contemporary politics of relations between Indigenous and non-Indigenous Australians without a historical analysis, the *version* of the past offered by those students participating in the discussion – in particular, the construction of a softened, 'even-handed' and non-specific account of 'white settlement' – does crucial ideological work.

The historical narrative explains away and rationalizes existing social relations and inequities. The 'even-handed' emphasis on past 'lifestyle differences' warrants the downplaying or denial of the view that contemporary dominant social practices and institutions – controlled by the non-Indigenous majority – reproduce oppression and inequity. Further, the imperialist narrative serves to deflect both moral accountability and political responsibility for the current circumstances of Aboriginal people away from contemporary Australians onto past generations, and also, with irony, onto Aboriginal people themselves.

Like McCreanor's 'standard story', this historical narrative is not replete with historical detail – events, people, dates, places – but is a non-specific account of the 'arrival' of the British who 'naturally' displaced and superseded a backward and primitive culture with modernity, technology and civilization. Of note, perhaps, is the same studied use of vagueness in contemporary Australian political discourse on matters pertaining to 'race'. Rapley (1998) has drawn attention to MP Pauline Hanson's careful characterization of the British colonization of Australia, in her maiden speech to the Australian parliament, as merely 'something that happened over 200 years ago'. Likewise, Prime Minister Howard's speech to the Reconciliation Convention in 1997 consistently deploys the vague and non-specific categories of 'past injustices', or 'blemishes' in Australia's past history when specifically referring to the forced removal of Indigenous children from their families and communities.

The above analysis also identified two recurring and interrelated metaphors around which the student groups structured their talk of Aboriginal people. These two metaphors of hierarchy and fit are reminiscent of social Darwinism, the ideological and 'scientific' doctrine that rationalized and justified imperialism during the nineteenth and early twentieth centuries. Social Darwinist discourse invoked the racial inferiority of 'coloured' and Indigenous peoples as a legitimation of their domination and oppression by imperial European powers. Indeed, the assumed inferiority of Aboriginal people pervaded Australian State and Federal government policies well into the 1970s. Government policies of assimilation were specifically predicated on the desirability and necessity of Aboriginal people adapting to the dominant white culture and in the consequent eradication of Aboriginal culture and identity.

While the students did not explicitly espouse beliefs in a racial hierarchy and, indeed, eschewed notions of inferiority and superiority based on race (see Augoustinos *et al.*, 1999), it is clear that their talk was framed by notions of a cultural hierarchy. While Aboriginal people as a group were not necessarily constructed as *biologically* inferior, they were constructed as *culturally* inferior. Aboriginal problems were represented largely in social Darwinist terms as problems of fit and adaptation to a superior culture. Moreover, failure to fit or 'gel' with this dominant culture was viewed primarily as preventing Aboriginal people from improving their social status through upward social mobility (see

Augoustinos *et al.*, 1999). As Essed (1991) has emphasized, the replacement of the metaphor of a biological hierarchy of groups with that of a cultural hierarchy is central to the covert and subtle nature of contemporary racism. We see here how the metaphors of hierarchy and fit conceptually articulate a coherent ideological position, and construct Aboriginal people as culturally inferior, as failing thereby to survive in a superior culture, hence as suffering the plight of social and economic disadvantage for which they themselves remain accountable.

12 On saying 'sorry': repertoires of apology to Australia's Stolen Generations

Amanda LeCouteur

EDITORIAL

One central topic that has been taken up in DP is 'the development of a critical analysis of the practices that sustain racism'. The impetus of this work is to treat racism as something other than a 'trait' (for example) or a 'personality type' deeply buried within the internal workings of some individuals and, by extension, not others. Instead, discursive psychologists orient to the construction *of social and psychological 'facts' – such as racism itself – in a way that considers how such a thing is actively brought about in quite material ways: via the talk-in-interaction of mundane actors.*

In this chapter, Amanda LeCouteur takes up this position but switches focus from face-to-face conversation and towards the genre of the e-mail letter. Turning to the question of whether the Australian Federal government should apologize to Indigenous Australians for past mistreatments, LeCouteur looks at postings to a public internet site. Via a careful analysis of the texts she finds there – and using forms of analysis common to DP and applied CA – she offers some significant findings about how everyday racism is discursively constructed.

That is, using the concept of 'interpretative repertoires', LeCouteur shows how the idea of apology can be mobilized in two sub-forms: as an expression of sympathy *and as a form of* healing. *'Treating racism as a matter of discursive social practice, at both the institutional and local, interpersonal levels', as the author puts it, can reveal a great deal. For it would be, perhaps, rather obvious to find that the* anti-*apology texts embody racist formations. Instead, in this chapter, LeCouteur finds much the same politico-discursive structures in* pro-*apology postings.*

At first sight, these letters seem reasonable, laudable, anti-discriminatory, and so on: many on the left, in the centre and even those of traditional liberal persuasions would probably agree with similar sentiments. But what forms of discourse *actually carry them off? LeCouteur's conclusion is both surprising and salutary. In this respect, she shows how a DP approach to politically sensitive texts can be, equally, a contribution to CDA.*

INTRODUCTION

In broad terms, this analysis of discourse-in-action looks at the construction of social realities around an issue that has been at the forefront of national concern in Australia for a considerable time. This issue concerns the question of whether a national apology should be given to the Indigenous peoples of Australia for the long-term institutionalized practice of forcible removal of their children from their families and communities. Talk and text about the appropriateness of this apology – about saying 'sorry' – have constituted an ongoing national debate in Australia in forums as diverse as State and Federal parliaments, national and local print and broadcast media, organized community meetings, as well as everyday discussions between people. Indeed, it is hard to imagine that any Australian could have remained untouched by this issue, or would not have been involved in the debate at some level over the past several years. Investigation of the action that such discourse between people achieves is the subject of this chapter. By 'action', I am referring to the setting up and knocking down of social realities (Antaki, 1994); the social practices involved in the ongoing struggle to construct 'the truth' around this key social and political issue of apologizing to Australia's Indigenous peoples.

Broadly, I want to look at some of the ways in which people construct what it means to apologize in this particular context. What concepts or repertoires of apologizing do people make use of in this debate, and to what ends? At another level, I will be focusing on the strategies, manoeuvres or rhetorics that organize accounts of the appropriateness of apologizing. Specifically, I will look at the discursive practices in terms of which social actions of categorization and identity are achieved in the context of this debate.

Methodologically, this analysis represents a continuation of the work of Wetherell and Potter (1992; Potter and Wetherell, 1987) on the development of a critical analysis of the practices that sustain racism. In particular, with their analyses of the talk of Pakeha New Zealanders, Wetherell and Potter show how racist legitimations can work through social reformist, humanitarian or liberal discourse. I will extend their argument to the practices deployed in texts arguing in favour of a national apology in this Australian debate. In the texts written in support of apologizing that I have chosen to analyse, I will argue that it is possible to read the versions of social reality that are constructed as functioning to sustain existing oppressive power relations between Indigenous and non-Indigenous Australians. Before presenting an analysis of this discourse-in-action, a brief overview of key aspects of the social context surrounding the development of the debate about apologizing in Australia is provided in the following section.

APOLOGIZING IN CONTEXT

In 1995, the Australian Federal Attorney General of the then Labor government requested that a national inquiry be conducted into the past laws, policies and practices that had resulted in the forcible removal of Aboriginal and Torres Strait Islander children from their families and communities over the period 1910 to 1970. The subsequent report of the Human Rights and Equal Opportunities Commission (HREOC, 1997) concluded that forcible removal of Indigenous children had been a widespread and commonplace activity in Australia. It was estimated that between one-in-three and one-in-ten Indigenous children had been separated from their families to be placed in institutions, missions, foster homes and adoptive families. The Commission described the systematic separation of generations of Indigenous children (who came to be referred to as the 'Stolen Generations') as 'a gross violation of . . . human rights' and 'an act of genocide contrary to the Convention of Genocide ratified by Australia in 1949' (1997: 27). Among the many recommendations included in the Report was the statement that 'everyone affected by forcible removals should be entitled to reparation [including] the children who were forcibly removed, their families, communities, children and grandchildren' (1997: 29). Specific recommendations for reparation included that all Australian parliaments:

- officially acknowledge the responsibility of their predecessors for the laws, policies and practices of forcible removal;
- negotiate with the Aboriginal and Torres Strait Islander Commission to find a form of words for official apologies to Indigenous individuals, families and communities, and extend those apologies with wide and culturally appropriate publicity; and that
- the Aboriginal and Torres Strait Islander Commission, in consultation with the Council For Aboriginal Reconciliation, should arrange for a national 'Sorry Day' to be celebrated each year to commemorate the history of forcible removals and its effects. (HREOC, 1997: 36)

These recommendations generated considerable debate and controversy, not only among members of the presiding conservative coalition government, but also among the wider Australian polity. Adding fuel to the debate was the Prime Minister, John Howard's, persistent refusal to offer a public and official apology to Indigenous people on behalf of 'the nation'. The Federal government's resistance on this matter was made more salient when conservative coalition governments in several states delivered formal apologies in their respective parliaments. It was within this context of continuing prime-ministerial refusal to offer an official apology that the texts under analysis were generated.

Subsequent to the time at which these texts were generated, and after two years of resisting HREOC's recommendations, the Prime Minister moved a parliamentary motion in which he expressed his 'deep and sincere *regret* that indigenous Australians had suffered injustices under the practices of *past* generations' (Hansard, 1999: 9205; emphasis added). Later, in April 2000, the government's formal submission to a Senate Inquiry into the HREOC Report controversially disputed the existence of a 'generation' of stolen children, arguing that only 10 per cent of Indigenous children had ever been removed from their families.

In my analysis of the local codes of argument and practices of rhetorical organization that constitute calls for an apology in the selected texts, I hope to demonstrate the fruitfulness of a discursive approach to apologizing. This is an approach that is grounded in the empirical – in the study of texts and talk *in situ*; in everyday practices of reasoning, negotiation and struggle over sense-making. The value of such an approach lies in its ability to lay bare the fragmentary, flexible, and contradictory nature of, in this case, apologizing-in-action. What I hope to show here is the ongoing struggle and negotiation that is involved in constructing locally contingent versions of what it means to apologize, and how these versions entail a range of different, and sometimes unexpected, consequences for political action.

THE DATA

This investigation is based on a set of 35 e-mailed texts sourced from a website, *The Australian Online Survey*, controlled by News Limited. Under the general heading, 'The stolen children: APOLOGY', this site invited readers to 'Have your say' on the issue of whether 'Australians [should] apologise for the treatment of Aborigines'. Respondents were instructed to limit their responses to 250 words, although this prescription was not always followed. The site also provided information on responses to the online survey: 48 per cent of respondents had voted 'Yes', and 52 per cent 'No'. One hundred and four responses were available for perusal at the site, with 69 (or 66.3 per cent) being representative of the 'No' case, and 35 (or 33.7 per cent) representing the 'Yes' case. For the purposes of analysis, these texts were corrected for spelling and any names appended to responses were removed. Some analyses of this material are reported elsewhere (LeCouteur and Augoustinos, in press a,b; LeCouteur *et al.*, in press). This chapter is a complementary analysis focused specifically on the discursive practices used in texts written to support the case for a national apology.

ANALYSIS

Extract 1

1. We apologised to our Vietnam Veterans for the injustices committed against them by Australian citizens upon their return home. This national apology and 'Welcome Home' by the government

of Australia, on behalf of the people of Australia, brought tremendous healing for many veterans, including myself.
It enabled us to get on with our lives and put the past behind. Prior to this, life was a seemingly endless battle with hopelessness and despair at past injustices not yet put right.
2. How much more then should we apologise for the far more terrible injustices done against the original Australians, unless of course we see this situation as different because of differences in skin colour?
3. Some say I shouldn't apologise because I didn't do anything wrong! Many who apologised to Vietnam Veterans personally never did them any harm, but it was nationally recognised that these men and women needed this national recognition to set them free from the past. How is this different, or any less significant, for indigenous people?
4. Perhaps the reason some white Australians do not want to apologise is fear; fear of admitting the truth and thus destroying our national identity as being a land of the 'fair go', 'the land of the Anzacs', the strong and the free? It takes courage to say you were wrong and stand up and say so. It takes a strong and secure person (or nation) to do this; maybe we aren't there just yet.
5. Further, I have spoken with white men of our generation who have boasted to me of so-called 'coon hunts' in the north of QLD and WA, where they have taken part in going out, drunk, and shooting Aboriginals. I was actually invited to do this from an aeroplane. Whether these stories are true or the figment of alcohol affected egos, it is certain that the ideas are still endemic in certain sections of our community.
6. Recently in Bourke, NSW, I was told of a young Aboriginal man being tied by a rope and towed behind a car by white youths. Racial prejudice is not dead and most Australians would feel abhorred by these things, abhorred by them because they are a disgrace to our nation, even though only a few might actually indulge in these things.
7. I would think nearly everyone would agree, that when certain members of any community, society or nation do anything disgraceful, somehow every other member of that community, society or culture is tainted by the few. I hold this is no different with modern Australia.
8. We are now presented with a unique opportunity to confess the past (whether or not we had any direct part in it), seek the forgiveness of both God and the people who have been wronged. Then we can be free of the past once and for all, and get on with the future, free of any accusation. The longer we put this off, the longer and more bitter will become the aggrieved parties, just like Vietnam Veterans and HMAS Voyager survivors. When will we learn the lessons of history?

Here, an apology is constructed as an action that permits movement forward and away from the past. The writer calls on personal experience to illustrate how apologies let us 'get on with our lives and put the past behind'. In a pattern that was repeated in the pro-apology texts, there is acknowledgement of an injustice (point 2), followed by an account in which injustice is neatly contained in the past, in history (point 8). In this account, there is a psycho-dynamic emphasis – people can be locked in the past by virtue of a lack of acknowledgement from others; an apology can 'set them free'. The idea of an apology as a form of psychological 'healing' is explicitly drawn upon. The injustice or offence that the apology is designed to remedy is objectified in terms of its emotional effects: 'hopelessness and despair' (point 1). This form of sense-making around apologizing, its construction as a remedy or palliative for some form of psychological trauma or emotional pain, was also repeated in many of the pro-apology texts.

Extract 1 also highlights the way in which commonplace, apparently undeniable, arguments could be organized in the service of arguably oppressive ends. Here, the author draws on the commonplace that 'injustices should be righted'. However, this argument is developed in the context of another taken-for-granted assumption of empowered, non-Indigenous group members – that injustice is a thing of the past; somehow inevitably absent from the future. The subtle mobilization of these 'clinching arguments' (Wetherell and Potter, 1992) becomes a means by which inequality is continually reproduced by the very discursive practices that maintain their authors as liberal and caring. Other investigations have shown how constructions of 'tolerance' and refutations of feelings of prejudice form part of the standard identity work of contemporary racist discourse (Blommaert and Verschueren, 1992, 1993, 1998; Rapley, 1998; Wetherell and Potter, 1992).

Extract 1 also displays considerable rhetorical work to do with the construction of subject positions for various actors in the debate. The author establishes a positive, authoritative identity for himself as a war veteran, and as someone who has experienced both injustice and the healing power of apology. In arguing for an apology, he draws on the commonplace that everyone should be treated equally: 'How is this different, or any less significant, for indigenous people?'. Those who will not apologize are positioned negatively in terms of their psychology. They may be prejudiced or they may be 'afraid', lacking the strength of character to admit 'the truth'. In a positioning common in the pro-apology texts, those who would apologize are portrayed, by contrast, in terms of their psychological integrity and maturity (courage, strength, security).

The author goes on to incorporate two personal anecdotes; in both cases with the geographical location specified with sufficient detail to bolster the authenticity of the account (points 5 and 6) and yet with sufficient vagueness to permit qualification, re-specification or retraction if challenged. These anecdotes work to reproduce the general view that racism is something that is restricted to a minority in contemporary Australia. The people involved are depicted as deficient or impaired; either by virtue of being alcohol-affected or by virtue of their youth. They are also resident in places that are widely considered 'redneck' territory. Furthermore, the very extremity of the racist acts described in these anecdotes contributes to the reproduction of the view that Australians, generally, are not racist. This notion is reinforced when the author draws on a corruption metaphor (point 7). He calls up a consensus here to bolster the strength of his position, contrasting 'nearly everyone' with the 'few' who can 'taint' the whole by virtue of their actions. These actions are constituted as being wrong in terms of the 'disgrace' that they can bring to 'our nation'. Thus racism is individualized; it is depicted as a problem of deficient individuals and as involving extreme, disgraceful acts of brutality and physical violence. There is no space for the consideration of racism as a matter of the systematic institutionalized and everyday practices by which a dominant group reproduces its power.

In the sections that follow, I want to take up some of the themes identified in this initial extract, providing further empirical support for my reading of some pro-apology texts as involving discursive practices that sustain continuing inequality and oppression. In analysing these texts, I found it useful to identify two different constructions of the act of apologizing, or two different repertoires of apology, that were drawn upon with different implications. By 'repertoires of apology', I am referring to the analytic category, 'interpretative repertoire', developed by Potter and Wetherell (1987; Wetherell and Potter, 1992) to refer to 'broadly discernible clusters of terms, descriptions and figures of speech often assembled around metaphors or vivid images' (1992: 90).

One repertoire of apology that was common to the pro-apology texts I examined involved its construction as a *conventional expression of courtesy* that should be offered to anyone who had suffered sadness or misfortune. This is a repertoire in which the question of responsibility for the offence can be sidestepped. Here apologizing is not so much a matter of admitting an offence, but of demonstrating civility, consideration, good manners. Another repertoire involved the construction of apology as an *act of emotional healing.* This construction was developed in the context of descriptions of Indigenous peoples' suffering and grievance as a matter of psychological damage. It is important not to give the impression, here, that these repertoires of apology could be found as pure types in the texts. Indeed, in many texts, both forms were present, as we shall see.

CONSTRUCTING SUBJECTIVITIES: THE MOBILIZATION OF EMOTION/PSYCHOLOGY

In the pro-apology texts, racist acts that involved the systematic, institutionalized removal of Indigenous children from their families are repeatedly described or marked out in terms of emotional trauma or psychological damage. Potter (1996a) uses the term 'ontological gerrymandering' to refer to this aspect of the central business of descriptions. By this he means the selection of one realm of phenomena as relevant, and the avoidance of other potential ones. Indigenous peoples in these pro-apology accounts are repeatedly positioned, not as having justifiable claims for economic compensation and warranted grievances against an oppressive institutional system, but in terms of their emotional needs. They are described as experiencing 'sorrow' or as 'hurting'. The appropriate response, in such circumstances, is presented as the customary expression of feelings of sympathy or empathy. The apologists are positioned, in this type of account, as being proper, benevolent, societal members, and as superior members in the sense that they are the ones who can dole out the resource of consideration to those who need it; there is an aspect of condescension involved here.

Apology as a customary expression of sympathy/empathy

Extract 2
If a great deal of harm is caused of course the civilised thing is to apologise. Even if one inadvertently causes some discomfort one apologises. Let alone something as devastating as taking away children from their families, whether or not it was done with (patronising) good intent.

This extract draws explicitly on the hierarchical notion of 'civilization'. Those who apologize are fulfilling an obligation that follows implicitly ('of course') from their membership of a 'civilized' society. The assumption is that civilization carries with it humanitarian obligation. The implicit understanding – that civilized societies, by definition, are not racist societies – then also becomes available. The argumentative framework that is developed here centres around the construction of an unspoken contrast between being civilized and being uncivilized, and between the present and the past. The past, by virtue of the discursive constitution of its practices – 'taking away children from their families' – does not qualify as civilized, regardless of the unenlightened 'good intent' of its members. In the civilized present, such practices would not happen; they would be 'patronising', 'devastating':

Another example of this repertoire of apology as civility or courtesy can be seen in the next extract.

Extract 3
It's simple courtesy. By custom, we express sympathy in another's sorrow. Many Aboriginal people are still living in their sorrow.
We can help, just a little, by saying sorry. Perhaps then we will be better able to work together in trust, to seek solutions to the problems of a dispossessed people.

Apologizing is constructed here as a matter of 'simple courtesy' or 'custom'. People who are courteous are understood as committed to social harmony; they are benevolent and respectful of others. In this account, Indigenous people are positioned as experiencing 'sorrow' and 'problems' that 'we' (non-Indigenous) people can 'help' them 'seek solutions to'. Notably, 'we' are not constructed as the cause of their problems, but as people who, having demonstrated our sympathy for them, they can 'trust', and with whom they can 'work together'. The prospect of a utopian future is held out, with an emphasis on togetherness or unity. The possibility of a future characterized by indigenous self-determination, independence or separatism finds no space in this repertoire of understanding.

The customary aspect of apologizing when one has caused offence is also illustrated by the two extracts below. These extracts display shared cultural knowledge about the meaning of apology:

Extract 4
The (so far) negative results of your poll astound me. When did we become so arrogant, so unfeeling,

so utterly trapped in our white Christian European belief system that we can't even say sorry when someone is hurting?
I wonder if these same people who voted 'no' to apologising to Australia's Aborigines would also refuse to apologise for standing on their mother's foot or reversing into someone in a car park?
Saying sorry has absolutely nothing to do with admitting guilt (heaven forbid, Mr Howard), and thinking that it does merely reflects a paranoid level of self-interest.
Saying sorry has everything to do with feeling empathy towards other human beings. I really pity those who can't do this.
Funny isn't it? Once upon a time empathy used to be considered innate in humans. Looks like we've successfully bred it out of our genes. Still, maybe this means that one day we can also breed out that insidious gene that causes racism.
Yours with a very waning sense of patriotism.

Extract 5
When someone dies we say: 'I'm sorry', meaning: sorry for your loss and your grief. It is an expression of empathy, whereby we can comfort and console those still hurting from a painful and traumatic experience. Within this definition of sorry, pride has no place.

These extracts assume that everyone knows what should be done when one wants to communicate 'empathy' with others who are 'hurting'. Both the surprise expressed by the author of Extract 4 that others in the culture don't share this view – using what Pomerantz (1986) refers to as an extreme case formulation that strengthens the case: '*astound* me' – and the axiomatic status conveyed by the author of Extract 5 in his description of an apology ('When X happens, we say Y, meaning Z'), are indicative of the sense of basic accountability that the authors assume is carried by this repertoire of apology as customary expression of sympathy/empathy.

Considerable rhetorical work is accomplished in Extract 4 by the construction of those who will not apologize as incomprehensible (astound[ing]) and extreme – in the form of a three-part list (that incorporates extreme case formulation, '*so* arrogant, *so* unfeeling, *so utterly* trapped'), a device that Atkinson (1984) identifies as signalling the special comprehensiveness of what is being claimed. As Wetherell and Potter (1992) point out, if the position of those with whom one disagrees can be presented as inexplicable then, by contrast, one's own stance denotes moderation and realism. Indeed, in Extract 4, empathy is constituted as an innate emotional quality; and, hence, as a taken-for-granted, defining feature of being human. It is also represented as an organizing feature of another positive social category: 'the patriot'. Forms of construction like these, in which the reason for not apologizing is constituted in terms of some people's inability to show that they care about the psychological damage experienced by others, have the effect of rendering indistinct the specific nature of the injustices suffered by Indigenous peoples, and their discontent with their continuing exploitation and oppression.

These extracts draw on classic liberal humanist constructions. The authors position themselves as kind and caring in their attitude to Indigenous peoples. Furthermore, they position themselves in contrast to specific others on the opposite side of the debate. As Billig (1987, 1991) demonstrates, when a particular version or account is designed to make an argument, it is also designed to undermine competing versions. Here, then, we see negative subject positions constructed for those who refuse to apologize. They are also constituted primarily in terms of their emotions. They are portrayed as driven by wrong (or even sinful) emotions ('arrogance', 'pride'), or as emotionally deficient (they are 'unfeeling'). In this repertoire of apology, where the remedy for injustice is worked up as a matter of people being 'civil' or 'courteous' to each other, and where injustice is presented as a matter of 'harm', 'hurt' and 'sorrow', rather than in terms of discrimination and exploitation, issues of systematic inequality need not be addressed.

Apology as healing

The second repertoire of apology involves the construction of apology as a means of emotional healing for damaged psyches. In this apology-as-healing repertoire, the focus of descriptions is on the psychological and emotional damage caused by the forced removals, not on other issues that are potentially relevant, such as issues of basic human rights, or issues to do with continuing discrimination and disadvantage in, for example, areas of economics, criminal justice, education and health. By constructing Indigenous peoples' suffering as a matter of psychological and emotional damage, issues to do with their ongoing social, political and economic oppression can be avoided. One consequence of the use of this interpretative repertoire is that if Indigenous peoples can be 'healed', psychologically and emotionally, by the act of apology, then there is no reason why they should not assume an equal place in society. Framing apologizing as a matter of emotional healing does not result in major disturbances to existing power relations. Rather, it emphasizes the benefits of apologizing for both the givers and the receivers. Typically, these benefits are constructed in terms of personal growth or psychological well-being.

In Extract 6, for example, a contrast is presented between the 'large effect' that an apology can have on 'emotional healing', and the smallness and ease of the act required. Those who would apologize are positioned positively in terms of a personality or character trait as 'humble'; so by implication those who would not do so are taken as exhibiting pride. Indigenous peoples are also positioned in psychological terms as being made to feel 'worthless' and 'inferior'. The assumption is that they need to be made to feel better about themselves, and that non-Indigenous Australians are the ones who can do this for them:

Extract 6

Surely saying 'sorry' can't be such a difficult task. If such a small and humble action can have a large effect upon the emotional healing of a group of people continually reminded of their worthlessness and inferiority, then LET'S DO IT.

Let us acknowledge the stupidity and bigotry of the past so we can all move forward TOGETHER.

I feel embarrassed that Howard cannot apologise for the nation as a whole but what can you expect from such a man.
He represents just over half of Australians' choice of leader: he does not act on my behalf or that of millions of other Australians.

As indicated before, there is an emphasis here on the benevolence of those who would apologize. Non-Indigenous Australians have the power, by virtue of a small act of courtesy and recognition, to 'heal' injured Indigenous peoples. The idea of moving forward together was also repeated many times in these texts, in the sense of the non-Indigenous drawing the Indigenous peoples along with them in a unified and inevitable movement forward. In this extract we can also see another manoeuvre that is repeated many times: the practice of acknowledging some injustice ('stupidity and bigotry') while locating it explicitly in the past, not the present or the idealized, shared future.

In the next extract we can trace the development of an argument that draws on an ideology of humanistic psychology.

Extract 7
In 1787, this land was full of culture, wealth, beauty, and innocence. It stood in marked contrast to the hatred, fear, and power plays of Europe. The people who had lived here for many millennia had established a way of life to be admired.
That many of us today cannot understand the great loss of life, love and happiness over the past 200 years is in itself a national tragedy. The original inhabitants of this country have much to offer those of us with European backgrounds. We are not the winners, nor they the losers. Sadly, we are all losers. And as soon as we come to realise it, to apologise for what we as a people have done, not just to the Aboriginal people (although they have suffered the most terrible crimes) but to ourselves as well, the sooner we can get on with building Australia as a truly great nation.
The alternative is a nation divided, a people without purpose or vision, an environment of unease and hidden guilt, a vastly unspiritual nation. A very sad nation indeed.

Here, non-Indigenous people are positioned as needing to apologize to – and, by implication, forgive – *themselves*, as well as apologizing to Aboriginal people. They need to tend their psyches in order to become functionally whole again (to have 'purpose or vision'). Without this form of self-actualization afforded by an apology, they will suffer the psychological consequences of 'sadness', 'unease', 'guilt'. Accordingly, Indigenous and non-Indigenous Australians are positioned as being equally diminished by racist acts ('we are all losers'). The emphasis then shifts from the injustices experienced by Indigenous peoples to the task of nation-building that lies ahead. It is taken for granted that apologizing will bring about national unity, and a return to the spirituality and happiness that characterized the pre-colonial, utopian past. This conclusion to the account is achieved within the context of an initial explicit contrast between a utopian version of pre-colonial Australia and its fallen, colonial state. In addition to accomplishing a neat act of rhetorical organization, this construction also functions to locate the injustice, once again firmly within a historical past.

A similar construction can be seen in Extract 8. Here the concept of self-actualization is drawn upon in the form of a focus on the benefits of apologizing to the givers; they will 'grow as human beings'.

Extract 8
Most Australians, to some extent, empathise with the Aboriginal people, but saying sorry means so many different things to so many people.
For some an apology signifies a personal admission of guilt, perhaps arising from the guilt associated with misguided racist beliefs inherited from our ancestors.
For me it's an acknowledgement of suffering, and expression of empathy for those who suffered, both black and white, at the hands of our righteous forefathers.
To be truly one nation we must get past this blockade to unity.
Why is this such a controversial issue anyway? To grow as human beings we've got to do whatever is necessary to learn and benefit from each other. Let us show the world how fair dinkum we really are and get on with it.

The use of the category 'most Australians' at the outset of this extract accomplishes the rhetorical work of denying racism in contemporary Australia: it is not that most Australians don't empathize with Aboriginal people, it is that apologizing means different things to different people. So this is not a matter of racism but of semantics. Again we see the development of the notion that other, 'white', people have suffered as well as Indigenous people and, again, this suffering is located in the historical past (in the time of 'ancestors' and 'forefathers', not, for instance, 30 years ago as described in the HREOC Report). Again, too, in this extract, we see an author expressing surprise that others do not share his view about the meaning of apology, about what 'must' be done, what 'we've got to do'. This rhetorical resource, together with the use of imperative formulations, reinforces the rightness of his argument. Who could not agree with the self-sufficient claim that 'we've got to do whatever is necessary to learn and benefit from each other'?

CONCLUDING REMARKS

What I hope to have shown is another example of the ways in which discourse that justifies, sustains and legitimates oppressive power relations – in Wetherell and Potter's (1992: 70) words, 'racist discourse' – can be liberal, reformist or humanitarian in form. However, as Wetherell and Potter note, the key insight of the discourse-analytic approach is that arguments and interpretative resources can be mobilized in a range of different directions. My point is not, then, to argue simply that the authors of these pro-apology texts were 'really' racist; that underneath their benevolent platitudes could be detected their true, prejudiced, attitudes and opinions about Indigenous Australians. Indeed, humanitarian and social reformist argumentative resources that draw on the liberal principles of equality, individual rights and justice are occasionally used in these texts in ways that could be read as serving anti-racist ends. And, although I have presented a reading that emphasizes the oppressive forms of some pro-apology repertoires, this is not to say that these repertoires – of apology as sympathy/empathy, and apology as emotional healing – could not also be used to further liberatory ends, or in the service of effective struggle and resistance.

What I have tried to emphasize here is that the authors of these pro-apology texts could be seen to be doing a range of different kinds of things with their recruitment of liberal, humanitarian discourses, their use of the social category of 'nation' and their emphasis on the idea of moving forward into the future. These discursive resources, like all others, can be worked subtly and flexibly to effect argumentative ends with social and political implications that span the spectrum from liberal to illiberal, from egalitarian to oppressive. The social and political consequences of pro-apology texts were not uniformly reformist, nor were they necessarily oppressive. They were not authored by individuals who could fruitfully, from a critical perspective, be described as more or less tolerant or prejudiced. Rather, what we have seen is the importance of treating racism as a matter of discursive social practice, at both the institutional and local-interpersonal levels. To challenge racism, we need to focus not at the level of individual psychology, but at the level of the ongoing *discursive* reproduction and legitimation of unequal power relations.

13 Far from the madding crowd: psychiatric diagnosis as the management of moral accountability

David McCarthy and Mark Rapley

EDITORIAL

By this stage in the collection, readers will no doubt be aware of the overlapping nature of the various approaches to the study of talk in institutional settings. David McCarthy and Mark Rapley provide what is perhaps the clearest instance of this so far. They work from an EM/CA base, turning to, and amplifying, the forms of MCA already encountered in Rhyll Vallis's contribution (Chapter 7). They then move into a more DP-based frame and show how MCA can analyse the dilemmas faced by lay and professional members alike when it comes to accounting for a mass killing via its perpetrator's 'mental condition' and his concomitant moral status. Finally, they suggest how such an EM/CA/DP combination can contribute to CDA by, equally, contributing to the anti-psychiatry movement.

McCarthy and Rapley illustrate how 'institutional' talk can be widely understood as referring to both talk and texts *– for the institution they are most concerned with here is the press and its uptake of both commonsense understandings and professional psychiatric 'diagnosis'. To set this in place, they rely on Sacks's notion that cultures display 'order at all points'. That is, cultures are such that their features can't simply be aggregated or counted. Instead, even very small fragments of them (particular 'cultural objects'), according to Sacks, must (as with holograms) display the order inherent in the whole. One aspect of this order is the* explanatory *work cultures can do with categorization devices (MCDs) and their predicates (CBAs). So by taking only a few fragments (extracts from news texts), McCarthy and Rapley show how finely powerful CA can be with regard to important, real-worldly, political events and public dilemmas. As the racing driver Stirling Moss once put it:* multum in parvo *(a lot in a little space).*[1]

INTRODUCTION

Extract 1
'Violence the resort of young, disturbed men'
(*The Australian*, 30 April 1996)
The Port Arthur massacre has raised the expected queries of what manner of person would go berserk in this fashion and how far the crimes could have been anticipated. Without wishing to pre-empt later legal findings the report thus far is that the killer is a young man believed to have had a history of mental illness. How is it possible that such an apparently disturbed young man has escaped scrutiny for so long?

In November 1996, Martin Bryant was sentenced to life imprisonment on 35 counts of murder for which he had been indicted after the shootings at the historic site of Port Arthur, Tasmania, in April of the same year. In sentencing him, Chief Justice Cox told the court that consideration of the prisoner's mental condition at the time of the shootings was at the 'forefront' of the case. Under the provisions of Tasmania's Criminal Code, for Bryant to be held criminally responsible for his actions – despite his change of plea to 'guilty' during the trial – the court had to be satisfied that two conditions were met: that he knew what he was doing at the time of his actions, and that he knew they were wrong. If found to be 'insane' (s381) or a 'natural imbecile' (s16(4)), the Code provides for a verdict of 'not guilty by reason of insanity'. Such a verdict (and the disposal options so afforded) turn as much on the *moral* as the *legal* status accorded to the accused. The 'insane' and the 'imbecile', by virtue of their membership in these categories, are excluded from the category 'accountable actor' and are, as such, exculpated from moral responsibility for their actions.

Three forensic psychiatrists and a forensic psychologist were given the task of making the assessment of Bryant's psychological condition and, although there was disagreement among the psychiatrists as to the correct diagnosis, all agreed that while Bryant 'suffered' from a 'significant personality disorder', he was not insane. Other (psychological) evidence suggested that, while Bryant had an IQ of 66 (sufficient to place him in the 'borderline intellectual disability' category), this level of intelligence did not imply that he was sufficiently impaired to satisfy the condition of 'natural imbecility'. The judge accepted the psychiatric account, acknowledging Bryant to have been 'grossly disturbed from early childhood' and describing him as having 'developed into a pathetic social misfit which called for pity and understanding'.

The Port Arthur massacre caused an avalanche of global media interest. In the Australian press, journalists were unanimous that Bryant was a culpable agent deserving of the severest punishment; but most conceded that they could not answer their own most pressing question: 'Why did he do it?' The shootings placed heavy demands on the news media for explication of the event and what 'manner of a person' its perpetrator was. As the editorial in *The Australian* (Extract 1) shows, the fourth estate was well aware both of its institutional role in rehearsing society's 'expected queries' about such momentous happenings and of its (self-appointed) responsibility for offering definitive accounts of them. As is further apparent from Extract 1, in the immediate recourse to the category 'mental illness' as explanatory resource, the media draw upon (and in so doing reproduce) the 'institutionalized' common sense of the culture on which they report.

The matter-of-fact tone of reporting adopted in the editorial (re)presents and naturalizes the mundane notion that only madness could account for Bryant's actions: however, despite (or perhaps *because of*) its seeming transparency and taken-for-grantedness, this is not a notion which can be left unexamined.[2] The flexibility and fluidity of psychiatric diagnostic categories – and their local and contingent deployment to manage the moral status and moral accountability of Bryant in the print media – form the focus of this chapter.

THEORETICAL APPROACH

We draw upon work in EM/CA, particularly MCA (Hester and Eglin, 1997; Jayyusi, 1984) and DP (Edwards and Potter, 1992a), to examine the ways in which the notionally scientific categories of psychiatry and clinical psychology can be understood not as the 'objective', value-free and morally neutral descriptions that their proponents claim them to be (APA, 1994), but rather as an apparatus for the moral management of unwanted conduct and as an institutional explanatory resource for the moral categorization of troublesome social actors. As such this chapter employs the theoretical and technical tools of DP and EM/CA to contribute to a project sometimes described as 'antipsychiatry' (see Boyle, 1990; Newnes *et al.*, 1999; Sarbin and Mancuso, 1984) that would perhaps be seen as more in keeping with the socio-political commitments of CDA.[3]

We start from two observations made by Harvey Sacks (1992a): first Sacks's insight that, in coming to understand a culture, one may profitably assume that cultures show *order at all points* and, secondly, *that descriptions of activities and persons may be* 'correct' in infinite ways. Schegloff puts the Sacksian position on the issue of 'order' very clearly:

> Sacks points out that [sampling] depends on the sort of order one takes it that the social world exhibits. An alternative to the possibility that order manifests itself at an aggregate level and is statistical in character is what he terms the 'order at all points' view. This view . . . understands order not to be present only at aggregate levels and therefore subject to an overall differential distribution, but to be present in detail on a case by case, environment by environment basis. A culture is not then to be found only by aggregating all of its venues; it is substantially present in each of its venues. (Schegloff in Sacks, 1992a: xlvi)

With regard to the matter of description, Sacks, in contrast to the naive 'picture theory' of categorization adopted by psychiatry and psychology, argues that there are infinitely many 'correct descriptions' of persons. Their correctness is not the point, however. The point is that *particularly selected* correct descriptions can do, among many other things, *explanatory* work:

> [O]ne whole range of ways that identifications get picked turns on category-bound activities. In the first instance, *a* way that you go about selecting an identificatory category – given, say, that some action is going on, done by some person – is to determine if there is a category-bound activity of that sort, and if that person is a member of that category, then use that category to identify them. Now these kinds of things are not just 'correct descriptions', they're correct descriptions in quite powerful ways. . . . Whereas lots of category-and-activity combinations will pose problems like 'Why in the world did that happen', 'Gee, isn't that unusual', in the specific cases where you've got a category-bound activity and the category for that is applied to some scene, *why* the thing happened is not a question. That it happened is explained by the very characterization. (Sacks, 1992a: 588–9)

We follow Sacks's lead in assuming that, in the examination of *fragments* of a culture, that which operates *across a culture as a whole* will come clearly into view. What we seek to do here, then, is to examine the way in which a limited sample of the Australian print media's reporting of the Port Arthur massacre deploys characterizations of Bryant in the service of explanation; reproduces and underpins the interpenetration of commonsense and psychiatric 'thinking'; and, simultaneously, exposes the contingent – and inescapably moral – functions which such 'psychiatric' categorization serves.

MANUFACTURING THE 'PSYCHIATRIC CASE'

The focus of this analysis is on the descriptions of Bryant in newspaper texts which attend to the necessity of accounting for the events at Port Arthur, or which report on the consequences of those events. Accordingly, we examine what journalists, as members of a shared social order, deem to be valid descriptions of the nature of persons and the reasons for their actions, and the work such identifications accomplish (see Smith, 1978). We briefly outline the candidate membership categories offered by the media over one year's reporting of the events and then examine, in more detail, specific instances of the deployment of psychiatric membership categories.

While initial reports of the shootings offered a variety of candidate membership categories in their accounts of Bryant, all converged on commonsense understandings of deviance. That is, acts understandable a priori as non-normative (here, engaging in multiple killings of perfect strangers) were characterized by the presentation of complementarily deviant identity categories. While many specific candidate 'micro' category memberships were offered, all could be heard to share the MCD of 'deviant' when applied to an adult male. For example Bryant was variously characterized as 'a Jekyll and Hyde', 'a man who sleeps with his pet pig' and 'a child'. Indeed, over the course of 1996, and particularly during the trial, the initially fragmented media characterizations of Bryant coalesced around the three categorisations: 'monster', 'madman' and 'child'. Here we restrict ourselves to an examination of the delicate discursive production of Bryant's membership in the category 'psychiatric case'.

SOME DATA

Our interest here is in the use and interpenetration of 'lay' and 'formal' membership categories in accounting for Bryant's actions between the social institutions of psychiatry and the media. In characterizing Bryant, the print media employ each genre of categorization dialogically to bolster the other: both everyday and psychiatric accounts converge on the explanation of the shootings by virtue of Bryant's categorization as a 'nut'. In the following case, a former neighbour of Bryant's describes his experience of the day:

Extract 2
'Explosion of a violent loner'
(*The Australian*, 30 April 1996)
'I had to stop a couple of times and think was this real. Then I realised the mongrel on the killing spree was the joker who had lived next door. He was a nut, a psycho' said Mr Featherstone.

There are a number of points of interest in this extract. First, we observe the direction given to the reader of the sense to be made of the story in the headline: that 'violent explosions' are the natural predicates of the (unnatural, asocial, odd) membership category 'loner'. Secondly, we observe that the immediacy and factuality of this account of Bryant and his actions is heightened by the adoption of the device of direct reported speech (Holt, 2000): these are not the speculations of the journalist, but the vivid recollections of an eyewitness. We further note the careful contrast worked up by Mr Featherstone between his status as an observer and checker of the facts (stopping not once, but 'a *couple* of times' to check the 'reality' of the 'unreal' events) and Bryant's status as careless (he was on a 'spree'), out of control and, by implication, out of touch with the 'reality' Featherstone has so meticulously checked. Such positioning (as well as his avowal of membership in the category of 'neighbour' – one who may thereby be expected to *know*, more intimately than a stranger would, about the actuality of Bryant's character) works both to provide a warrant for the veracity of Featherstone's account and also to produce him as a normative comparison against which Bryant may be understood. We further note that, as well as the direct invocation of the commonsense proto-psychiatric membership categories of 'nut' and 'psycho', these categories are preceded and hence framed by those of 'mongrel' and 'joker' – which are unequivocally (negative) moral judgements. That Bryant is also described in the past tense ('"He *was* a nut, a psycho" said Mr Featherstone') further serves to underpin the 'fact' that he has *always* been a 'nut', and to cement the commonsense view that, in the long run, 'violent explosions' are normatively to be expected of those incumbent in the (extraordinarily overdetermined) membership categories of 'psychos', 'loners' and 'nuts'.

Our third extract, like Extract 1, works in its headline to establish a *temporally sustained* 'otherness' as characteristic of Bryant. This furthers the project of the concatenation of commonsense and psychiatric membership categorizations to produce another version of Bryant grounded in the experience of those who may be seen to have a particularly strong epistemological warrant for the claims they make about him.

Extract 3
'Young man dogged by tragedy'
(*The Age*, 30 April 1996)
Bryant, variously described by acquaintances and former friends as slow, mentally ill and schizophrenic, became friends with a woman in New Town who lived in a mansion on Clare Street.

Bryant is 'variously' described by 'acquaintances and former friends' (members of categories that have intimate first-hand knowledge of the man as essential category predicate) in terms of *his* membership in both lay and psychiatric categories: 'slow', 'mentally ill' and 'schizophrenic'. The range of cited categories, and the implication of a broad *array* of sources, suggests that though there may be dispute about the specific 'type' of 'mental illness' afflicting Bryant, general agreement exists about problems of a psychiatric nature that have been observed independently by a number of people close to him. We note, however, that the headline here implies indeterminacy as to *cause*: Bryant is a *young man* (not, say, as would also have been a correct categorization, a 'mass murderer' or 'deranged killer') who has been 'dogged by tragedy'. This exemplifies the central paradox inherent in the entire media coverage of the Bryant case: the juggling of the possibility of Bryant's simultaneous membership in competing categories (sane vs. mad; of us vs. not of us) with very different moral implications. If Bryant is indeed a 'young man dogged by tragedy', he is a member of a shared social order and is morally (and legally) accountable for his actions. If he is a 'slow, mentally ill, schizophrenic' he is not. But if he is indeed one of us, the explanation of the shootings accomplished by and through his membership in the category 'madman' collapses.

Of course lay people can be wrong about their appraisals. Institutionally 'mental illness' requires an official diagnosis by those with specific knowledge entitlements such as psychiatrists and psychologists. However, members of *other* categories may be deployed by the media to enhance lay diagnoses; for example category members with 'expertise' on 'mass killers' are produced to ratify what may be seen as speculative commonsense categorizations:

Extract 4
'Police portrait of a mass killer'
(*Sydney Morning Herald*, 30 April 1996)
The gunman responsible for the massacre was aged 29, possibly a schizophrenic, who had planned the murders and probably knew one or two of his victims, police said this morning.

Here the 'portrait of a mass killer' loses any personal identification, becoming 'a gunman' who is possibly 'a schizophrenic' rather than a person, Martin Bryant, who possibly has schizophrenia (see Leudar and Thomas, 2000). As with Extract 1, where violent explosions are normatively bound to the category 'loners', here the *Herald* binds schizophrenia *per se*, rather than a specific individual, to violence and killing. 'Massacre' and 'murder', then, are natural predicates of the category 'schizophrenic'. The explanation of 'killing' is accomplished by characterizing the 'killer': mass killing is what schizophrenics *do*. As Sacks suggested: '*Why* the thing happened is not a question. That it happened is explained by the very characterization' – and the warrant of the reporting category 'police' works further to give the proffered characterization a sanctionable 'truth'. Yet again we see the tension inherent in the accounting: inasmuch as the *Herald* deploys the category 'police' to do some work in establishing 'senseless' killing as a predicate of insanity, so psychiatry tells us that the essential predicates of the membership category 'schizophrenics' are loss of reason and of contact with 'reality': such attributes sit uneasily with the characterization of the 'mass killer' as having carefully planned his actions. Similarly 'murders' are, in law, committed by those with *mens rea*, with agency and with volitional control, predicates normatively understood as outwith the category 'schizophrenic'.

We have seen that in reports of everyday characterization members produce intrinsically adequate accounts of the shootings by drawing upon, and blending, commonsense categories ('nut', mongrel', 'slow') with proto-psychiatric ones ('psycho', 'schizophrenic', 'mentally ill'). But, in terms of the requirements of *institutional accounting*, there is a problem: how can psychiatry characterize Bryant in such a manner that does the work of explanation (expertise in the explanation of inexplicable or unwanted conduct being psychiatry's self-appointed bailiwick), but which simultaneously retains his membership in the category of accountable moral actor? This is how:

Extract 5
'No Motive, No Mercy, No Remorse'
(*Sydney Morning Herald*, 23 November 1996)
Martin Bryant, in the months following the Port Arthur tragedy, was examined by four psychologists and psychiatrists. They all concluded that, while he suffered from a personality disorder and was, according to intelligence tests, in the borderline range between intellectual disability and the 'dull normal individual', he was not criminally insane, and did not suffer from serious mental illness – such as depression or schizophrenia. In other words, in the opinion of those psychologists and psychiatrists who examined him, Bryant was capable of distinguishing between right and wrong, and understood, in the words of Paul Mullen, a forensic psychiatrist from Monash University, 'what it meant to be guilty and to be not guilty'.

We see here a skilful resolution of the essential tension between Bryant's candidate memberships. He is constructed by psychiatry and psychology in terms of 'diagnostic' categories which essentially place him in no-man's land: he is 'personality disordered' but not insane; he is intellectually deficient but insufficiently retarded to be exculpable; he is both of us and not of us. Enough is retained of commonsense members' understandings of the characterization 'psycho' to do the work of explanation. (The shootings are explained by Bryant's institutionally ratified membership in the category 'psychologically disturbed'.) Yet he is simultaneously not 'nuts' enough to be 'let off the hook': he is, again via the ratification of institutional psychiatry, sufficiently 'of us' to be held accountable.

IN CONCLUSION

We have seen that media reporting of social life is an important and rich source of data for the understanding of the workings of a culture. But further: *how* professionalized knowledges (specifically the classificatory systems of psychiatry and clinical psychology) are brought into play in these reports can show us, following Sacks, that the deployment of characterization can and does, in and of itself, do the work of explanation. The repertoires of identity constructed by the Australian print media for Bryant (as 'monster', 'psychiatric case' and 'child') turn upon the category-bound activities associated with such identities, and are organized to accomplish the difficult task of producing an account of Bryant and his actions which retain his status as an agentic, accountable, moral actor – and hence liable to the full force of the criminal law – but which also manage the production of an 'explanation' of the inexplicable. Thus Bryant was produced as 'monstrous', but capable of human kindness; as 'childish' – but as a child of an age to know right from wrong; as psychologically disturbed, but not as entirely 'mad'.

It can be seen here, then, that not only can characterization do the work of accounting, but also there appears to be no *principled* way of separating out (as somehow epistemologically distinct) the candidate category of 'psychiatric case' from the others made available in these media accounts. Rather, the manner in which both popular media and the professions draw upon these MCDs suggests that they are not the dispassionate, objective, scientific nosologies that the disciplines claim them to be. Rather, as Sarbin and Mancuso (1984) suggest, they are powerful and contingent devices which can be – and here are – pressed into local service in public discourse not to accomplish *medical diagnosis* but rather to pass *moral verdict.*

Notes

1. Many thanks to Rod Watson for passing on this phrase, albeit that he will no doubt be less than happy with its misuse in this context.
2. Our analysis of stories in the quality press suggests that four discursive themes are drawn upon to construct the identity of Martin Bryant, and to secure an individual-

ized, psychologized, account of the shootings in terms of Bryant's personal 'pathology'. Bryant is variously constructed as a 'Peter Pan' figure, as a 'monster', as a 'psychiatric case' and, finally, as 'unique'. The analysis further suggests that variation in the temporal salience of these competing identity categories – with early reports focusing on Bryant's essential 'otherness' and later reports emphasizing his shared, but flawed, membership in the category of 'accountable actor' – can be understood as strategically organized in order to manage his criminal culpability.

3. See Fairclough (Chapter 3) and the debate on the relationship between 'pure' CA and post-structuralist approaches broadly termed 'critical discursive social psychology' (Wetherell, 1998; Schegloff, 1998).

PART III

Theory and Method

14 Two lines of approach to the question 'What does the interviewer have in mind?'

Angela O'Brien-Malone and Charles Antaki

EDITORIAL

In this chapter, Angela O'Brien-Malone and Charles Antaki raise the question of the praxis *as against the* mentality *of the interviewer in a case of psychological testing. Unlike other contributions, this analysis of a dialogue is itself composed as a dialogue with each of the authors offering a distinct 'take' on the matters of whether we can tell what an interviewer 'has in mind' and, more importantly, whether such a question is material to an understanding of the everyday discursive business of 'institutional' interviews.*

Angela adopts a cognitivist position and argues that we can't make sense of the interview event itself unless we make reasonable and grounded decisions about the interviewer's internal mental state. At first, this assumption appears relatively trouble-free since, as Angela puts it, it seems only fair to say that 'we (the reader) could infer that [the interviewer] held an intention with respect to the conversation he was about to have with [the client] – he intended to ask her the standardized questions'.

Charles's response, however, is that such matters may or may not be pertinent to these two actual participants in the talk, and that we can discern such (im)pertinence by a close inspection of the interview data itself. His argument is not that persons don't have mental states (far from it); rather it is that such matters are not universally relevant to talk and that sometimes (perhaps even in a majority of cases) participants do not have to work with assumptions about what the other has in mind. If this is true for participants, then all the more so for analysts.

The consequences of this debate for CA and related disciplines, and for the distinction between CA-based work and cognitive approaches to language and discourse, are wide-ranging. In the end, the reader is invited to make up their own mind (mind?) about the criticality of cognitivist assumptions about everyday language use – whether lay or professional. But what's perhaps more important in this chapter is that two previously distinct traditions of psychological-institutional analysis are brought together for the first time that we know of. They are not, however, brought into direct confrontation. Rather they talk together in a way that displays both possibilities of mutual benefits and great openness to hearing and understanding the positions adopted on either side of the debate.[1]

INTRODUCTION

It's a sad truth that when families split, members stop talking to each other (although they may be quite happy to talk *about* one another). Academic families are no different. Over these pages we shall try to mend our ways a little by having a dialogue about one piece of data which can, at least at first glance, be taken as 'institutional'. One way of looking at it is, broadly, as a demonstration of people's cognitive powers in remembering and having intentions; the other is (equally broadly) as a demonstration of their discursive practices in bringing off certain ways of asking and answering questions. We have organized the chapter as a commentary that shuttles between the cognitive reading of what's happening (written by Angela) and a more discursive, conversation-analytically informed reading (written by Charles). We shall try to pick up each other's worries and say something to make ourselves clear to each other – even if we do end up disagreeing.

EXTRACT[2]

MI	°ok°
	(0.4)
MI	just thinking about ↑this for a minute (.) ↓Anne (0.4)
	are most the things that happen (0.8) re↑warding (.) ac↓ceptable
	(.) or disap↓pointing
AN	I like to go to the ↑family ↓'ouse
	(0.4)
MI	yeah (.) ↑can can we just ↓do these ↑questions (0.4) and ↓then
	we'll have a chat about (.) the ↑other ↓things
	(0.8)
MI	yeah?
	(0.8)
MI	hm?
AN	av ↑'ad me ↓pills
	(2.0)
AN	↓love
MI	yeah?
	(2.0)
MI	ok .hh (.) ↑is ↑most the ↓thing are ↑most the ↓things in life (0.4)
	good (.) ↓ok or (.) ↑not so good
	(6.0)
AN	yes (.)
MI	which one
AN	it's al:↑right
MI	it's al↓right
AN	you can book it ↓down
MI	ok

28 (0.8)
29 MI ↑how ↓happy are you with (1.5) living ↓here
30 AN I ↑like to live ↓here

Charles: A working gloss of all that is to say that one participant (MI) is asking questions of the other (AN), and pursuing answers to a series of alternatives. AN's answers are not always smoothly executed, and often seem to occasion checking and reformulation. Certainly there is enough to suggest, prima facie, that the interaction is 'institutional' in at least two of the terms suggested by Drew and Heritage (1992a) – first that at least one participant seems to be working towards some official goal (the determination of answers among a pre-given set), and secondly that both participants treat certain aspects of the exchange as being constraining (perhaps the most obvious one here is that AN does not ask the questions). If we take this as a point of departure, what can we say about the interaction from a cognitive and from a discursive position? Let us start out with a cognitive point of view. This will always be expressed by Angela, and I will respond and raise my own points as we go along.

ON SUPPOSING 'THINGS IN THE HEAD'

Angela: Let's begin with the opening lines from the extract (1–5). The first thing to note is that MI begins with an utterance which seems to make sense to him. MI is not producing random noise; he's producing something that we – the reader – recognize as words. Now while there is little in the transcript to indicate that MI necessarily understands the words (a video might have been of more use here), what is clear is that there is no accompanying utterance that indicates that he doesn't.

Of course, we can cheat a bit because, as it happens, we have a bit more available to us than that – we have a copy of the standardized questions MI was supposed to be asking.[3] We can read the transcript, and the record of the required standardized questions, and decide that Question 4 was the question that MI 'had in mind'. That could provide an interesting line of analysis.

Charles: I can see that Angela is working towards a reading of MI as 'having a question in mind' and opening up discussion of what that question was, and what institutional purposes it serves and so on. But although we might eventually get to that discussion, I'm wary of reaching it on a path that starts with an observation of the sort that MI is 'producing an utterance that has meaning for him'; surely that is something we can take on trust? But I do see that once you put it like that, it becomes a thought-provoking observation. What it provokes is the realization that we don't always extend such rationality to people; so this speaker must be doing something to make him pass as normal. So I take this as a useful note that 'being meaningful' is an accomplishment, which is perhaps far from what a cognitivist reading would want to say. But let us proceed on the bearing that Angela has struck.

Angela: Let's think about MI's cognitive capacities a bit more. First, we (the reader) could infer that MI held an intention with respect to the conversation he was about to have with Anne – he intended to ask her the standardized questions. This inference of an intention is supported by the evidence, namely, the sequence of events: there was a set of standardized questions which were formulated before the interview took place, and MI used these when he actually spoke to Anne. Since MI behaves in a way that is consistent with prior events – with events that were removed in time – we also have some evidence of him using memory. So, we have evidence of MI holding an intention, and also using memory. Since MI didn't appear to make up sounds on the spot which just happened to correspond to words, and his verbal transcript is consistent with his utterance being meaningful for him, we also have evidence that MI had knowledge of word meanings; that is, that he had a lexicon, and that he was using it in constructing this utterance. So far, so good: we see in MI intention, memory and evidence of a lexicon. So MI is using 'things in the head' when he begins his conversation with Anne.

Charles: Slow down! There's an awful lot there that wants thinking about. I may not persuade you, but I just want you to think about what expressions like 'using memory' mean (at least in everyday use). 'We have evidence of MI using memory' is an odd phrase. It would be all right if MI was the codename for a mouse or an insect about whose possibility of having such a thing as 'memory' there were genuine doubts. But we don't have such doubts about ordinary people.

Angela: That's an interesting thought. I had guessed – wrongly, it seems – that you held the position that there was no such thing as 'things in the head'. Hence my opening with an address to that issue. But having said that, while I am more than happy to assume MI is a cognitive being, what exactly constitutes his (our) cognitive abilities, and how they work, are matters for investigation, and some cognitive faculties which we have been purported to have, or explanations for how they operate, have failed when empirically investigated.

Charles: 'Ordinary language' philosophy, and the ethnomethodological (EM) study of people's everyday practices, sets us straight here. It's not a matter of empirical discovery that people have the faculty of memory. It's not that we've noticed something curious about people (or some people) that wants a label attached to it, like the discovery of allergy to pollen ('hay fever'). It's the other way about. (There's a lovely exposition of the argument in Derek Edwards's *Discourse and Cognition.*) People (any people) have ways of talking about things (the world, themselves, other people) which presume and imply things in the past. We call that 'memory' and can use it (like we can use any assumed human attribute) in various ways. Famously, of course, memory is usable as a resource to account for faults, and as a fault in itself. One's memory lapse is a (possible, alleged, and so forth) empirical discovery, but the fact that you have the faculty of memory – if you are not an ant or a mouse – can't be.

So I'm not much moved by your demonstration that MI is 'using memory' here, or that he's 'using things in the head'. That's just the way we talk about people (and not ants, and the rest), by definition. I'd be more interested if there was evidence that having a (good, long, unreliable, faulty . . .) memory was a live matter for either MI or Anne at this point (and whether that gives us any purchase on institutional practice), but we'll come to the notion of something being a 'live matter' later on.

Angela: So are we actually disagreeing about what *can* be investigated? – about the kinds of questions it makes sense to ask? Or are we disagreeing about what we should *assume* about people? I think these are questions that potentially raise issues about the limits of the discipline and the limits of knowledge.

As a cognitive psychologist, I am unwilling to assume that people can necessarily *always* tell us correctly about their own cognitive processes and faculties – like memory, learning, and so on. The debates in the cognitive tradition about introspective access go back quite a long time (for instance, Nisbett and Wilson worked in the 1970s on introspective access to cognitive processes – their 1977 paper is a review), but the question is still hotly debated, for instance, in the literatures about consciousness and implicit learning by people like Dienes and Berry (1997), Shanks and St John (1994), or Stadler (1997), and others (see, for example, the *Psychonomic Bulletin and Review*'s 1997 special issue on implicit learning). So I don't think that the only thing that ought to be investigated is people's use of language to describe themselves. But in saying that, I don't mean to imply that people's use of language to describe themselves should *not* be investigated.

Charles: I'd better jump in quickly here because I don't want you to run away with the idea that I think people should be asked to describe their own mental processes. That's a charge often levelled at discourse analysts of various stripes, and is always misplaced. What I want is for us to look and see what MI and AN actually *do* with each other – how they treat each other as 'understanding', 'missing the point', 'answering appropriately', 'misremembering', and so on.

Angela: I think I'll take you up on that in a minute – but back to 'memory' for a moment. I also think that 'memory' is a problematic word, mostly because it has more than one meaning. When a cognitive psychologist says 'memory', he or she is usually alluding to one or more of a swag of theoretical constructs – short-term memory, long-term memory, working memory, and the like. All these ways of talking about memory are born of some particular way of thinking about it. (There are a number of such ways; see, for instance, Koriat and Goldsmith (1996).) But when I say 'memory' in this chapter, I simply want to denote the ability to organize our behaviour over time, in particular, to organize our conversational behaviour. The fact that conversation does not become incoherent – that local meaning and communication can be made – requires, minimally, that the previous utterance be taken into account. And I am not merely asserting that MI could organize his behaviour over time; there is evidence to support this statement. For instance, in a number of places in this dialogue, what MI says implies that he holds some record about his previous utterance(s). The question of memory is not 'live' for either MI or Anne in this conversation, but that doesn't mean they didn't use it – merely that they didn't discuss it. I agree with you that the word 'memory' does form part of the way we talk about people, part of our discursive practice. But, inasmuch as it also refers to our ability to organize our behaviour over time, then I think it is also an empirical issue. We might have to agree to disagree on this! Anyway, let's see what happens next by returning to lines 6–30.

An odd thing happens from line 6 on. Anne's response (6) doesn't appear to be a response to the question MI has asked (1–5). MI doesn't seem to think it's a response to his question either, because he says 'yeah, can can we just do these questions and then we'll have a chat about the other things, yeah?' (8–11). It may be that AN has understood the question in some way other than MI, but the transcript suggests that MI held a working hypothesis that AN did not understand, since he repeats the question (19–20), and he does so in a simplified form. MI says: 'are most . . . things in life good, ok, or not so good'. (The standardized question was: 'Are most of the things that happen to you: Rewarding; Acceptable; Disappointing'.)

After a pause (21) Anne says (22) 'yes'. MI appears to believe (more evidence of 'things in the head') that AN is now replying to his question because he says (23) 'which one', where 'which' appears to apply to the options listed at line 20 ('good, ok, or not so good'). AN replies 'it's alright'. MI repeats 'it's alright'. Perhaps Anne now gets impatient with MI because she says: 'you can book it down', at which point MI seems to take this ('it's alright') as the answer to his question ('ok' (27)), and introduces the next question.

Charles: I think Angela would agree with me that her defence of the status of MI as a cognitive being isn't strictly necessary for her analysis of the lines above. She, like the rest of us (and especially and principally, the two people in the interaction), has to go on the organization and content of the speakers' words and how they relate to each other. General statements about people (whether cognitive, biological, psychodynamic or any other) aren't much help.

Angela: My point exactly! I think that 'the organization and content of the speakers' words and how they relate to each other' *reveals* that MI is a cognitive being, or is at least supportive of this hypothesis.

TALKING ABOUT ANALYSIS

Charles: I think we might as well drop the issue of whether MI needs 'revealing' as a cognitive being. It comes down, ultimately, to whether one sees cognition and cognitive faculties as a matter of empirical discovery, or as a presumption about humans. Instead let's progress by keeping with Angela's account of the organization of MI and Anne's turns. In taking the lead on analysis for a moment, I'll slip in some jargon (and try to say why what it represents is useful).

CA takes up the venerable EM distinction between, on the one hand, 'participants' orientation' to each other and, on the other, our own, social-scientific ideas about what's going on. The cautious recommendation is to prefer people's own, first-hand, then-and-there displays of sense-making (their 'orientation' to what's going on) over whatever theoretical speculations we might come up with as a Johnny-come-lately. In CA terms, it is the relativist notion that (for example) something is a question if it's so treated, a satisfactory answer if it's so treated, and so on. (Or nearly so; there are certain prerequisites, namely that the action be recognizable to any competent member as being at least potentially a question or answer and so on.)

So rather than say, with Angela, that 'Anne's response at line 6 doesn't appear to be a response to the question MI asked', I'd rather we stuck with the next observation that Angela herself immediately makes, which is that MI doesn't treat it as one. Presumably, it was always open for him to have done so; indeed, there are other things she says (not in this extract, I admit) which are equally 'off-target' but which nevertheless get dealt with as if they were quite proper. Who are we to say? It is the participants themselves who must decide what is and isn't a proper question and answer (or invitation, summons, noticing, informing, news announcement and so on ad infinitum). If we don't have that as a limit on interpretation, then where would one ever draw the line?

Angela: May I interject here, Charles? If it were only the participants who were able to interpret the conversation, wouldn't the appropriate method of analysis be to ask them what it meant? This is the point I wanted to take issue with a while back. I agree that the participants do have a privileged insight into the meaning of the conversation (largely because of the 'things in the head' which are not recorded in the transcript, but which they remember thinking, feeling, attending to, and so on). But allowing that the participants have a privileged status with respect to interpretation is not the same as saying that it is necessarily uninterpretable for the rest of us. And, when we analyse a transcript like this, all we have in the end is our valuation of what we believe (or can argue) to be the participants' valuation, not the thing in itself.

Charles: I'm taking the familiar EM line of saying that the participants don't sit down and analyse these things, in the way that a professional analyst can do afterwards, but rather that they *do* them then and there, without any feeling of having to strain at 'working it out'. A person needs to analyse their conversation as much as an oak leaf needs to analyse its photosynthesis. Speakers do what they do, making their actions intelligible to each other, but we have the luxury and time to play and replay a record of it and see *how* they do it. There's not much point asking them to reflect on it, either, because what they have access to are their patchy memories of what they did, soaked in folk-theories of why they did it, and compromised by whatever business they want to promote in giving a sensible, silly, complete, newsworthy, amusing (and so on) reflection to us now, in retrospect.

What interests me is what makes Angela (or any of us) understand what MI says (8) as being enough for her to conclude that he doesn't think what Anne said is an answer to his question. This is surely where the action is – how exactly human beings communicate such things as 'not thinking something is an answer' (whether he *really* thought that or not of course is beyond us, and irrelevant to the interaction). One shouldn't gloss over it as if it were either trivially done (after all, not being able to do things like this would make a person look incompetent and barely human) or so ineffably subtle as not to be analysable (it must be analysable, since the communicated-to person presumably 'analyses' it). Note a few things about it.

First, it is preceded by a brief pause (about 0.4 seconds). Not only is it a pause, it is a pause at a point where MI might be expected to speak; after all, Anne has just completed a turn – the accumulated canon of CA has lots to say about how people shape their talk into turns, but let's leave it like that for the moment and return to lines 6–13.

The sort of turn AN has produced at line 6 is in the space set up by MI's previous question, so it is hearably produced as an 'answer', just as a summons calls forth a response, or one greeting calls forth another. And the sequence question–answer can lead, in smooth conversation, to a number of next turns: an assessment of the answer ('good, right'), a receipt of it as news ('oh really?'), a further question, a new topic, and so on. All of these, to count as 'smooth', would be done without missing a beat or drawing attention to themselves. But that's not the way MI does it. The pause does take a beat and his 'yeah', while ambiguous, is followed by a dysfluent 'can can we just' which marks off what he's saying as not any of those smooth uptakes. In other words, by simply doing something as tiny as waiting for 0.4 seconds, 'stumbling' over a word and designing the very start of his turn as a request which wants mitigation, MI gets across that something untoward is happening. In CA jargon, he is marking his turn as 'dispreferred', and a commentary on the acceptability of what he is reacting to.

Angela: These are great points! But there are aspects of this conversation that remind me of the play-within-the-play in *Hamlet.* You have just analysed this data and, as you say, the participants must also be able to analyse it (although the status of their analysis with respect to consciousness could be an interesting question . . .). Where does the analysis occur, if not 'in the head'? Can the existence of an analysis – such as you have just given us – be anything except evidence for a cognitive life?

Charles: There are two activities going on. One is what we, the social scientists, are up to, and the other is what the people in the extract are doing. On the first count, anything which wants to claim allegiance to EM will distance itself from the sort of 'analysis' that converts one set of phenomena into another, or into signs or symptoms of something else, including internal cognitions. A discursive psychology (say) will not be like psychoanalysis, or inferential statistics, or literary criticism. The phenomena stay the same after our dealings with them – we explicate them, lay them out, see how they work, but we neither explain them nor transform them. On the other hand there is what the speakers are doing – for them, the talk is what it visibly and hearably is, and it may be that sometimes they themselves will test each other out as to their cognitive capacities. If they do that, then, of course, we can look on and observe what they construe such capacities to be (and we might do so with the dialogue between MI and AN). But it's they who call the tune. They get on and do what they do, and we arrive (late) and say how they did it.

Angela: For me, these points highlight issues we thought about earlier: what is it we ought to analyse and what is it we ought to assume? As you say, 'the communicated-to person presumably "analyses"' the conversation, but needs to do so 'as much as an oak leaf needs to analyse its photosynthesis'. This is an interesting issue for a cognitive psychologist, since processes seem to vary on how automated they are, and also on how (accurately) reportable they are, and these differences may tell us something about consciousness. So, if I have understood correctly, you want to assume something that I want to analyse. But is this necessarily a problem?

There is something else about the nature of analysis that your last points raise for me – this is a point I have alluded to already. It seems to me that, when we analyse a transcript of a conversation, we always convert 'one set of phenomena into another, or into signs or symptoms of something else'. First, what we have is a transcript, not the conversation itself. Even videotapes and audiotapes are not the thing itself. Then we overlay that first step away from the 'thing itself' with our thoughts about the transcript. No matter how carefully we try to keep to what can be ascertained from the data, it is always *our* thoughts about that data. It is never the 'thing itself'. I think analysis of any kind *necessarily* implies a one-step-removed process that converts one thing, one 'phenomenon' (the conversation), into 'signs and symptoms of something else' (our analysis of the phenomenon).

Reflecting on our discussion of this point leads me to wonder whether we have another fundamental question to discuss. I think that, in order to interpret 'what they do', we need to take account of a larger set of behaviours and events – in other words, we need to recognize that the behaviour in question is larger than the utterance produced. So, in order to understand this conversation, I want to include knowledge of past events (for example, that there were standard questions selected prior to the interview), and I also want to include word-knowledge and social knowledge (for example, what a clinical psychologist is and what sort of roles he or she might hold). What do you think?

Charles: Taking the EM/CA line, a discursive psychologist would fight shy of using her or his own knowledge of such things as the roles of the speakers or their past histories, or even of things in their surroundings which seem obviously to be relevant (that they might be in a hospital rather than a private house and so on). It is perhaps easiest to see why such obviously arguable things as speakers' past histories are very dubious sands on which to base analysis but the same principle, expressed most pithily by Schegloff (1997), applies to roles, genders, ages and all such 'analysts' categories' as Sacks put it. Put crudely, I would rather we wait and see what the participants do to see what they treat as 'context'. Don't think this condemns us to thin pickings; there is evidence in bucket loads, and it is at first hand.

INSTITUTIONALITY

Charles: This brings us squarely back to the motivating force of this exercise: what, if anything, can be said about the institutionality of this stretch of talk? The first-hand evidence is clear enough, even on a bare pass. One speaker has the monopoly on questions, and both participants allow him to pursue them beyond the 'normal' first candidate answer, a pattern thoroughly infused with institutional regimes of expertise and asymmetric rights to inquire. So far so good. But if we look more closely we see things which only show up at fine-grain, and which are nicely captured by Drew and Heritage's (1992a) third element in their suggestive list of features of institutional talk: that it selectively (but not uniformly) exempts speakers from what would, in other times and places, be the obvious implications of their actions.

This is perhaps most obvious in MI's talk. Normally (I mean, when the speakers are not heard to be doing 'institutional business'), responses to the sort of personal questions being asked here get some sort of assessment before a next question is asked; not to do so would open the questioner to the implication that he or she is 'cold', 'impersonal' or even 'callous', and would make trouble in the interaction (visible, perhaps, by the respondent challenging the questioner's actions). The fact that this doesn't happen here is evidence that the standard expectations must be in abeyance. Let us return, then, to the extract.

We notice (7–8) that MI passes on the opportunity to treat AN's replies as newsworthy – with an 'oh really' and 'do you' and so on; see the account in Heritage (1984a). This is a common feature of institutional talk, where non-appearance of such things does not carry the same implication as it does in other places – or rather, it *marks* what is being done as not like what happens elsewhere, and that the speaker is not bound by normal expectations. We could then go on, with that observation under our belt, to analyse AN's reaction, to see how MI recycles the question, and so on, all contributing to our understanding of this particular slice of institutional talk. But rather than do that, let us see what Angela makes of that same stretch.

Angela: I would take those lines as evidence of the theme I've been pursuing throughout – that MI has something in mind. The way I see it is that lines 7–20 show MI (a) offering an explanation for why he can't talk about going to 'the family house' just now, and (b) entertaining the hypothesis that Anne didn't understand the question the way he asked it the first time, since he repeats the question in a simplified form. In these lines, I would argue, we see the effect of MI's thoughts; we see him making an adjustment to the wording of the question, working 'in-the-moment' of the interaction to keep the meaning (or what he presumably thinks is the meaning) of the question, while simplifying the language in a way that – he hopes? – will make it more comprehensible to Anne. This implies, of course, that he has some construct or judgement 'in-the-head' about what it is that Anne is likely to understand. So, the 'in-the-moment' interaction is affected by constructs or expectations 'in-the-head'. Further, we see MI seem to form another hypothesis (22–28): namely, that Anne's answer to his question about what most of the things that happen to her are like, is that they are 'alright'.

There's another point that the transcript of the conversation we have looked at so far raises questions about. This is the use of standardized questions. Line 29 sees MI introduce Question 5: 'how happy are you with living here'. The 'official' standardized question was: 'How satisfied are you with your current home or living arrangements? Very satisfied; Somewhat satisfied; Unsatisfied; or Very unsatisfied'. When we use standardized questions, we should ask ourselves what it is we are attempting to standardize: the words, the whole interaction (including tone, prosody, body language, and so on), or the communication of meaning? Look at what MI does: he abandons any attempt at giving the exact wording of the question, and goes immediately to a simplified version: 'how happy are you with living here'. One interpretation of MI's use of this simplified form of words is that it is an attempt to keep the meaning of the question standardized – in the sense of being adequately communicated to AN. This could be a laudable change, or not, depending on what the actual purpose of the study was. The issues of *what* it is that is being standardized when we use so-called standardized questions, *how* this is being standardized, and *for whom*, are generally more complex than has been acknowledged within the cognitive tradition.

SUMMARY

Angela: Clearly we could carry the discussion on, but I think we can draw a line here and reflect on what we have been saying to each other. When we started out, I thought that the position you were taking was that there was no such thing as 'things in the head'. Now, reading what you have written, I think I was mistaken. I am happy to assume that humans are cognitive beings. But I think that the details about what cognitive abilities we have, and how they work, are matters for investigation. But that we have a cognitive system – well, I wouldn't normally see that there was any need to argue that. But I have argued it here, because of the position I thought (initially) that you were taking. So I see that there has been a change in my understanding of your position which has grown out of our interaction over this data. The other thing I've learned from our conversation is that many of our disagreements seem to lie in the areas of what ought to be assumed, and what ought to be analysed. We also seem to have a different concept of what analysis means.

Charles: My ideas have changed too – or rather, I was banking on you putting your analytic spotlight not on the interviewer MI but rather on the interviewee AN, who (one might say) seemed to be most 'interesting' cognitively in the way she seemed to have trouble coping with the questions. I was going primly to say that, for an EM-minded analyst, all participants contribute to the action so all are fair game, and remind you that psychologists pretty well universally edit themselves out of the picture of what they are explaining (thus, in this case, MI's contribution to the interaction simply disappears at the end of the session when all is left is a numerical record of AN's answers). But you took the wind out of my sails there. We ended up on the same side, treating the occasion as being in the hands of both parties, and its institutionality jointly achieved.

I agree with Angela on one thing: that 'the details about what cognitive abilities we have, and how they work, are matters for investigation' – but with a qualification. I think that EM and CA – especially as they converge in the discursive psychology of Edwards and Potter (1992a) – have opened up the vastly attractive prospect of investigating such things *as they matter*. That is, as people challenge, invoke, hint at, congratulate or query each other's cognitive abilities in going about their everyday business.

Angela: I completely agree with you on this. Mainstream cognitive psychology has concentrated heavily on laboratory-based studies. It is certainly time that we turned more of our attention to gaining an understanding of the cognitive system as it is used and operates in everyday life, be that in conversation, or in other activities.

Notes

1. *Editors' note:* Further ways forward, following the debate offered in this chapter, might be to reconsider: (a) Sacks's analysis of how what looks like 'mind reading' can be a completely ordinary, everyday practice (Silverman, 1998: 10–11) and (b) core EM work on the everyday use of mental predicates (Coulter, 1979).
2. Notation follows the Jefferson system used, with some exceptions, throughout this book, but note that timings are only approximate.
3. These are the official questions printed on the interview schedule (held by the interviewer) which most closely resemble what he actually says:

   - Question 4. Are most of the things that happen to you:
     Rewarding; Acceptable; Disappointing?
   - Question 5. How satisfied are you with your current home or living arrangements?
     Very satisfied; Somewhat satisfied; Unsatisfied; Very unsatisfied.

   We are grateful to Mark Rapley for providing us with the original tape and the printed questionnaire used by the psychologist.

15 Methodological issues in analysing talk and text: the case of childhood in and for school

Helena Austin, Peter Freebody and Bronwyn Dwyer

EDITORIAL

Reflecting on a larger research project (Austin et al., *in preparation), the authors of this chapter offer a methodological insight into how to handle texts and talk as they are produced and come to be modified over time in a primary-school setting. Here, they aim to make good what they discern as a relative neglect of texts (by comparison with talk) in the EM/CA literature. In particular, they are interested in how a novel is read; how teachers and students (in whole-class and small-group situations) then discuss their readings; how students compose pieces of writing based on that* text-and-talk nexus *(see Ann Kelly's chapter, earlier); and finally, how teachers talk (in class, to students and in interviews) about their achievements in this process. As they put it, this constitutes 'the web of sense that resonates between data sets' and, so, takes us beyond conversational fragments to local negotiations of identity.*

How these processes work (and are worked at *by the participants) turns out to be critical for how the category of 'Child' operates. That is, Austin* et al. *find that 'what it is to be a child' is imbricated in how children are expected to read, talk and write. They find there to be a form of competent childhood that, peculiarly perhaps, consists in being audibly and visibly* pre-*competent (with respect to adulthood). And that pre-competence is clearly displayed in the kinds of 'interpretive frame' expected in children's readings and writings.*

Some specific instances of this are analysed 'in the breach'; that is, where some children display in*competence by displaying* over-*competence. They, therefore, present themselves as being too much like adults. Hence: 'the over-competent are, ironically, categorized as "immature"; or taken to be inappropriately using exclusively adult devices'. This finding is interesting because, as the authors show, it corroborates some of the speculative macro-theorizing of previous sociological work on childhood – except that, here, as with all CA-type approaches, the finding is grounded in actual, everyday materials and transcriptions thereof.*

Helena Austin, Peter Freebody and Bronwyn Dwyer

INTRODUCTION

This chapter aims to demonstrate and extend some analytic features of conversation analysis (CA) and membership categorization analysis (MCA), drawing on instances of talk and text from various sites within an institution. Our substantive interest is in the institutional construction of the category 'Child' in and for school as that category is effected through the selection and production of certain texts and talk about those texts. Here, we specifically address several methodological issues, the first of which is the scope of the data set. To date, the scope of studies of talk-in-interaction has been, in the main, precisely focused analyses of brief transcripts or segments of text. This chapter, by contrast, tracks through a large body of varied data (talk and text) and aims to achieve coherence in method and analytic outcomes, to explicate the web of sense that resonates between data sets and between the analyses, and to demonstrate the delicacy and precision of the analysis with specific examples.

Our second point of analytic interest concerns text analysis. Watson (1997a: 80) has commented that 'there is a relative paucity of studies which deal with texts as mundane phenomena, as a routine part of our everyday activities', and has further noted that 'texts have seldom been treated as analytically significant phenomena in their own right, as comprising self-contained data in themselves . . . as objects of attention on their own behalf' (1997a: 85). These observations are critical for applied ethnomethodologists interested in schooling – partly because of the heavy reliance of schooling processes on the reading and writing of printed materials and – a related point – because so much talk in classrooms is centrally interested in mediating students' reading and writing.

Here we deal with the analysis of different types of texts: a published novel, Colin Thiele's *Magpie Island* (1974), and students' writing in reaction to classroom work on and around that novel. Because what students write in school is consequential for their success there, a text on or around which they produce their writing can be seen to have 'a structuring effect, that actively organises a course of social action and that is consequential for that action, directing it in its course' (Watson, 1997a: 85).

This understanding leads to a third domain of interest in this chapter: the nexus between talk and text. We draw on Heap's (1986) research on the organization of talk in elementary classroom lessons. One of Heap's concerns was the reciprocal construction of the conjoined authority of both the teacher and a text. He was partly interested in interrogating reading lessons to explore how it is that teacher-endorsed readings of a text are made available to students, and are given interpretive privilege in classroom talk. He concluded that reading lessons can be examined for the ways in which they endorse particular forms of propositional knowledge, and also for the ways in which they are effectively lessons in the 'comprehension of culture and the logic of its organisation and possibilities. The text is simply the site for launching that comprehension' (Heap,

1985: 265). Drawing on these ideas, Baker and Freebody (1989a) showed how teachers ask questions that are apparently aimed at making classroom talk about texts more 'student-centred'. They noted that 'the location of such techniques in a teacher-centred, evaluative organization of talk in the classroom may serve to expand the *legislative boundaries* of schooling into personal and social areas of the child's life which may bear no apparent relevance to the child's acquisition of skills such as reading' (1989a: 282; emphasis added).

One outcome of the discussion here is to demonstrate the material reality and consequentiality of these understandings of the text–talk nexus, in this case with respect to the expansion of 'the legislative boundaries' pertaining to what it is to be a member of the category Child in and for the workings of school life generally, and particularly in reading lessons. Wilson (1991: 39) has noted that 'the fundamental justification for a classification of occasions must be that the participants orient to it as a type of situation and, moreover, orient to the present interaction as an instance of that type'. The general substantive question is thus: what consistencies and contrasts are visible in the ways in which the category Child is purpose-built in these school-based materials? From an EM perspective, the warrant for this question derives from Baker and Freebody's (1989a, 1989b) work, but also from the analyses themselves during which it became evident that the category Child was a powerful and continual topic and resource for the management and accomplishment of lessons for school.

THE CATEGORY 'CHILD'

We can take our starting-point from Jenks (1996: 2–3):

> Despite a long commitment to the good of the child and a more recent intellectual engagement with the topic of childhood, what remains perpetually diffuse and ambiguous is the basic conceptualization of childhood as a social practice.

By taking this statement as a challenge, we seek to make less 'diffuse and ambiguous' the 'social practices' that constitute the child. In a search for the 'patterning of action' (Jenks, 1996: 3) that constitutes the category Child we address the theoretical and practical challenges presented by Jenks's observations by situating our study in the school – a social location that is a powerful institution and, equally, relies on deeply naturalized and, at the same time, generally unformulated theories of childhood.

Two attributes were found to be consistently made relevant to being a student in the primary classroom. Here we take up one of these, and one that may be familiar: *pre-competence*, as explicated by Freebody (1995), after Speier (1976). In brief, children are commonsensically described by taking adults as the contrastive standard (James and Prout, 1990a; Jenks, 1989) thereby focusing attention on what children *do not have* in relation to what adults *do have* (Dewey, 1944; Mackay,

Table 15.1 Characterizations of the categories 'Child' and 'Adult'

Children are:	**Adults are:**
carefree	serious
non-productive	productive
immature	mature
irrational	rational
incompetent	competent
acultural	cultured
asocial	social
inadequate	adequate
asexual	sexual
simplistic thinkers	complex thinkers

Sources: Jackson, 1982; James and Prout, 1990a,b; Kleinig, 1982; Mackay, 1974

1974; Watson, 1992). The concept of children as 'adults in the making' has been variously described in the literature. For example, children have been described as 'candidates' and as 'placed on the waiting list' for adulthood (Dewey, 1944: 54). Table 15.1 summarizes these lay and professional characterizations of the categories Child and Adult. Children are conventionally understood, then, as provisional, inadequate or pathologized in relation to the fixed standard of an 'adult', and childhood is largely theorized as a rehearsal for adult life and as important only in terms of that future.

Accordingly, with regard to the notion of competence, we found the construction of *pre*-competence rather than *in*competence in our data. Freebody (1995), after Speier (1976), has argued that children's displays of 'trying' or 'learning' or 'developing' (1995: 5; see also Freiberg and Freebody, 1995) – integral to the successful participation in the business of being children – in effect, display children's 'pre-competence' as opposed to either total incompetence *or* competence *simpliciter*. Such displays incorporate a sense of movement, development and transition. For example, childhood has been referred to as 'something to be grown out of, the start of the road to adulthood' (Kleinig, 1982: 198), as 'a highly complex and engineered trajectory towards adulthood' (James and Prout, 1990b: 226); as a 'stage of life that builds preparatory mechanisms' (Speier, 1970: 188); as a 'period of apprenticeship' (James and Prout, 1990a: 10) and as a 'passing phenomenon . . . on the way to . . . adult rational life' (Jenks, 1995: 2). In early childhood education, pre-competence is projected by teachers making mystery and surprise relevant to classroom activities. It is enacted in children's displays of a susceptibility to and interest in fantasy, suspense and guessing (Baker and Freebody, 1989a; Freebody, 1995; Freiberg and Freebody, 1995).[1]

THE WHOLE-CLASS DATA AND SMALL-GROUP DATA[2]

We found the students in the whole-class materials were routinely oriented to by each other and the teacher as neither *in*competent nor fully competent, but as developing into competency. They are taken to be in the business of observably developing those capacities (Baker and Freebody, 1989a; Freebody, 1995; Freebody and Dwyer, 1992; Freiberg and Freebody, 1995). Children were reconfigured as pre-competent in the course of ordinary classroom interaction in three interrelated ways: 1) as not incompetent but not *yet* competent – for example, through orientation to their actions as displays of 'trying', 'learning' or 'developing'; 2) as possessing a predilection for pretending and serendipity – for example, through being directed to 'imagine' and 'pretend' as routine ways of achieving and organizing classroom tasks; and 3) as possessing a proclivity for being kept in 'suspense' and excitable – for example, through 'wait-and-see' techniques which orient to the students' knowledge as partial and pre-competent compared to the teacher's competent and authoritative knowledge (see Freiberg and Freebody, 1995: 322; Baker and Freebody, 1989a).

There were, however, systematic differences between the enactments of pre-competence in the small-group child-for-school and the whole-class child-for-school. In the groups, students demonstrably acted, and coordinated their actions, on the assumption of having sufficient skills to engage in and to complete the student-group activities – for example, by not providing provisional answers and by hearing each other's talk-in-interaction as purposeful and reasoned. We found students in the small groups accomplished their identities as capable and competent in the matter of doing the set task, rather than as *pre*- or *in*-competent.

THE CHILD THE NOVEL ASSUMES

Having considered the child's pre-competence as differently enacted in whole-class and small-group settings, we looked to the novel itself for versions of the child described and enacted there. In the first instance, MCA revealed that the Child described in the text – both through the ascribed and implied attributes of the child characters alone and in paired partnerships with adult characters – essentially reflected the characterizations in Table 15.1 above. Attributes of the Child characters were such things as 'gabbling', headstrong and squabbling by contrast with the calm, serene and tolerant adult attributes that the Child characters had yet to attain.

However, certain interpretive requirements of the novel complicate a simple reading of the Child in terms of the continua represented in Table 15.1. There is also a Child assumed by the text. As this novel was written and marketed especially for children, and brought into a classroom for children, we can ask: what sort of Child can read and make sense of this novel? Baker and Freebody

(1989a) have detailed the appropriate interpretive competences of the Child readers called upon, for example, by the interleaving of fantasy and reality commonly found in texts for children. In the novel *Magpie Island*, at least three broad categories of interpretive competence are called for – we call them 'interpretive frames':

- *Realistic Narrative Frame* – requiring the reader to call on the relevances of the real world when making sense of the text;
- *Anthropomorphic Narrative Frame* – requiring the reader to call on the relevances of the anthropomorphized world of animals which act, talk, think and feel as humans when making sense of the text;
- *Representational Tale Frame* – requiring the reader to call on the relevances of allegory and parable when making sense of the text. (See Austin, 1996.)

A feature of this novel is not only the co-existence within it of these three frames but also the slippage between them. Sometimes a paragraph will draw on one frame (for example, realistically discussing the habitat and life-cycle of an animal) and then the next will draw on another (for example, anthropomorphically giving the bird human-like thoughts, hopes and dreams). Such slippages assume particular and capable interpretive competence of the Child reader. The denouement of the novel provides a pivotal example of such slippage: realistic, anthropomorphic and representational readings are interleaved in such a way that the overall reading of the novel is made ambiguous. The child who can make sense of this novel, then, is assumed to:

- have the capacity to interpret within realistic, anthropomorphic and representational frames;
- be capable of 'slipping' from one interpretive frame to another in order to read the novel as sensible and coherent; and
- tolerate ambiguity in interpretation; that is, accept parallel final renderings of the story, a 'real' ending, a 'sad' ending *and* a 'symbolic' ending.

The reader of this novel, then, is assumed to have considerable interpretive competence and the capacity to accept ambiguity in the final reading of the narrative. We can speculate that the Child assumed by this novel is more competent than the one described in it.

CLASSROOM TALK

We return to the classroom talk to take a specific analytic path in interrogating the way(s) the Child in the novel – both the conventionally pre-competent one it describes and the competent one it assumes – was enacted in the classroom talk. The classroom talk is the public display of the reading of this book as relevant to the classroom. It is in the talk that students both learn, and participate in, the interactive procedures that constitute displays of the propositional and procedural knowledges that are taken to count as 'interpretation' in the context of the classroom literature lesson (Heap, 1985, 1987; Bruner, 1975). In analysing the classroom talk, we found it achieved pre-competence in the ways briefly described above. We also examined the routine categorization work of the participants in establishing the category Child as an explicit and unproblematic category in the talk. Further, the category Child was assembled in the talk in terms of the membership categorization device 'stage-of-life' and category attributes were assembled both directly and by the inferential logic of standardized relational pairs (SRPs) in terms comparable to the novel and the characterization in Table 15.1 (see Austin, 1997).

To elaborate our purpose in this chapter, we will briefly review the working of the novel's denouement in the classroom talk. In doing so, we see the working of a text through talk and we see a more restricted version of childhood pre-competence reasserted. The novel closes with an image of the central character, 'Magpie', alone on an island, with no hope of rescue, having just experienced the destruction of his mate and their eggs. In class, the discussion begins with the sadness of this ending:

Extract 1

96	T	Umm (.) do you think the author does that with a purpose what's he trying, he he knows his story is very sad, what do you think he leaves (.) his readers with a feeling of what. Anita?
97	Anita	Well so they can work out what happens the way, what they want to happen?
98	T	Yes, there's a feeling there I, I think, June.
99	June	Suspension? About
100	T	Yes?
101	S	Look what they have done to the magpie kind of thing?
102	T	Y:es? (.) Ok? Joshua? What do you think there's a feeling of at the end? I'd like you to really concentrate and try and think. Carol?
103	Carol	Sorrow.
104	T	Sorrow? Is there another feeling other than sorrow, Toni?
105	Toni	Well at the end how it says BUT IT WAS DARK OUTSIDE and he said it was going to be a bright new day tomorrow, well it was gonna like sort of begin all again? The next day?
106	T	Right. Does anyone feel that the author has left the reader
107	S	( )
108	T	Does the author feel, do you think at least, does anyone feel that he's left you with perhaps a feeling of hope?
109	Amy	Yeah.
110	T	Why?
111	Amy	Becau:se well umm he says that bit about all the fishermen?
112	T	The fishermen going past and seeing Magpie. So he is going to survive and perhaps [just
113	Amy	[Yeah, kind of think that
114	T	Yeah, I think perhaps there's a slight feeling of hope there, I think the author's also trying to tell us something else, that people? (.) as well as Magpie but I think he's really giving us a message about ourselves. That we are able to (.) do what. (.) What are

people capable of doing. (0.4) I think he really tries to give us this message through (0.3) the magpie. (.) What do you think (.) even though, I'll phrase it in another way. Even though people have losses (.) and hardships (.) and dreadful periods of sorrow (.) what's he actually telling you at the end, Colin?

115 Colin That it doesn't really matter that there are people that do, I mean, that do (.)

116 T I'd like you to pay a bit more attention

.

.

.

119 Amy Like you shouldn't, I think he might be trying to say that you shouldn't feel sorry for yourself you should just try and get on with everything?

120 T I think that you do survive and life goes on, even though at the time it seems as black as black. Do you think? Yeah.

There had been a discussion earlier which hinged on the notion that novels, especially for children, *usually* have a happy ending. And the teacher here works to achieve some such ending. Magpie, stranded and alone, is brought off as having a 'happy ending' using a representational interpretation that reads the magpie as a symbol of hope and survival. Toni's restatement of the final words of the novel (105) is reformulated by the teacher into a 'feeling of hope' (108), and she then explains this in representational terms (114) and, a few turns later, a student renders a version of the 'moral' of the story (119) and again the teacher confirms this representational rendering (120).

Later in the lesson, the teacher and students are discussing the 'feeling' that the 'images' in the text evoke. The students talk of the emotional tenor of the conclusion of the novel in terms of sadness, sorrow, disappointment and depression. The teacher asks for more feelings (159) and Toni provides 'hope' (164) which the teacher had suggested earlier in the lesson (108):

Extract 2

159 T there's also a tremendous feeling of something else at the end I felt

.

.

.

164 Toni Hope? So that it might happen maybe he'll

165 T Maybe he'll be happy and survive. Yes.

The teacher interrupts Toni's answer (164) to state her own version (165), explicitly stating her preferred representational interpretation of the novel. The teacher, it seems, works hard in the talk to establish a 'hopeful' reading of the text in the face of the students' insistence on quite different readings. In a comment to the researchers, the teacher offered the following:

Extract 3

358 T Umm, there are a few questions, obviously, obviously why Magpie wasn't given a name, because he wants it to be universal that (.) this is what all people do and endure and this is people's life. I don't know how much of that they're going to get.

Here, the teacher predicts that many of the students are not capable of the representational interpretation. Her talk implies that her prediction is based on a developmental theory of childhood whereby the representational interpretation is privileged as the more 'mature' or 'developed' interpretation. Paradoxically, the teacher employs a representational interpretive frame – that is an allegorical reading – to achieve a 'happy ending' enacting the theory that the Child requires a happy ending. So considerable interpretive competence is called upon in requiring that the students enact themselves as children by engaging in an interactive competence which has been articulated by the teacher as beyond them.

STUDENTS' WRITING

We now turn to the students' writing as being itself textually mediated in Watson's (1997a: 96) sense of the 'textually mediated social event'; that is, this writing emerges from the context of the novel itself and the classroom talk about it. As we saw above, the talk and the novel are reflexively related to meaning-making in this site; the interpretive possibilities of the novel are made salient (or not) in the talk. The students' writing is a further element of this reflexivity; it is both the product of, and a component of, the classroom as an interactive event. Again through MCA, we found the students wrote in terms of a standardized adult–child pairing and relied on these attributes in terms articulated in the classroom talk and the novel. One question students were asked was:

What do you think were the main differences between the Magpie and the Eagle? Don't just think about the physical differences . . . try to think what else made them different.

Students' answers included the attributes shown in Table 15.2. The students described the characters in terms of categorical polarities; for example, 6 students made an age comparison and 22 students made a size comparison (both suggested earlier by the teacher in classroom discussions). Other comparisons were made in terms of physical prowess, flying capacity, flying style, voice, size and habitat.

The students' writing is available not only as a record of the categories they used to make their writing sensible. It is also available as a material record of their production of a 'competent reading' (Watson, 1997a: 88). The students' writing, that is, is available to the teacher as a measure of their competence. Then, the teacher's assessments are available to the analyst as a record of the criteria by which the writing is assessed. If we return to the question of pre-competence, taking the writing as an artefact used to gauge competence by some criteria, we can look to those pieces of writing that attract censure and identify the criteria by which they do so. For, as Heritage (1984b: 16) reminds

Table 15.2 Students' descriptions of characters

Magpie	Eagle	Magpie	Eagle
squawky little baby bird	large patient strong	small weak fly short distances flapped	fly long distances smart quick-witted big strong glided
extremely young very daring	older tolerant	younger adventurous eager to prove himself	tolerant larger smarter patient
small noisy weak panicky impatient straight beak	huge quiet powerful calm tolerant curved beak	quite small courageous adventurous	large strong tolerant patient content casual

us, 'breaches of norms are commonly more revealing about the attitudes, motives and circumstances of other people than is conformity'.

One case in point is the following task: 'Imagine that the two magpies are able to talk. Write a conversation of what might have been said between them when they first meet.' One student's response (Phillip) is possibly designed to be humorous and reads (we preserve the original spelling and formatting):

'What's your name?' asked Magpie inquiringly
* 'I don't know,' she replied.
* 'I've an idea,' Magpie spoke again.
* 'What is it? Come on out with it.'
* 'Do you want to do it?' Magpie asked.
* 'Do what,' replied the female bird.
* 'You know,' hinted Magpie with a wink.
* 'No. I'm afraid I don't.'
[next page]
'Don't you even know what 'Do it' is?'
'Oh, yeah, I know youre [you're] going to
show me around – aren't you.'
'Yes, of course. You didn't think I ment
[meant] anything fo [foul] did you?'

Phillip's writing attracted censure; the teacher noted in the margin: 'I really feel this conversation is getting out of hand Phillip – don't you?' And the final teacher comment on Phillip's unit of work is: 'A very good unit of work Phillip

– don't spoil it by careless, rude writing please!' In discussion with the researchers, the teacher elaborated on this evaluation:

16	T	And it's interesting. Phillip, who is at camp this week, you know how he wrote three different endings, just look at the last one
17	R	((reads out Phillip's writing, above))
18	T	I didn't really think it was suitable
19	R	No::
20	T	No:: so he's feeling his oats a bit isn't he?

Here, the teacher expresses the writing's unsuitability and the criterion upon which it is unsuitable: he is 'feeling his oats', an allusion to sexual exploration. Phillip's writing is hearable by the teacher as unsuitable through its reference to sexuality, evidenced by the terms 'feeling his oats' and 'rude'. The 'unsuitability' can be described on the basis of Phillip's 'childness'.[3]

In another example, Dillon's writing was assessed in terms of his choice of vocabulary. His uses of the words 'butt' and 'crap' were questioned by the teacher in a written comment:

Although I was happy for you to put your own feelings and opinions into answering this question I feel you have gone 'off the track' too much. I would like to see slang and swearing left out of your work please.

The teacher's written assessment of Dillon's vocabulary was repeated in the classroom talk. Here the teacher addresses Dillon, with the class as over-hearing audience:

5	T	Also umm some of the words that you used I don't think are suitable for using in stories. Ok, it was very, you've got a wonderful sense of humour

In some senses, Dillon and Phillip have been *over*-competent in that they have used language and ideas culturally reserved for exclusively adult use. They have, perhaps, incompetently enacted their expected pre-competence.

CONCLUSION

The attributes of the Child and the Adult categories in these textual sites – in the novel, in students' writing and in the classroom talk – support the cultural devices characterized in Table 15.1. The participants in these scenes work together, smoothly, across many textual sites, to create and sustain such versions of childhood and adulthood. We also found that pre-competence is firmly embedded in the category of Child as defined by the purposes of school, whereas the child-for-school that is not under the direct scrutiny of the institution (in the small group) is not necessarily assumed to have this same pre-competence. Further, considering the children's competence as children-for-school, we note that an important criterion available for their assessment was their occasional *over*-competence, in terms of vocabulary and adherence to culturally delicate matters. Children who display as over-competent, who, in other words, contest or challenge pre-competence, are redefined as careless, rude, out of hand, off the track, unsuitable, and the rest.

Perhaps we see here a rendering of Jackson's (1982: 27) argument that contemporary children are actively maintained *as* children and that 'children who behave like adults are regarded as at best amusing and at worst thoroughly obnoxious'. The over-competent are, ironically, categorized as 'immature'; or taken to be inappropriately using exclusively adult devices. Certainly we see that both adults and children are constrained by a strongly normative theory of the Child; and this constraint is especially evident in the breach. These breaches can be heard as challenges or attempts to negotiate those normativities; but they also, and thereby, attract moral disapproval. These analyses, then, have implications for our understanding of the moral ordering of schooling and its construction around strongly enacted notions of stage-of-life. There are therefore further consequences for the institutional organization of the school, for practices in classrooms and, more broadly, for our culture's characterizations and treatment of young people.

Using the tools available to us through applied EM/CA, we have tried to show that category incumbency does not somehow reside *in* the individual, *in* child-students or adult-teachers, but in the *activities* that frame the interactive 'working space' between party partnerships – in this case, reader–writer and speaker–speaker pairs. It is in this sense that adults and children constitute intertextual sites. So, if we are searching for answers about cultural practice, it is unproductive to explore the category contrasts Child–Adult or Teacher–Student via an interrogation of, for example, the biology and psychology of individuals. Tyler (1993: 41), who studied childhood construction in kindergartens, concluded from her research on the history of schooling, together with its supportive human sciences, that they 'have produced norms of performance as a child, institutionalizing the possibility that some children operate more successfully as children than others, are better children, better at being children'. To 'be better at being children' is essentially to operate in the talk-and-text connections that make up much of classroom activity. The task of applied EM/CA has been described as rendering 'some activity or course of reasoning transparent in its structure and consequences' (Heap, 1990: 45). This is done so as to 'recover and formulate the functions served by some sets of practices', to formulate 'how those practices foster, facilitate and limit the formulated functions' (Heap, 1990: 46–7). Lessons (such as those analysed here) have as their formulated functions students' increased understanding of textual materials and their increased ability to write about these materials and their reactions to them. One of the things we have shown is that such formations rely crucially on certain cultural understandings – in this case about generational categories, not just as implicature, but as the explicit topics and resources for answering teachers' questions and writing for the teacher. Students with diverging understandings of the SRP 'Adult–Child' will not be on the same footing as those with views that converge with the teacher's. This will be consequential for the ways in which the latter can participate in classroom talk and write to the satisfaction of the teacher.

Notes

1. It is important to note that recent research (see Hutchby and Moran-Ellis, 1998) has engaged seriously with 'social competence' in children, recognizing that social competence is something that children themselves negotiate and struggle over in local occasions of activity. Our data reveals this struggle over definitions of pre-competence as well as displays of competence – at times, paradoxically, competence in enacting pre-competence (after Mackay, 1974).
2. This section summarizes more detailed and grounded analyses in the larger study (Austin *et al.*, forthcoming).
3. The 'unsuitability' can further be described on the basis of *both* Phillip's 'childness' and his 'studentness'. That is, the criteria of this writing's unsuitability are enacted at the intersection of the relevances of the Child and the public forum of the school. This point is elaborated by Austin and Freebody (in press).

16 Demystifying discourse analysis: theory, method and practice

Keith Tuffin and Christina Howard

EDITORIAL

Working against the oft-held (but mistaken) assumption that discourse analysis in general and discursive psychology (DP) in particular are forms of naive empiricism without theoretical grounding, Keith Tuffin and Christina Howard set out, in this chapter, to detail some of the 'ontological and epistemological commitments' on which DP is based. In line with Edwards and Potter's chapter, Tuffin and Howard argue for an anti-individualist and social constructionist approach to traditional psychological 'objects' such as attitudes, emotions and trauma. For DP, they note, such objects are pragmatically constructed by participants in everyday settings, including, here, institutional settings. That is, they are 'forms of social practice produced in and through conversational interaction'.

To exemplify these general orientations and commitments, Tuffin and Howard offer us a meta-analysis (an analysis of an analysis) so as to show the novice 'what to actually do *with the data at the point of analysis'. The study in question was an analysis of interviews with police officers about problems of 'emotion' and 'trauma' in their daily institutional life (Howard* et al., *2000). Revisiting that study with their meta-analysis, the authors are concerned to show how interview transcripts can be coded and analysed.*

Importantly, what we find here is that 'emotions' and 'emotion talk' are not separable. That is, we have to take into account the pragmatic fact that the type of talk involved here is an interview. To put this another way: the interview may well be a research instrument in its own right (at least in more traditional versions of social psychology), but it is also a form of institutional talk which, as it turns out, accomplishes *emotions as 'talkable' and 'doable' objects. For example, and non-paradoxically, police officers were found to* talk *about emotions as 'unspeakables' as far as their institutional culture was concerned. Hence talking about emotions is not a simple means of entry into 'real' emotions as such; rather, in their daily institutional life as well as in a series of interviews, officers have to discursively construct what come, after the fact, to count as having been emotions 'all along'.*

Readers will also notice that the methodological 'take' offered by Tuffin and Howard in this chapter is quite distinct from the firmly EM/CA-based DP discussed in Edwards and Potter's chapter. The approach taken here (for example, in its consideration of the quantity *of data that may be held to warrant analysis) comes, in its distance from canonical Sacksian principles, somewhat closer to the variant of CDA known as 'critical psychology'.*

INTRODUCTION

As DP approaches to investigating psychological subjects have become more widely accepted, more students have become interested in conducting discursive research. However, applying existing literature to their own research is often problematic. In particular, they have difficulty in understanding the importance of the alternative philosophical underpinnings of discursive methodology. Also, they find that discourse analysts often fail to provide an adequate account of their research practices, and this lack of detail is unhelpful. In response, this chapter has two primary purposes. First, we aim to provide an argument which positions the methods of DP as being inextricably linked to underlying assumptions concerning ontology and epistemology. Secondly, we provide an example of the intimate workings of discursive methodology in the context of a study of police talk of trauma and associated emotions. As teachers of DP, we are aware that students not only are keen to learn *about* discursive research, they also want to learn how to *do* it. Our goal is to make this project more accessible.

BACKGROUND

It would be a mistake to assume that DP was simply another outgrowth of social psychology. Social psychology has spawned a number of sub-disciplines, which are featured as illustrations of *applied* areas in textbooks. Baron and Byrne (1997) provide a recent example of this practice and include legal, organizational, health and environmental applications. However, readers of the mainstream social psychological literature will be disappointed if they expect to see DP appear in a similar fashion. The reason for this is that, in its short history, DP (Edwards and Potter, 1992a) has demonstrated itself to be more a challenge to mainstream social psychology than a readily integrated (and about to be adopted) new area of study.

The discursive perspective is founded partly on critiques of mainstream practices within social psychology and, in this regard, is clearly aligned with the critical movement within social psychology (Spears, 1997). Such criticality formed an important part of the seminal work by Potter and Wetherell (1987) who argue for a functional approach to discourse analysis. This work has become especially well known for its searching attack on the notion of *attitudes*. In particular, Potter and Wetherell air three lines of concern. First, they are critical of traditional measurement techniques (Kline, 1988). Second, they question the assumptions that attitudes are enduring and stable entities. These assumptions become difficult to sustain in the light of data variability which, at times, approaches dramatic levels. People may say one thing on one occasion and precisely the opposite on another. Indeed, one of the established canons which informs the work of discursive psychologists is the prevalence of variability.

Unlike 'positivist' approaches, DP is interested in such variability and seeks to understand its importance at a functional level, rather than suppressing, aggregating or ignoring it. Third, Potter and Wetherell stress the importance of contextual sensitivity. Context informs organizational understanding which, in turn, clarifies the action orientation of talk. One of the cornerstones of DP is the action orientation of text (Edwards and Potter, 1992a). The suggestion here is that talk and writing are constructed with attention to the facilitation of particular tasks. These tasks include explanations, justifications, blamings, denials, accusations, excuses, and describing events in such a manner as to subvert negative attributional interpretations. From this (albeit inexhaustive) list, the inherently social and active nature of these tasks becomes apparent.

In addition to providing a challenge to existing understandings in social psychology, DP has made an impressive beginning in terms of its variety of research topics. Examples of the diversity of topics include: majority group representations of race relations (Wetherell and Potter, 1992); the justification of gender inequality in broadcasting (Gill, 1993); political advertising in health reforms (Morgan *et al.*, 1994); and the construction of trust within intimate relationships (Willig, 1997). Indeed, discursive psychologists have provided provocative analyses of a wide range of data including interview material, focus groups, newspaper reports, television documentaries, personal diaries, political speeches and telephone conversations. This work (of which the above is only a small sample) has taken place within the last two decades of the twentieth century and, as such, signals the beginning of an emerging new tradition of social psychological research.

THEORY, KNOWLEDGE AND RESEARCH PRACTICE

While discursive psychology is interested in the study of everyday language and takes a critical perspective on traditional research practice, it has also been involved in the theorization of the role of language. Such theorization is at the heart of both the guiding principles and the research methods used in DP. It makes little sense to study language use, without having first developed some theoretical notions about the ways in which language works.

As discursive psychologists, we have taken heed of the critiques of psychology's long-standing ontological assumptions regarding individualism (Sampson, 1989). In this regard, we have attempted to incorporate assumptions regarding the social nature of the human condition into our approach to doing research. We want to argue that the choice of method should follow directly from the understandings which the researcher holds about the nature of the social world and how we may come to know this world. The ultimate choice of method must be seen as a consequence of the assumptions which guide the researchers' understanding of what their practices involve, and the knowledge claims which result from their research. More bluntly, research-based questions are best answered within a framework which clearly identifies the ontological and epistemological assumptions informing research practice. Our work owes much to the social constructionist movement within psychology (Gergen, 1985). For social constructionists – for example Kitzinger (1992) – research involves treating the subjects of inquiry (for example, emotion and trauma) as socio-political constructions. A constructionist ontology argues for examining the ways in which language contributes to our shared understandings of how such categories are put together in particular ways, with particular effects. In short, such categories are not treated as ontological givens, but are regarded as topics for analysis in their own right.

Social constructionism moves beyond psychology's visually mediated adherence to positivism and promotes a linguistically mediated epistemology which places knowledge within particular historical and cultural frameworks. As social constructionists, we approach psychological knowledge not as something to be extracted from the interior (mind, personality, identity), but as something to be studied interactionally, conversationally and relationally. As Burr (1995) suggests, knowledge is something which occurs between people in their daily interactions with one another. In this regard, emotions come to be studied not as descriptive labels for internal processes within the individual, but as forms of social practice produced in and through conversational interaction (Edwards and Potter, 1992a).

These ontological and epistemological commitments have direct implications for the use of particular methods within constructionist psychology. Discursive work is developed out of specific understandings which inform both the research 'questions' which may be asked and the methods which may be deployed. In this regard, we strongly resist the suggestion that research methods may be regarded merely as 'tools' to be applied to different research problems at will. For these reasons, discursive work is not readily portable across differing ontological research frameworks. Indeed, our theoretical claim is that the 'tools' approach neglects important issues which researchers should be encouraged to consider as they go about the business of asking questions, collecting data and analysing discourse.

MYSTIQUE, CRAFT SKILL AND ANALYSIS

Discursive analysis is often characterized by practitioners as a somewhat mysterious 'craft skill' (Potter and Wetherell, 1987) which is difficult to describe or teach. Wooffitt (1993) talks about analysis as being conducted without hard-and-fast rules, and of an 'analytic mentality', acquired through practical experience. In contrast, quantitative statistical methodologies, in which the actual work of analysis is done by mathematical 'machines' (such as formulae and computers) is seen as being relatively straightforward. The impression often gained by readers is that analytic skills are difficult and time-consuming to learn. This may discourage some newcomers to the area who would otherwise be interested in attempting this style of research. A number of different instructive or demonstrative texts have appeared to guide novice analysts (Potter, 1996c; Potter and Wetherell, 1987; Wooffitt, 1993). These give some excellent advice on the different stages of the research process and other general issues. For example, Potter and Wetherell's (1987) ten analytic stages deal thoroughly with issues such as developing a research question, gathering data and transcription.

The area in which most of these texts fall short, however, is in describing what actually to *do* with the data at the point of analysis (Burr, 1995). Somewhat ironically, Potter and Wetherell (1987: 168) announce 'Words fail us at this point . . .'. Even more detailed attempts to delineate the process of analysis (Potter and Wetherell, 1994) invoke unsatisfactorily vague comparisons to both 'chicken-sexing' and 'bicycle-riding'. While we acknowledge that doing discourse analysis may not be as straightforward as plugging numbers into a formula, we believe there are a number of ways into analysis that can be explained and illustrated more clearly, for the benefit of students. To that end, we present the following description and commentary on the process of an analysis (Howard *et al.*, 2000) which examined police talk about emotion in relation to the organizational culture of the police force.

As mentioned above, the preliminary stages of the research process are well covered in existing texts, and will not be reiterated here. However, some brief background information about the study may be useful. The data consisted of twelve interviews with police officers on their experiences of trauma. These interviews were initially undertaken as part of an earlier study (Stephens, 1996) in which participants gave permission for their data to be used for further research if required. Interviews were loosely structured around a series of open-ended questions. The questions ranged over officers' experiences of trauma, how they dealt with these experiences, and the adequacy of organizational policy and practice following trauma. Interviews were recorded and transcribed using the conventions of standard orthography. The decision to undertake further analysis was prompted by a recognition of the linguistic richness of the data, especially with respect to emotion. Specifically, most respondents mentioned fear, but allusions to grief, anger and frustration were also prevalent. Drawing on a constructionist understanding of the performative nature of language, a broad research question was developed to guide the analysis: how do police officers 'do' emotion?

Preliminary coding

Armed with this question and around 130 pages of double-spaced interview transcripts, it was time to begin the analysis. Potter and Wetherell (1987: 167) suggest that the next methodological step is coding the data into categories, in order to 'squeeze an unwieldy body of discourse into manageable chunks'. Yet exactly how the process of coding should be carried out is not made clear. They do suggest a preliminary coding stage in which material which is not related in any way to the topic of interest is eliminated. The extent to which this process will 'cut down' the body of data is obviously variable. When dealing with text which is closely focused around a topic of interest, the amount of irrelevant data may be small. In respect to the current analysis, it was decided to undertake a process of preliminary coding which isolated and retained all instances of talk which seemed to deal in some way with emotions. Because the focus of the original interviews was not exclusively about emotion, there was a significant amount of text which was discarded, such as information about organizational policies and hierarchies.

In practice, there are two ways in which the process of preliminary coding can be undertaken. The first is to use the 'search' or 'find' feature available in word-processing programs. The computer can be instructed to scan the transcript, and find instances of particular words or phrases. The sections of text containing these can then be placed in a separate preliminary coding file (see Augoustinos, Tuffin and Sale, 1999; Potter and Wetherell, 1994). Computer coding is used primarily because it greatly reduces the time- and labour-intensiveness of the project.

The second method of preliminary coding is very similar to the first, except that it is the analyst who reads and selects pertinent instances for retention. This 'manual' process of preliminary coding is useful for two key reasons. Firstly, it engages the analyst in the practice of 'close reading' of the text, which is widely acknowledged as an essential element of discursive research (see Lovering, 1995; Wooffitt, 1993). This process may already have begun if the analyst has spent time transcribing their data. Indeed, we routinely recommend that analysts undertake this task themselves, for this very reason. But if this has not occurred, the manual coding process may be the first attempt the analyst makes to thoroughly scrutinize and engage with the data. Secondly, preliminary manual coding serves as an opportunity to revisit one's own understandings of the topic of interest, in relation to the actual data. Close reading as part of this process may reveal additional aspects of the topic which were not originally considered by the analyst, but which emerge in participants' talk. Therefore it is important for the analyst to remain flexible and open. In the case of the police data, preliminary coding criteria specified that direct expressions of emotions, along with both specific and general references to emotions and/or feelings, should be included. However, while reading the transcripts, two additional (and previously unconsidered) forms of emotion talk were identified and retained: instances where participants talked about 'talking about emotions' (which was prevalent in the data), and instances where participants talked about 'trauma' or 'stress' as synonymous with emotional response.

Coding

Once this preliminary coding stage is completed, the next step is to organize the data into discrete coding categories. The importance of these categories cannot be over-stated as they form the backbone of the analytic process. Careful categorization of data encourages analytic focus, and highlights broad similarities and differences within the data. The most important point to be aware of here is that categories should *emerge* from the text, rather than being imposed upon it. The coding categories must not be decided by the analyst before coding takes place, with individual instances of text then being 'dropped in' to these pre-existing categories. Instead, similar instances of talk should be identified and grouped together.

In the case of the police data, the following process was employed to code the text into categories. Preliminary coding had resulted in the original data being broken down into discrete 'passages' of text which said something about emotion. Most of the passages consisted of question-and-answer pairs, though there were some longer exchanges. To begin, the first passage was read slowly and carefully, in order to 'get a feel' for what the text was saying (What is it about? What does it mean? What is the central concern?). This passage of text became the first member of the first category.

The next passage was read in the same fashion, and evaluated in relation to the first. Was it the same type of statement, or something different? Each subsequent passage was considered in terms of whether it was similar to others which had already been read, or whether it said something new. If the passage could not be placed in an existing category, a new one would be created. Each category was given a label indicating the content of the passages it contained. Occasionally, a passage would be found which did not seem to fit any existing category, and yet did not have any easily identifiable features on which to base a new category. These passages were left to one side.

Following Potter and Wetherell's (1987) principle of inclusivity, passages which had similar features to two coding categories were placed in both. When the entire set of transcripts had been read through once, the process was repeated looking at all the passages which had earlier been put aside. This was continued until we felt that as much of the data as possible had been coded. The small amount of data remaining was excluded from the analysis.

By the end of this process, seven coding categories had been developed, each containing similar instances of text. They were labelled as follows: 'emotions are unspeakable', 'emotions are uncontrollable', 'controlling emotion', 'emotions and humour', 'emotions enhance performance', 'emotions are detrimental to performance' and 'emotions are weakening'.

The next step required an examination of the content of coding categories in order to decide whether they were well supported by the data. Where it was considered there were insufficient examples in a category for it to be analysed in any depth, the category was discarded (such as the 'emotions enhance performance' category, which contained only four excerpts). On examination, the categories referring to emotions as 'detrimental to performance' and as 'weakening' were found to be very similar, and were amalgamated. And the 'unspeakable emotion' category, which ended up containing excerpts relating to both suppressing and *expressing* emotion, was divided into two categories. The end result was six categories, the smallest of which ('controlling emotion') contained fourteen excerpts.

Analysis

Following coding, the formal analysis was undertaken. Potter and Wetherell (1987) suggest that analysis involves two phases. The first is the search for systematic patterns in the data (which may be patterns of similarity or difference). The second is the search for functional effects and consequences. Across these two phases, the concepts of construction, variability and function can be applied. Indeed, Potter and Wetherell (1994) identify variation as the single most important principle in guiding analysis. However, it is important to remember that these three concepts operate in an interrelated manner. For instance, the process of coding provides a starting point for the analysis of patterns of similarity in the text. We acknowledge the reflexive point that this process relies on the reading which the analysts bring to the text. Nonetheless, excerpts of talk are grouped together by the analyst on the basis of similarity. This similarity often lies in the way the texts are constructed – by drawing on the same linguistic resources and commonsense understandings. Or, in other cases, the texts have a similar action orientation and serve similar functions. We can then ask whether these same functions are also served by other constructions. Patterns of variability may be identified by comparing different coding categories, or by examining contrasting accounts provided by the same participant. Variability is evident if differing constructions of a 'concept' are identifiable. A close examination of the context of these constructions is necessary to gain an understanding of this variability. Such variability is often related to the functions that particular constructions may serve.

A consideration of construction, function and variability should give rise to more specific research questions. For example, in relation to the general question 'How do police officers "do" emotion?', some very interesting variability was obvious in the data. There was an entire category of talk (unspeakable emotion) which suggested that participants tended *not* to do emotion in any in-depth way, alongside talk that indicated emotional disclosure was common and accepted in the police force. The following extracts illustrate this:

Q: So, do you think that um, they would be able to talk to each other or you about being afraid, say an emotion like fear.

Hugh: I don't think you'd get many policemen who'd talk about fear. After an incident where you've had a helluva fright, someone's been assaulted or someone's, you know, fear – they might say 'hell that scared the hell out of me' – probably not.

Q: Right, so that's part of the job too. You have to get on top of that fear afterwards, if they weren't alone in most cases if you did have a partner, or you came back and were with a group, would it be acceptable to talk about that?
Hugh: Yes, it would be. That would be acceptable, to talk about it afterwards. Well, again with anyone on the staff that's with them. Generally, you talk about it now, whereas years ago you wouldn't.

This dramatic variability raised questions about its purpose, its function and what it achieved. An examination of the context of this talk (including the interviewer's questions) indicated that the two different constructions were deployed to serve different functions. On the one hand, when questioned about the behaviour of *others* or about police culture in general, talk about emotional disclosure allowed participants to present themselves and their organization as culturally competent and aware (through acknowledging the 'fact' that expressing emotions is necessary to maintain mental health). However, when asked about their *own* behaviour, participants indicated that emotions were not something they needed to talk about. This downplaying of emotionality at the individual level provoked a further question regarding the reason for its occurrence. One of the coding categories contained passages relating to emotions as potentially contributing to poor job performance. Analysis of these texts revealed that emotions were constructed as extreme, uncontrollable and irrational. In contrast, good officers were required to be decisive, firm and in control at all times. What became clear was that emotion was constructed as a threat to professional competence (see Howard *et al.*, 2000).

Further variability was evident in passages of text which indicated that police officers *did* talk about emotions to their colleagues. These were analysed as 'deviant cases' (Potter, 1996c), in relation to the pattern evident in the rest of the data. An examination of these passages indicated that, in the instances where emotion was discussed, this was rarely a simple or straightforward procedure. The time, place, confidante and form of the emotional disclosure were all strictly selected according to set criteria. These criteria were all based upon the emotional disclosure being potentially damaging to the police officer concerned, and therefore needing to be restricted to a trusted individual in a private setting. Rather than supporting the ideal of an emotionally open police force, these passages reinforced the general 'unspeakability' of emotions in the organizational culture.

These examples show the relationship between construction, function and variability in analysis. They also indicate how different coding categories can be analysed in relation to one another in order to develop an integrated analysis. This goes beyond the mere identification of 'interpretive repertoires' which is sometimes seen as being the goal of discursive analysis (Harré and Gillett, 1994). It attempts to make sense of these linguistic resources in terms of the work which they can be called upon to do for participants, and provide the type of coherent analytic structure which is crucial for the validation of this type of research (Potter and Wetherell, 1987).

CONCLUSION

Consistent with the title of this book and its broad thematics, we have attempted to clarify important aspects of an analysis of talk which was produced within a particular institutional setting. We have offered some suggestions regarding the pragmatics of conducting analysis, and have illustrated this process with interview data drawn from a study of police talk about emotion. In addition, we have grounded our approach to doing discursive work within a social constructionist framework, and argued that this is essential, given that methodological considerations are informed by epistemological and ontological assumptions.

We acknowledge that this approach to discursive work is only one of many. Different ontological and epistemological assumptions will result in differing orientations, emphases and analyses. We have offered our understanding of an approach with which we are familiar and which provides an accessible introduction to the field. As teachers of DP, we are aware of the problems which students encounter. The suggestions and guidelines offered here have been developed in response to these problems and we trust readers will find them useful.

17 Is institutional talk a phenomenon? Reflections on ethnomethodology and applied conversation analysis

Stephen Hester and David Francis

EDITORIAL

What Stephen Hester and David Francis attempt in this chapter is at once self-explanatory – their title asks it all – and slightly more advanced than the previous chapters. Their discussion is advanced because it deals with some recent and trenchant methodological issues in the field of applied CA; and it is self-explanatory in that it questions the very idea of a program *of research on institutional talk (IT) and, in particular, any such program based on the idea that* particular turn-sequential forms alone *can anchor each variety of institutional talk.*

This is interesting, at this final point in the book, for two reasons. The first is that our collection opened with Paul ten Have rightly noticing that 'variations' and 'restrictions' on the local-allocational resources of 'ordinary conversation' were the initial impetus for applying CA to non-conversational and/or quasi-conversational types of talk in institutions such as courtrooms, schools and interview settings. But if Hester and Francis are right in this 'final analysis', then that starting point has, at the very least, to be questioned. Because, if they are *right, then both the central tenets of applied CA and some of the 'pure' CA criticisms of them (Schegloff, 1991, 1992) may well miss what instances of 'institutional' talk are,* as phenomena in their own right, *according to CA's ethnomethodological roots. That is, while most applied CA workers have wanted to invoke certain versions of 'context' (against purer appeals to the talk and nothing but the talk), Hester and Francis now suggest that both camps miss the phenomenon and that some mainstream applied CA is actually '*not "institutional" enough*'.*

The second reason is that this methodological reflection opens on to a final question for us as editors and, we hope, for our readers. The question is: to what extent do the various contributions to this collection tangle with the problems raised by Hester and Francis? We don't presume to answer this question, but leave it to the reader to decide. At the end of the day, having now moved from Paul ten Have's 'bookend' to this one, is *institutional talk a phenomenon? And if so, where in the book is it?*

INTRODUCTION

During the past twenty years, CA has focused increasingly upon what has come to be referred to as 'institutional talk'. A steady stream of studies has sought to apply CA to the social organization of talk in settings such as courtrooms (Atkinson and Drew, 1979), classrooms (McHoul, 1978; Mehan, 1979), medical consultations (Silverman, 1987), interviews (Greatbatch, 1988) and emergency services (Whalen and Zimmerman, 1987; Zimmerman, 1984). Such studies nowadays would seem to constitute the dominant strand of work within CA. They have made a major contribution to sociological understanding of how 'official' activities of one kind or another are accomplished in and through talk. However, attempts have also been made to draw such studies together and provide them with an explicit programatic rationale. This is evident in the work of Heritage (1984b) and, most notably, in two foundational collections: Boden and Zimmerman (1991) and Drew and Heritage (1992b). These collections not only include a range of CA studies of interaction in various bureaucratic or professional settings, they also seek to provide a general rationale which articulates the aims and assumptions of the IT program.[1] Such attempts to draw together the varied range of studies mentioned above, as a coherent and systematic program of inquiry, presuppose several things. Firstly, they presume a contrast between 'institutional' and 'non-institutional' talk. Secondly, and relatedly, they assume that there are generic properties that distinguish the first from the second. And thirdly, they presuppose that such properties of talk-in-interaction as may be located there are foundational for the recognizable production of given institutional settings.

It is these presuppositions that we will critically address in this chapter. Our argument will be (a) that the analytic burden imposed upon the structures of talk-in-interaction as distinctive with respect to, and definitive of, particular institutional settings is more than they can intelligibly bear and (b) that the attempt to then define the generic structures of institutional talk simply compounds this error. We are not arguing that it is inappropriate to seek out structures of talk-in-interaction for particular institutional settings, nor that particular structures of talking together may not be found in such settings. Rather what we find to be deeply problematic is the foundationalist character of the claim that such structures provide for the recognizable production of such institutional settings and action.

The basic assumption of the institutional talk program (ITP) is that the concepts and methods of CA can be extended beyond the study of 'ordinary conversation' to the investigation of various forms of 'institutional talk' in order to show that such interaction differs from ordinary conversation *in systematic ways*. At the heart of ITP is the claim that the sequential organizational characteristics of 'ordinary conversation' comprise a 'bedrock' to which other 'speech exchange systems' are tied as specific modifications of that 'paramount system'. These adaptations have the consequence of limiting both the range of turn types available to participants and the distribution of turns. In this sense, institutional talk comprises more 'constrained' ways of talking than ordinary conversation – much that is 'open' to utterance-by-utterance ordering in ordinary conversation is 'pre-structured' in IT. Thus, allocation of speaking rights in terms of the distribution of turns and what may be done in them – matters which are organized contingently in the utterance-by-utterance production of ordinary conversation – are tied to institutional identities and tasks, and thus subject to 'pre-allocation' in IT.

Besides extending CA into 'institutional contexts', ITP also seeks to elucidate the relationship between the social organization of interaction and the social order of institutions. The significance of ITP for its proponents is that it will show how 'institutional order' and 'institutional' relations, including social distributions of knowledge, power and authority, are underpinned by and realized through 'talk-in-interaction'. ITP, then, promises some rapprochement between CA interests in the organization of interaction and those of mainstream sociology in the forms and processes of 'social structure'. Indeed, part of the motivation for such work, arguably, is to demonstrate that such a rapprochement is possible without sacrificing the distinctive analytical orientation and methodological strengths of CA. The ITP promises to demonstrate how central sociological topics (such as the nature of institutional order and the social organization of relations of knowledge, power and authority) can be addressed from an EM/CA point of view while retaining the distinctiveness of the latter. Proponents of ITP have taken considerable care to emphasize this distinctiveness, reiterating that EM/CA's conception of social order diverges markedly from that of conventional sociology, that it provides for a different way of conceiving the relations between interactional activities and their institutional 'context', and that such differences must be kept in view if one is to avoid the pitfalls awaiting the theoretically incautious. The central issue, as Psathas (1995) points out, is that of 'reification', conventional sociology's practice of conceiving of 'social structures' as independent of members' practical actions.

WHAT IS 'INSTITUTIONAL' TALK?

Since the concept of 'institutional talk' is coined by Drew and Heritage (D&H), one might expect from them some explication of its reference. While they are reluctant to be definitive, they make it clear that it involves a contrast with 'ordinary conversation':

> We will address some aspects of interaction which often are cited when analysts seek to distinguish 'institutional talk' from 'ordinary conversation'. We stress that we do not accept that there is necessarily a hard and fast distinction to be made between the two in all instances of interactional events, nor even at all points in a single

> interactional event. Nor do we intend to offer a definition of 'institutional talk', nor to make any attempt at synoptic distinction. (1992a: 21)

Such caution about defining their key concept would make sense were it unproblematic and in common currency. However, neither is the case, as D&H implicitly recognize when they go on to discuss some of its difficulties. By way of clarification, they list a number of things to which the concept is *not* intended to refer. Firstly, IT is not to be defined in terms of physical location; in other words, the mere fact that a piece of interactional conduct occurs in, say, an office, a school or a courtroom is not *in and of itself* sufficient to make that interaction 'institutional'. Secondly, the fact that the parties to an interaction may be describable in terms of one or more social identities is also an insufficient basis on which to regard their activities as constituting a specific kind of IT. After all, as Sacks pointed out long ago, persons are 'correctly' describable in an infinite variety of ways, not all of which will be *situationally* appropriate. Thirdly, the 'institutional' in IT is to be distinguished from conventional sociological conceptions of 'social institutions'. Thus D&H remark that 'notwithstanding the standard sociological usage within which the family is also a social institution, we will also avoid using the term to describe activities that would be glossed as family dinners, picnics and the like' (1992a: 59). Fourthly, and finally, it is talk which falls outside the realm of 'ordinary conversation'.

More positively, D&H identify three general features which, they claim, are characteristic of institutional talk. These are: (a) that 'institutional talk is goal-oriented in institutionally relevant ways'; (b) that there are '*special and particular constraints* on what one or both of the participants will treat as allowable contributions to the business at hand'; and (c) that 'institutional talk may be associated with *inferential frameworks* and procedures that are particular to specific institutional contexts' (1992a: 22). However, since points (a) and (c) make reference to the concept of institutionality – 'institutional goals', 'institutional contexts' – to elucidate the concept of institutional talk, they get us little further forwards in the clarity department. Similarly unhelpful, for the same reason, is what D&H say about 'institutional interaction': 'interaction is institutional insofar as participants' institutional or professional identities are somehow made relevant to the work activities in which they are engaged' (1992a: 4).

These difficulties, we would argue, reflect the fact that 'institutional interaction' or 'institutional talk' are not notions with an intuitively clear reference, firmly enshrined in everyday discourse and demonstrably oriented to *as such* by members.[2] The terms 'institution' and 'institutional' are, rather, sociological terms. As such, they come trailing clouds of (conventional) theory. In using them as they do, D&H invite the assumption that they are being employed in something like their standard sociological sense. Yet this is precisely what is problematic. We take it that, from an EM point of view, if 'institutional and professional identities' are being 'made relevant' in interaction, then this is a *members' accomplishment*; participants are making such identities relevant to and for other participants. If 'institutional talk' refers to the ways in which work identities and activities are accomplished in and through talk, then the phenomenon for which IT is a gloss is through-and-through a *members' phenomenon*; the term 'institutional' is not being used in anything like a conventional sociological way.

The underlying problem here is whether or not D&H intend 'institutional talk' as a technical concept. They are remarkably slippery about this – some of the characterizations they give strongly suggest that institutional talk is any and all talk in which persons engage while enacting work identities and performing work activities. If this is what it means, then the concept *cannot be* a technical one identifying a systematic phenomenon. 'Work' is many things, and 'talk' can be involved in work in many different ways. There is no reason to suppose that the immense variety of these ways will be connected such that 'institutional talk' could be the object of general theorizing and systematic description. Yet such generalization is just what D&H seem to have in mind. What Wittgenstein (1969: 18) called 'the craving for generality', so it seems to us, lies behind this contrast between 'institutional talk' and 'ordinary conversation'. It leads D&H to concentrate upon sequential form as the key to the phenomenon of 'institutional talk'.

IDENTIFYING THE FORMAL STRUCTURES OF INSTITUTIONAL TALK

The contention that institutional talk consists of distinctive, definitive and identifiable formal structures, amounting to a unique 'fingerprint' for each institutional context, is expressed most clearly in the following passage from Drew and Heritage (1992a: 26):

> To the extent that the participants' talk is conducted within the constraints of a specialised turn-taking system, other systematic differences from ordinary conversation tend to emerge. These differences commonly involve specific *reductions* of the range of options and opportunities for action that are characteristic in conversation and they often involve *specialisations* and *respecifications* of the interactional functions of the activities that remain. The ensemble of these variations from conversational practice may contribute to a unique 'fingerprint' for each institutional form of interaction – the 'fingerprint' being comprised of a set of interactional practices differentiating each form both from other institutional forms and from the base-line of mundane conversational interaction itself.

Thus, the claim that 'institutional talk' consists of distinctive sequential structures centres around two points. The first is that certain *sequential* forms comprise institutionally specific and *distinctive* adaptations of the turn-taking organization of ordinary conversation. The second is that the distinctive forms of turn-taking organization associated with specific institutional settings are *constitutive* of the *recognizable* 'institutionality' of the conduct which marks such a setting. We consider these in turn.

Sequential distinctiveness

Analysis of the 'speech exchange systems' constitutive of forms of institutional talk has centred around the concept of 'adjacency pairs'. Numerous studies have sought to analyse the distinctive features of adjacency-pair structures in different social (usually work) settings. Notable studies in this regard are those of the 'instructional sequence' (McHoul, 1978; Mehan, 1979), of the 'perspective-display series' in the communication of medical diagnoses (Maynard, 1989, 1991, 1992) and of the sequential organization of media news interviews (Greatbatch, 1988; Heritage and Greatbatch, 1991).

For example, Maynard proposes, in his studies of the communication of medical diagnoses, that a particular three-part modification of the adjacency-pair format, which he calls the 'perspective-display series' (PDS), is routinely employed. The parts of this structure are 1) clinician's opinion-query or perspective-display invitation, 2) recipient's reply or assessment, and 3) clinician's report or assessment. However, in terms of its formal sequential properties, there is nothing about the PDS as described in Maynard's work that is specific to this particular setting and thereby 'institutionally' distinctive. This is something which Maynard himself recognizes in the opening section of his paper where he cites examples of 'bad news delivery' in ordinary conversation which have the same three-part sequential structure. More explicitly, in his conclusion, Maynard (1992: 355) remarks that:

> The perspective-display series is not characteristic of clinical talk alone. Just as the clueing-guessing-confirming mechanism for telling bad news occurs in ordinary conversation and in clinical environments, so too does the perspective-display series appear in both contexts.

We take it that Maynard is here acknowledging the difference between two very different analytic claims. On the one hand is the claim that a sequential structure that is used in a variety of interactional environments has a particular relevance for the delivery of medical news, especially where that news is 'negative'. On the other hand there is the far more questionable claim that such a structure is essential for the production for a given institutional activity. Clearly, there is a considerable difference between arguing that a sequential structure is *useful* for the accomplishment of a certain task and arguing that the task in question *can only* be done via such a structure.

Heritage and Greatbatch (H&G) have no time for such analytic caution. In their studies of news interviewing, they argue that news interview turn-taking consists in a 'pre-allocated' and normatively ordered distribution of turn types between interviewer (IR) and interviewee (IE): IRs pose questions and IEs supply answers. They argue that this 'base structure' takes an institutionally specific form. By comparison with ordinary conversation – in which the turn-taking machinery described by Sacks *et al.* (1974) 'exerts a systematic pressure towards the minimization of turn size' – news interview talk is characterized by an imbalance in turn size; IRs' questions typically are relatively brief by comparison with IEs' extended answers. Furthermore, whereas in ordinary conversation lengthy turns by one speaker are 'broken up' by 'continuers' and 'response tokens' by the other ('hmhhm', 'yeah', 'mmm'), such actions are specifically absent from news interviews. Since IEs typically produce utterances containing many 'possible completion points', at which locations in ordinary conversation one finds continuers placed, H&G argue that, in news interviews, such speech actions are systematically 'withheld' by the IR, thus giving news interview talk a sequential pattern quite distinctive from ordinary conversation.

In our view H&G might profit by exercising some of Maynard's caution. Arguably, the sequential structures described in their studies are not institutionally distinctive, nor are they constitutive of the particular institutional character of the stretches of talk cited as data. The non-distinctiveness of these sequential structures calls into question D&H's claim that they amount to 'unique institutional fingerprints'.

Consider, for example, the claim that the institutionally distinctive character of news interview talk is manifest in the typically extended and uninterrupted nature of IEs' turns. While this feature is common in news interviews, it is by no means ubiquitous, nor is its absence necessarily treated as problematic by participants. Furthermore, it is questionable whether news interview talk is as distinctive from other talk in this respect as H&G claim. It is apparent to us that the primary task of the IR is to elicit comment on newsworthy matters from IEs. In this respect, the asymmetry of participation involved in news interviews is not dissimilar to that which marks other kinds of interviews, such as job and research interviews. It is also not dissimilar to the sequential features of story-telling in ordinary conversation, especially those occasions in which one participant tells an *invited story* at the behest of another (Cuff and Francis, 1978). If the formal structures identified in these studies are not distinctive then, by themselves, they cannot provide for the recognizable production of institutional talk. It might therefore seem reasonable to ask, if it is not sequential structures that provide for such recognizable production, then what does? However, posing the question in these terms is apt to mislead one into the assumption that, if not sequential order, then *some other property of the talk* must be sought to account for its intelligibility as institutional. To make such an assumption is to commit the *linear fallacy* which marks ITP, and which arguably is also committed by Schegloff (1991, 1992) in his several critiques of ITP. Thus, in seeking to identify formal sequential *foundations* of institutions, both practitioners of ITP and Schegloff assume a linear conception of the relation between talk and its context. In so doing, both misconceive the issue of how an 'institutional activity' is recognizable as such in the first place.

Constitutive recognizability

The recognizability of any stretch of interaction such as a news interview or, say, a medical consultation or a classroom lesson is not made available by any unique formal properties of talk's organization, although we would not deny that such formal properties as sequential ordering can support some sense of the activity being engaged in. However, such a sense is informed by many more things than sequentiality – most crucially it involves mundanely available commonsense knowledge of the connections between categorial identities and activities, knowledge which members, conversation analysts included, employ in situated and reflexive ways to make adequate 'global sense' of an occasion. In its analytic privileging of sequential form, ITP takes for granted and neglects this situated sense-making, *while at the same time relying upon it for its phenomena and its findings*.

Recognizability is a *situated accomplishment*, and involves a reflexive relationship between utterances, situated identities and other circumstantial particulars. In its pursuit of linear formality, ITP neglects this reflexivity and thus misses the accomplished intelligibility of the phenomena. For example, in Maynard's studies, the recognizability of the talk as 'medical talk' lies in what Maynard takes for granted: the identities of the participants and the recognizably medical character of the matters talked of by them. These circumstantial particulars are *presupposed* in the ways in which Maynard presents his data. In his description of the PDS, it is the 'clinician' who initiates the sequence by producing a first part in the form of a 'perspective-display invitation' and the 'patient', or patient's representative (for example, a 'parent'), to whom this invitation is directed and who is thus the proper supplier of such 'perspective-display' in the next utterance slot. The analyst's description of the PDS thus trades upon members' commonsense competencies in category analysis – competencies by which they are able to find that a certain utterance is performing a recognizable 'clinician's action' – and it is these same commonsense competences by means of which the analyst is able to provide his 'technical' description of the sequential structure.

Similarly, with respect to the H&G studies, the fact that news interviews are recognizable activities would appear to involve not so much a specific 'news interview turn-taking machinery' as (a) the topical 'content' of the talk (the omni-relevance of the notion of 'news'), and (b) categorial identities and associated category-bound activities. With reference to (a), we find it surprising that H&G make so little of the fact that a news interview is not just *any* interview, but one specifically concerned with some topic or issue *defined as news*. This fact goes a long way towards explaining both the 'pre-allocated' distribution of turn types between IR and IE and the typical imbalance in turn size. These sequential features, so it seems to us, are the product of the fact that it is the *IE* who is the 'newsworthy' participant, not the IR. Therefore it is the views, actions and knowledge of the IE that are the *focus* of the interview.

Furthermore, the fact that a news interview consists in utterances which are 'minimally recognizable as questions and answers' is to do with the reflexive relationship between utterances, identities and setting. The recognizability of questions and answers enables H&G to make empirical claims concerning the distribution of these 'turn types', to find that 'the overwhelming mass of news interview conduct is compatible . . . with this turn-taking system' (1991: 106). Yet nowhere do they pose the question of what the accomplishment of such recognizability consists in. It is simply presupposed and taken for granted in their analysis. Given that many IR utterances are not produced in a standardly grammatical interrogative format, hearing or recognizing them as questions is a *situated accomplishment*, one which involves, at least minimally, the fact that the speaker is relevantly identifiable as an 'interviewer'. Similarly with respect to 'IE answers', it is the fact that someone is identifiable and identified *as* an 'interviewee' which can be critical for applying the designation 'answers' to their utterances.

With reference to (b), it is notable that H&G *presuppose* categorial identities in the very ways they make their phenomenon available for analysis. Thus the institutionality of the talk is presupposed from the outset, both in the way the data is presented and in the very title of their paper. The reader is informed at the beginning that the paper is about 'news interviews'; the identities of the participants are given in the transcript extracts as 'interviewer' and 'interviewee'. The reader is effectively provided with a set of instructions to read these materials *as* a certain kind of institutional talk. What is never addressed is its *intelligibility* as 'institutional' in the first place. Addressing this issue demands examination of the *reflexive* relations between talk, identity and other circumstantial particulars as accomplishments of commonsense understanding. Such reflexive relations are available to H&G and to their readers, and account for how it is that neither we nor they have any difficulty in recognizing the talk for the activity that it manifests. However, the exclusively formal character of H&G's approach, wherein sequential organization constitutes institutionality, obscures the reflexive constitution of the phenomenon just as they simultaneously trade upon this as a resource. Thus, H&G replace a concern for *members'* commonsense analysis with a 'technical' concern for those features of situations that can be formalized. In their linear concentration upon the sequential form of talk and their desire to define institutional matters purely in terms of such form, H&G construct an analysis of news interviewing which is *not 'institutional' enough*. Their analysis takes insufficient account of the distinguishing institutional feature of their phenomenon – that news interviewing is, first and foremost, precisely that, *news* interviewing, conducted by persons properly and relevantly identifiable *as* news interviewers.

CONCLUSION

In this chapter, we have argued that deployment of the concept of speech exchange systems in conjunction with the claim that conversational structures comprise a 'bedrock' for institutional ones, effectively desensitizes analysts from the local specifics of institutional interaction. Ironically, we have seen that, in transporting the framework of CA to the analysis of talk in workplaces, in searching for differences in terms of that framework, and in allocating a primary and constitutive role to sequential structures, institutional analysts 'miss the phenomenon' they seek to explicate. The notion that the turn-taking organization of ordinary conversation constitutes a bedrock for the construction of forms of institutional talk involves a misleading emphasis upon sequentiality. Whilst we would not wish to call into question the significance of sequential considerations *for members* (and thereby for analysts), we *do* question (*pace* Watson, 1995, 1997b) the extent to which categorizational and sequential organizational features of talk can be separated, not only in ITP but also in CA as such. Thus, insofar as the rules for turn-allocation require recourse to such occasioned categories as 'first speaker', 'projected next speaker', 'story-teller', 'story recipient' and the rest, talk-in-interaction displays rights and obligations in relation to turn-taking. These rights and obligations are not tied to turns in themselves but to persons who, for just the time it takes to do whatever it is they're doing, occupy particular social positions relative to one another. They are incumbents, in other words, of particular membership categories. Such categories may be *locally and situationally* associated with other 'setting' identities, in as much as the activities which are done in and through the talk are setting-implicative.

It is even more ironic that the rigorous attention of CA to sequential matters has resulted in studies of institutional talk *some* of which unfortunately fall short of the very standards of analytic rigour which characterized classical CA. The basic reason for this is that ITP attempts to use CA to address precisely the kinds of phenomena which it *excluded* from its investigations. Such exclusion arguably was necessary in order to achieve rigorous attention to the formal sequential features of talk *per se*. There is a sense in which the pioneering studies of Sacks and others into the formal organization of talk deliberately disattended the institutional dimensions of such talk. Thus, much of Sacks's data consisted of talk that can be correctly described as 'calls to a suicide prevention centre' and 'therapy session talk', yet such descriptions in no way encompass everything that Sacks was interested in about this data. In examining such data for what it revealed about the endogenous organization of conversation, Sacks frequently disattended aspects of its contextual character. Such disattention, as practised by Schegloff, Jefferson and others as well as Sacks himself, enabled CA to build a rigorous, cumulative and systematic corpus of studies. ITP seeks to extend this corpus. However, whilst a focus on sequential ordering alone has produced the achievements of CA, such a focus will not allow the institutional analyst to adequately explicate the *in situ* social organization of 'institutional' talk and activities.

We remarked earlier on the 'craving for generality' that permeates ITP. The proponents of ITP, in pursuing the extension of CA's cumulative program of studies, have failed to appreciate the truly radical implications for the conduct of sociological inquiry of Garfinkel's famous injunction to view the orderliness of social life as available only 'from within'. The consequence of this failure is that, for all their self-positioning within the tradition of EM/CA, their studies display key hallmarks of what Sharrock and Anderson (1986: 82) refer to as 'Galilean science'. This 'seeks for similarity and generality, and in order to do so directs attention away from the specificities and particularities of things'. By contrast 'the inquiries of ethnomethodology go in a different direction, looking precisely for the distinguishing and identifying features of phenomena'.

To such a link between ITP and the framework of Galilean science it may be objected that CA has been from its outset a formalistic program of inquiry.[3] Its fundamental concerns are with *structures of interaction* and, as we have already suggested, in pursuit of rigorous description of these, classical CA consciously ignored particularities of 'content' – such as speakers' social identities, the location and avowed purpose of the interaction, and other contextual features – *except insofar as these were analytically relevant to the description of the structures under consideration.* All this is perfectly true, CA is and has always been a *formal* inquiry in these senses. What is also true, however, is that this formalist stance was wedded to another, more ethnomethodological one, involving a commitment to what Garfinkel and Wieder (1992) have referred to as the 'unique adequacy feature' of sociological inquiry. By this is meant the unavoidable tying of inquiry to the phenomenon upon which that inquiry is premised; inquiry itself is constructed 'from within', in the sense that the means by which inquiry is built are ones which the *phenomenon itself* makes available. In the case of conversation, for example, this means that sequential orderliness is not a *finding about* conversation, as in 'Galilean science', but something which the phenomenon itself *imposes* upon inquiry. To hear a stretch of talk as conversation is to hear it sequentially – speakers are talking to one another in a non-predetermined sequential manner, producing utterances which are sequentially related and which are *so intended and designed.* What CA does is to take this constitutive feature of conversation and transform it from something seen-but-unnoticed into a topic of self-conscious, systematic investigation. In so doing, the conversation analyst *extends* their members' knowledge (Coulter, 1983), formulating explicitly and systematically what is known ordinarily, practically and tacitly.

It follows from the unique adequacy feature that each inquiry must be distinct in significant respects; enormous caution needs to be exercised before assuming that an analytic approach taken in respect of one object of inquiry can be 'exported', as it were, from its original setting to studies in another. This exportation, or so it seems to us, is precisely what ITP attempts and is the key reason for its failure adequately to illuminate the phenomenon it seeks to address. In the course of its attempts to apply the methods and concepts of CA to the study of 'institutional' activities (where this term is a gloss for 'medical', 'journalistic', 'educational', 'judicial', and so forth) the very character of the phenomenon disappears from view. By treating such activities as variants of the activity of conversation, what it is that makes them the activities they recognizably are is largely passed over. On the evidence of ITP analyses such as those we have considered, it is hard not to conclude that proponents of ITP, in seeking what D&H (1992a: 21) refer to as 'institutional moorings', are at risk of losing their ethnomethodological ones.

Notes

1. Although these two books are the major statements of the program, they are not the only texts which attempt this task. For briefer statements, see Maynard and Clayman (1991, 1995) and Silverman (1993).
2. Perhaps sensing this difficulty, D&H go on a little later to offer a more extensive characterization of IT, in the form of a discussion of 'some features that may contribute to family resemblances among cases of institutional talk'. This seems on the face of it a somewhat strange claim; one is moved to ask how such 'cases' have been assembled *as cases* if D&H have no definite conception of what distinguishes a stretch of interactional talk as 'institutional'. However, for the sake of getting an overall picture of their views about IT, we will put this query on hold for the present.
3. We are not the first to note the 'scientism' of CA. Lynch and Bogen (1994) discuss Sacks's aspiration to build a 'primitive natural science' of conversation, based in certain respects on the model of biology. As they put it: 'Although conversation analysis is far from a dominant "paradigm" in the social sciences, it has been called a rare exemplar of a "normal science" research program in sociology (Law and Lodge, 1984). Accompanying such positive success, strong empiricist and scientistic tendencies have become established in conversation analytic discourse. While these tendencies are not necessarily incompatible with Sacks' prescriptions for a natural science of human behaviour, they are curiously at odds with the ethnomethodological conception of science that initially inspired Sacks and subsequently has been developed by ethnomethodological studies of practices in the natural sciences and mathematics.'

References

Althusser, L. (1971) Ideology and ideological state apparatuses. In: *Lenin and Philosophy and Other Essays*. London: Verso, pp. 121–73.

Antaki, C. (1994) *Explaining and Arguing: The Social Organization of Accounts*. London: Sage.

Antaki, C. (1998) Identity ascriptions in their time and place: 'Fagin' and 'the terminally dim'. In: C. Antaki and S. Widdicombe (eds), *Identities in Talk*. London: Sage, pp. 71–86.

Antaki, C. and M. Wetherell (1999) Show concessions. *Discourse Studies* 1(1): 7–27.

APA (American Psychiatric Association) (1994) *Diagnostic and Statistical Manual of Mental Disorders*, 4th edn. Washington, DC: APA.

Atkinson, J. M. (1982) Understanding formality: the categorization and production of 'formal' interaction. *British Journal of Sociology* 33: 86–117.

Atkinson, J. M. (1984) *Our Master's Voices: The Language and Body Language of Politics*. London: Methuen.

Atkinson, J. M. and P. Drew (1979) *Order in Court: The Organisation of Verbal Interaction in Judicial Settings*. London: Macmillan.

Auburn, T., S. Lea and S. Drake (1999) 'It's your opportunity to be truthful': disbelief, mundane reasoning and the investigation of crime. In: C. Willig (ed.), *Applied Discourse Analysis: Social and Psychological Investigations*. Buckingham: Open University Press, pp. 44–65.

Augoustinos, M., K. Tuffin and M. Rapley (1999) Genocide or a failure to gel? Racism, history and nationalism in Australian talk. *Discourse and Society* 10: 351–78.

Augoustinos, M., K. Tuffin and L. Sale (1999) Race talk. *Australian Journal of Psychology* 51(2): 90–7.

Austin, H. (1996) Reading positions and the student-of-literature in a year six classroom. *Australian Journal of Language and Literacy* 19(2): 144–153.

Austin, H. (1997) Literature for school: theorising 'the child' in talk and text. *Language and Education* 11(2): 77–95.

Austin, H., B. Dwyer and P. Freebody (in preparation) *The Educational Respecification of the Child: Ethnomethodological Studies of Language Interaction in Schooling*.

Austin, H. and P. Freebody (in press) Assembling and assessing the 'child-student': 'the child' as a criterion of assessment. *Journal of Curriculum Studies*.

Baker, C. D. (1983) A 'second look' at interviews with adolescents. *Journal of Youth and Adolescence* 12(6): 501–19.

Baker, C. D. (1997) Membership categorization and interview accounts. In: D. Silverman (ed.), *Qualitative Research: Theory, Method and Practice*. London: Sage, pp. 130–43.

Baker, C. D. and P. Freebody (1989a) *Children's First School Books*. Oxford: Blackwell.

Baker, C. D. and P. Freebody (1989b) Talk around text: constructions of textual and teacher authority in classroom discourse. In: S. de Castell, A. Luke and C. Luke (eds), *Language, Authority and Criticism*. London: Falmer Press, pp. 263–83.

Bakhtin M. (1986) *Speech Genres and Other Late Essays*. Austin: Texas University Press.

Barát, E. (1999) A relational model of identity: discoursal negotiations for non-oppressive power relations in Hungarian women's life narratives. Unpublished PhD thesis, Lancaster University.

Baron, R. and D. Byrne (1997) *Social Psychology*, 8th edn. Boston: Allyn & Bacon.

Baruch, G. (1981) Moral tales: parents' stories of encounters with the health professionals. *Sociology of Health and Wellness* 3(3): 275–95.

Benveniste, E. (1971) *Problems in General Linguistics*. Florida: University of Miami Press.

Berger, P. L. and T. Luckmann (1966) *The Social Construction of Reality*. Garden City: Doubleday.

Bergmann, J. R. (1992) Veiled morality: notes on discretion in psychiatry. In: P. Drew and J. Heritage (eds), *Talk at Work: Interaction in Institutional Settings*. Cambridge: Cambridge University Press, pp. 137–62.

Bergmann, J. R. (1998) Introduction: morality in discourse. *Research on Language and Social Interaction* 31(3/4): 279–94.

Bernard, J. (1975) *A Short Guide to Traditional Grammar*. Sydney: Sydney University Press.

Bernstein, B. (1990) *The Structuring of Pedagogic Discourse: Class Codes and Control*, Vol. 4. London: Routledge.

Bhaskar, R. (1986) *Scientific Realism and Human Emancipation*. London: Verso.

Billett, S. (1992) Towards a theory of workplace learning. *Studies in Continuing Education* 14(2): 143–55.

Billett, S. (1994) Situated learning: a workplace experience. *Australian Journal of Adult and Community Education* 34(2): 112–30.

Billig, M. (1987) *Arguing and Thinking: A Rhetorical Approach to Social Psychology*. Cambridge: Cambridge University Press.

Billig, M. (1991) *Ideology and Opinions: Studies in Rhetorical Psychology*. London: Sage.

Bjelic, D. and M. Lynch (1992) The work of a (scientific) demonstration: respecifying Newton's and Goethe's theories of prismatic color. In: G. Watson and R. M. Seiler (eds), *Text in Context: Contributions to Ethnomethodology*. London: Sage, pp. 52–78.

Blommaert, J. and J. Verschueren (1992) The role of language in European nationalist ideologies. *Pragmatics* 2: 355–75.

Blommaert, J. and J. Verschueren (1993) The rhetoric of tolerance, or: what police officers are taught about migrants. *Journal of Intercultural Studies* 14: 49–63.

Blommaert, J. and J. Verschueren (1998) *Debating Diversity: Analysing the Discourse of Tolerance*. London: Routledge.

Boden, D. (1994) *The Business of Talk: Organizations in Action*. Cambridge: Polity Press.

Boden, D. and D. H. Zimmerman (eds) (1991) *Talk and Social Structure: Studies in Ethnomethodology and Conversation Analysis*. Cambridge: Polity Press.

Boltanski, L. and E. Chiapello (1999) *Le nouvel esprit du capitalisme*. Paris: Gallimard.

Bourdieu, P. (1984) *Distinction: A Social Critique of the Judgement of Taste*. London: Routledge.

Boyle, M. (1990) *Schizophrenia: A Scientific Delusion?* London: Routledge.

Brown, R. and A. Gilman (1960) The pronouns of power and solidarity. In: T. A. Sebeok (ed.), *Style in Language*. New York: Wiley, pp. 253–76.

Brun-Cottan, F. (1990/1991) Talk in the workplace: occupational relevance. *Research on Language and Social Interaction* 24: 277–95.

Bruner, J. (1975) From communication to language: a psychological perspective. *Cognition* 3: 255–87.

Burr, V. (1995) *An Introduction to Social Constructionism.* London: Routledge.

Buttny, R. (1993) *Social Accountability in Communication.* London: Sage.

Buttny, R. (1996) Clients' and therapists' joint construction of the client's problems. *Research on Language and Social Interaction* 29(2): 125–53.

Buttny, R. and A. D. Jensen (1995) Telling problems in an initial family therapy session: the hierarchical organization of problem-talk. In: G. H. Morris and R. J. Chenail (eds), *The Talk of the Clinic: Explorations in the Analysis of Medical and Therapeutic Discourse.* Hillsdale: Lawrence Erlbaum, pp. 19–47.

Button, G. (1987) Answers as interactional products: two sequential practices used in interviews. *Social Psychology Quarterly* 50: 160–71.

Button, G. (1992) Answers as interactional products: two sequential practices used in job interviews. In: P. Drew and J. Heritage (eds), *Talk at Work: Interaction in Institutional Settings.* Cambridge: Cambridge University Press, pp. 212–31.

Button, G., J. Coulter, J. R. E. Lee and W. W. Sharrock (1995) *Computers, Minds and Conduct.* Cambridge: Polity Press.

Chafe, W. (1982) Integration and involvement in speaking, writing and oral literature. In: D. Tannen (ed.), *Spoken and Written Language: Exploring Orality and Literacy.* Norwood: Ablex, pp. 5–53.

Chouliaraki, L. (1998) Regulation in 'progressivist' pedagogic discourse: individualized teacher–pupil talk. *Discourse and Society* 9(1): 5–32.

Chouliaraki, L. (1999) Media discourse and national identity: death and myth in a news broadcast. In: R. Wodak and C. Ludwig (eds), *Challenges in a Changing World: Issues in Critical Discourse Analysis.* Vienna: Passagen Verlag, pp. 37–62.

Chouliaraki, L. and N. Fairclough (1999) *Discourse in Late Modernity.* Edinburgh: Edinburgh University Press.

Cicourel, A. V. (1968) *The Social Organization of Juvenile Justice.* New York: Wiley.

Clarke, V., C. Kitzinger and J. Potter (forthcoming) Lesbian and gay parenting and talk about bullying.

Clayman, S. E. (1988) Displaying neutrality in television news interviews. *Social Problems* 35: 474–92.

Clayman, S. E. (1992) Footing in the achievement of neutrality: the case of news interview discourse. In: P. Drew and J. Heritage (eds), *Talk at Work: Interaction in Institutional Settings.* Cambridge: Cambridge University Press, pp. 163–98.

Collins, S., I. Markova and J. Murphy (1997) Bringing conversations to a close: the management of closings in interactions between AAC users and 'natural' speakers. *Journal of Clinical Linguistics and Phonetics* 11(6): 467–93.

Coulter, J. (1979) *The Social Construction of Mind: Studies in Ethnomethodology and Linguistic Philosophy.* London: Macmillan.

Coulter, J. (1983) Contingent and a priori structures in sequential analysis. *Human Studies* 6(4): 361–76.

Coulter, J. (1989) *Mind in Action.* Cambridge: Polity Press.

Crystal, D. (1985) *A Dictionary of Linguistics and Phonetics*, 2nd edn. Oxford: Blackwell.

Cuff, E. and D. Francis (1978) Some features of 'invited stories' about marriage breakdown. *International Journal of the Sociology of Language* 18: 111–33.

Cushing, S. (1994) *Fatal Words: Communication Clashes and Aircraft Crashes.* Chicago: University of Chicago Press.

Darrah, C. (1997) Complicating the concept of skill requirements: scenes from a workplace. In: G. Hull (ed.), *Changing Work, Changing Workers: Critical Perspectives on Language, Literacy and Skills*. Albany: State University of New York Press, pp. 249–72.

Davis, C. (1986) The process of problem (re)formulation in psychotherapy. *Sociology of Health and Illness* 8: 44–74.

Dewey, J. (1944) *Democracy and Education: An Introduction to the Philosophy of Education*. New York: Free Press.

Dienes, Z. and D. Berry (1997) Implicit learning: below the subjective threshold. *Psychonomic Bulletin and Review* 4: 3–23.

Drew, P. (1992) Contested evidence in courtroom cross-examination: the case of a trial for rape. In: P. Drew and J. Heritage (eds), *Talk at Work: Interaction in Institutional Settings*. Cambridge: Cambridge University Press, pp. 470–520.

Drew, P. and J. Heritage (1992a) Analysing talk at work: an introduction. In: P. Drew and J. Heritage (eds), *Talk at Work: Interaction in Institutional Settings*. Cambridge: Cambridge University Press, pp. 3–65.

Drew, P. and J. Heritage (eds) (1992b) *Talk at Work: Interaction in Institutional Settings*. Cambridge: Cambridge University Press.

Drew, P. and M.-L. Soronjen (1997) Institutional dialogue. In: T. A. van Dijk (ed.), *Discourse Studies: A Multidisciplinary Introduction*. London: Sage, pp. 92–118.

Duranti, A. and C. Goodwin (eds) (1992) *Rethinking Context: Language as an Interactive Phenomenon*. Cambridge: Cambridge University Press.

Eagleson, R. D., T. Threadgold and P. Collins (1983) *Grammar: Its Nature and Terminology*. Victoria: Pitman.

Edwards, D. (1993) But what do children really think? Discourse analysis and conceptual content in children's talk. *Cognition and Instruction* 11(3–4): 207–25.

Edwards, D. (1994) Script formulations: a study of event descriptions in conversation. *Journal of Language and Social Psychology* 13: 211–47.

Edwards, D. (1995) Two to tango: script formulations, dispositions, and rhetorical symmetry in relationship troubles talk. *Research on Language and Social Interaction* 28(4): 319–50.

Edwards, D. (1997) *Discourse and Cognition*. London: Sage.

Edwards, D. (1998) The relevant thing about her: social identity categories in use. In: C. Antaki and S. Widdicombe (eds), *Identities in Talk*. London: Sage, pp. 15–33.

Edwards, D. (1999) Emotion discourse. *Culture and Psychology* 5(3): 271–91.

Edwards, D. (2000a) Analysing racial discourse: a view from discursive psychology. In: H. van den Berg, H. Houtkoop-Steenstra and M. Wetherell (eds), *Analysing Interviews on Racial Issues: Multidisciplinary Approaches to Interview Discourse*. Cambridge: Cambridge University Press.

Edwards, D. (2000b) Extreme case formulations: softeners, investment, and doing nonliteral. *Research on Language and Social Interaction* 23(4): 347–73.

Edwards, D. and N. M. Mercer (1987) *Common Knowledge: The Development of Understanding in the Classroom*. London: Routledge.

Edwards, D., D. Middleton and J. Potter (1992) Toward a discursive psychology of remembering. *The Psychologist* 5: 56–60.

Edwards, D. and J. Potter (1992a) *Discursive Psychology*. London: Sage.

Edwards, D. and J. Potter (1992b) The chancellor's memory: rhetoric and truth in discursive remembering. *Applied Cognitive Psychology* 6: 187–215.

Edwards, D. and J. Potter (1993) Language and causation: a discursive action model of description and attribution. *Psychological Review* 100: 23–41.

Eglin, P. and D. Wideman (1986) Inequality in professional service encounters: verbal strategies of control versus task performance in calls to the police. *Zeitschrift für Soziologie* 15(5): 341–62.

Elias, N. (1978) *What Is Sociology?* London: Hutchinson.

Errington, J. J. (1988) *Structure and Style in Javanese: A Semiotic View of Linguistic Etiquette*. Philadelphia: University of Pennsylvania Press.

Essed, P. (1991) *Understanding Everyday Racism*. Newbury Park: Sage.

Fairclough, N. (1992) *Discourse and Social Change*. Cambridge: Polity Press.

Fairclough, N. (1995) *Media Discourse*. London: Edward Arnold.

Fairclough, N. (2000) Discourse, social theory and social research: the discourse of welfare reform. *Journal of Sociolinguistics* 4(2): 163–95.

Fairclough, N. and R. Wodak (1997) Critical discourse analysis. In: T. A. van Dijk (ed.), *Discourse as Social Interaction*. London: Sage, pp. 320–48.

Faith, N. (1998) *Black Box*, 2nd edn. London: Boxtree.

Flight Safety Foundation (1996) Commuter captain fails to follow emergency procedures after suspected engine failure, loses control of the aircraft during instrument approach. *Accident Prevention* 53(4): 1–12.

Flight Safety Foundation (1997) Flight crew's failure to perform landing checklist results in DC-9 wheels-up landing. *Accident Prevention* 54(5): 1–15.

Forgacs, D. (1988) *A Gramsci Reader*. London: Lawrence & Wishart.

Foucault, M. (1977) *Discipline and Punish*. London: Allen Lane.

Fowler R., B. Hodge, G. Kress and T. Trew (1979) *Language and Control*. London: Routledge.

Freebody, P. (1995) Identity and pre-competence in early childhood: the case of learning literacy. *Australian Journal of Early Childhood Education* 20: 17–22.

Freebody, P. and B. Dwyer (1992) Classrooms as literacy-learning environments: the structure of participation. In: M. Carter (ed.), *Proceedings of the Second Learning Disabilities Association Annual Conference*. Sydney: NSW Department of Education, pp. 17–26.

Freiberg, J. and P. Freebody (1995) Analysing literacy events in classrooms and homes: conversation-analytic approaches. In: P. Freebody, C. Ludwig and S. Gunn (eds), *Everyday Literacy Practices In and Out of Schools in Low Socio-economic Urban Communities*. Canberra: Commonwealth of Australia, Department of Employment, Education and Training, pp. 185–372.

Friedrich, P. (1972) Social context and semantic feature: the Russian pronominal usage. In: J. J. Gumperz and D. Hymes (eds), *Directions in Sociolinguistics: The Ethnography of Communication*. New York: Holt, Rinehart & Winston, pp. 270–300.

Frith, H. and C. Kitzinger (1998) 'Emotion work' as a participant resource: a feminist analysis of young women's talk-in-interaction. *Sociology* 32: 299–320.

Garfinkel, H. and H. Sacks (1970) On formal structures of practical action. In: J. C. McKinney and E. A. Tiryakian (eds), *Theoretical Sociology: Perspectives and Developments*. New York: Appleton-Century-Crofts, pp. 338–66.

Garfinkel, H. and D. L. Wieder (1992) Two incommensurable, asymmetrically alternate technologies of social analysis. In: G. Watson and R. M. Seiler (eds), *Text in Context: Contributions to Ethnomethodology*. Newbury Park: Sage, pp. 175–206.

Gergen, K. J. (1970) *The Concept of Self*. London: Holt, Rinehart & Winston.

Gergen, K. J. (1985) The social constructionist movement in modern psychology. *American Psychologist* 40: 266–75.

Gergen, K. J. (1997) The place of the psyche in a constructed world. *Theory and Psychology* 7(6): 723–46.

Giddens, A. (1993) *New Rules of Sociological Method: A Positive Critique of Interpretative Sociologies*. Cambridge: Polity Press.

Gill, R. (1993) Justifying injustice: broadcasters' accounts on inequality in radio. In: E. Burman and I. Parker (eds), *Discourse Analytic Research: Repertoires and Readings of Texts in Action*. London: Routledge, pp. 75–93.

Gilsinan, J. F. (1989) They are clowning tough: 911 and the social construction of reality. *Criminology* 27: 329–44.

Goffman, E. (1955) On face-work: an analysis of ritual elements in social interaction. *Psychiatry* 18: 213–31.

Goffman, E. (1981) *Forms of Talk*. Oxford: Blackwell.

Goodwin, C. (1996) Transparent vision. In: E. Ochs, E. A. Schegloff and S. A. Thompson (eds), *Interaction and Grammar*. Cambridge: Cambridge University Press, pp. 370–404.

Goodwin, C. and M. H. Goodwin (1996) Seeing as situated activity: formulating planes. In: Y. Engeström and D. Middleton (eds), *Cognition and Communication at Work*. Cambridge: Cambridge University Press, pp. 61–95.

Goodwin, M. H. (1995) Assembling a response: setting and collaboratively constructed work talk. In: P. ten Have and G. Psathas (eds), *Situated Order: Studies in the Social Organization of Talk and Embodied Activities*. Washington, DC: University Press of America, pp. 173–86.

Goodwin, M. H. (1996) Announcements in their environment: prosody within a multi-activity work setting. In: E. Couper-Kuhlen and M. Selting (eds), *Prosody in Conversation: Interactional Studies*. Cambridge: Cambridge University Press, pp. 436–61.

Gramsci, A. (1971) *Selections from the Prison Notebooks*. London: Lawrence & Wishart.

Greatbatch, D. (1988) A turn-taking system for British news interviews. *Language in Society* 17: 401–30.

Greatbatch, D. (1992) On the management of disagreement between news interviewers. In: P. Drew and J. Heritage (eds), *Talk at Work: Interaction in Institutional Settings*. Cambridge: Cambridge University Press, pp. 268–301.

Greatbatch, D., C. Heath, P. Luff and P. Campion (1995) Conversation analysis: human–computer interaction and the general practice consultation. In: A. Monk and N. Gilbert (eds), *Perspectives on HCI: Diverse Approaches*. New York: Academic Press, pp. 199–222.

Habermas, J. (1984/1987) *The Theory of Communicative Action*, Vols 1 and 2. London: Heinemann.

Hak, T. (1998) There are clear delusions: the production of a factual account. *Human Studies* 21: 419–36.

Halliday, M. A. K. (1985) *An Introduction to Functional Grammar*, 1st edn. London: Edward Arnold.

Halliday, M. A. K. (1994) *An Introduction to Functional Grammar*, 2nd edn. London: Edward Arnold.

Halliday, M. A. K. and R. Hasan (1976) *Cohesion in English*. London: Longman.

Hanks, W. F. (1990) *Referential Practice: Language and Lived Space among the Maya*. Chicago: University of Chicago Press.

Hansard [Australia] (1999) House of Representatives, 26 August 1999.

Harré, R. (1998) *The Singular Self: An Introduction to the Psychology of Personhood*. London: Sage.

Harré, R. and G. Gillett (1994) *The Discursive Mind*. London: Sage.

Harré, R. and W. G. Parrott (1996) *The Emotions: Social, Cultural and Biological Dimensions*. London: Sage.

Harvey. D. (1996) *Justice, Nature and the Geography of Difference*. London: Blackwell.

Heap, J. L. (1985) Discourse in the production of classroom knowledge: reading lessons. *Curriculum Inquiry* 15: 245–79.

Heap. J. L. (1986) Cultural logic and schema theory. *Curriculum Inquiry* 16: 73–86.

Heap, J. L. (1987) Sociologies in and of education: a reply to Hammersley. *Curriculum Inquiry* 17: 239–42.

Heap, J. L. (1990) Applied ethnomethodology: looking for the local rationality of reading activities. *Human Studies* 13: 39–72.

Heap, J. L. (1997) Conversation analysis methods in researching language and education. In: N. H. Hornberger and D. Corson (eds), *Encyclopedia of Language in Education*, Vol. 8: *Research Methods in Language and Education*. Dordrecht: Kluwer Academic, pp. 217–25.

Heath, C. (1986) *Body Movement and Speech in Medical Interaction*. Cambridge: Cambridge University Press.

Heath, C. (1988) Embarrassment and interactional organization. In: P. Drew and A. Wootton (eds), *Erving Goffman: Exploring the Interaction Order*. Cambridge: Polity Press, pp. 136–60.

Heath, C. (1992) The delivery and reception of diagnosis in the general practice consultation. In: P. Drew and J. Heritage (eds), *Talk at Work: Interaction in Institutional Settings*. Cambridge: Cambridge University Press, pp. 235–67.

Heath, C. (1997) The analysis of activities in face to face interaction using video. In: D. Silverman (ed.), *Qualitative Research: Theory, Method and Practice*. London: Sage, pp. 183–200.

Heath, C. and P. Luff (1997) Convergent activities: collaborative work and multimedia technology in London underground line control rooms. In: D. Middleton and Y. Engeström (eds), *Cognition and Communication at Work*. Cambridge: Cambridge University Press, pp. 96–129.

Heath, C. and P. Luff (2000) *Technology in Action*. Cambridge: Cambridge University Press.

Helmreich, R. L. (1994) Anatomy of a system accident: the crash of Avianca flight 052. *International Journal of Aviation Psychology* 4(3): 265–84.

Hepburn, A. (2000) Power lines: Derrida, discursive psychology and the management of accusations of school bullying. *British Journal of Social Psychology* 39(4): 605–28.

Heritage, J. (1984a) A change of state token and aspects of its sequential placement. In: J. M. Atkinson and J. Heritage (eds), *Structures of Social Action: Studies in Conversation Analysis*. Cambridge: Cambridge University Press, pp. 299–345.

Heritage, J. (1984b) *Garfinkel and Ethnomethodology*. Cambridge: Polity Press.

Heritage, J. (1985) Analysing news interviews: aspects of the production of talk for an overhearing audience. In: T. A. van Dijk (ed.), *Handbook of Discourse Analysis*, Vol. 3. London: Academic Press, pp. 95–117.

Heritage, J. (1997) Conversation analysis and institutional talk: analysing data. In: D. Silverman (ed.), *Qualitative Research: Theory, Method and Practice*. London: Sage, pp. 161–82.

Heritage, J. and J. M. Atkinson (1984) Introduction. In: J. M. Atkinson and J. Heritage (eds), *Structures of Social Action: Studies in Conversation Analysis*. Cambridge: Cambridge University Press, pp. 1–15.

Heritage, J. and D. Greatbatch (1991) On the institutional character of institutional talk:

the case of news interviews. In: D. Boden and D. H. Zimmerman (eds), *Talk and Social Structure: Studies in Ethnomethodology and Conversation Analysis*. Cambridge: Polity Press, pp. 93–137.

Heritage, J. and D. R. Watson (1979) Formulations as conversational objects. In: G. Psathas (ed.), *Everyday Language: Studies in Ethnomethodology*. New York: Irvington, pp. 123–62.

Heritage, J. and D. R. Watson (1980) Aspects of the properties of formulations in natural conversations: some instances analyzed. *Semiotica* 30: 245–62.

Hester, S. and P. Eglin (eds) (1997) *Culture in Action: Studies in Membership Categorization Analysis*. Washington, DC: University Press of America.

Holstein, J. A. and J. F. Gubrium (1997) Active interviewing. In: D. Silverman (ed.), *Qualitative Research: Theory, Method and Practice*. London: Sage, pp. 113–29.

Holt, E. (2000) Reporting and reacting: concurrent responses to reported speech. *Research on Language and Social Interaction* 33(4): 425–54.

Houtkoop-Steenstra, H. (1995) Meeting both ends: standardization and recipient design in telephone survey interviews. In: P. ten Have and G. Psathas (eds), *Situated Order: Studies in the Social Organization of Talk and Embodied Activities*. Washington, DC: University Press of America, pp. 91–106.

Houtkoop-Steenstra, H. (1996) Probing behavior of interviewers in the standardized semi-open research interview. *Quality and Quantity* 30: 205–30.

Houtkoop-Steenstra, H. (2000) *Interaction and the Standardized Interview: The Living Questionnaire*. Cambridge: Cambridge University Press.

Howard, C., K. Tuffin, and C. Stephens (2000) Unspeakable emotion: a discursive analysis of police talk about reactions to trauma. *Journal of Language and Social Psychology* 19(3): 295–314.

HREOC (Human Rights and Equal Opportunities Commission) (1997) *Bringing Them Home: Report of the National Inquiry into the Separation of Aboriginal and Torres Strait Islander Children From their Families* (Chair: Sir Ronald Wilson). Canberra: Australian Government Publication Service.

Hull, G. (1992) *Their Chances? Slim and None: An Ethnographic Account of the Experiences of Low-income People of Color in a Vocational Program and at Work*. Berkeley: National Center for Research in Vocational Education, University of California at Berkeley.

Hutchby, I. and J. Moran-Ellis (eds) (1998) *Children and Social Competence: Arenas of Action*. London: Falmer Press.

Hutchby, I. and R. Wooffitt (1998) *Conversation Analysis: Principles, Practices and Applications*. Oxford: Polity Press.

Jackson, S. (1982) *Childhood and Sexuality*. Oxford: Blackwell.

Jakobson, R. (1971/1957) Shifters, verbal categories, and the Russian verb. In: *Selected Writings*, Vol. 2. The Hague: Mouton, pp. 130–47.

James, A. and A. Prout (1990a) Introduction: constructing and reconstructing childhood. In: A. James and A. Prout (eds), *Constructing and Reconstructing Childhood: Contemporary Issues in the Sociological Study of Childhood*. London: Falmer Press, pp. 1–6.

James, A. and A. Prout (1990b) Re-presenting childhood: time and transition in the study of childhood. In: A. James and A. Prout (eds), *Constructing and Reconstructing Childhood: Contemporary Issues in the Sociological Study of Childhood*. London: Falmer Press, pp. 216–37.

Jayyusi, L. (1984) *Categorization and the Moral Order*. Boston: Routledge & Kegan Paul.

Jefferson, G. (1985) On the interactional unpackaging of a 'gloss'. *Language in Society* 14: 435–66.

Jefferson, G. (1990) List construction as a task and resource. In: G. Psathas (ed.), *Interaction Competence.* Washington, DC: University Press of America, pp. 63–92.

Jenks, C. (1989) Social theorising and the child. In: S. Doxiades (ed.), *Early Influences Shaping the Individual.* London: Plenum Press, pp. 93–102.

Jenks, C. (1995) Historical perspectives on normality. In: P. Lindstrom and N. Spencer (eds), *The European Textbook of Social Paediatrics.* Oxford: Oxford University Press, pp. 78–91.

Jenks, C. (1996) *Childhood.* London: Routledge.

Jessop, R. (2000) The crisis of the national spatio-temporal fix and the ecological dominance of globalizing capitalism. Draft ms. University of Lancaster. <www.comp.lancaster.ac.uk/sociology/soc043rj.html>

Kelly, A. (1999) Representing oral complaints in a bureaucratic form in a council office. Paper presented at the National Centre for Vocational Education Research Conference ('Training Research Conference'), Toowoomba, Queensland, 6–8 July 1999.

Kitagawa, C. and A. Lehrer (1990) Impersonal uses of personal pronouns. *Journal of Pragmatics* 14: 739–59.

Kitzinger, C. (1992) The individuated self. In: G. Breakwell (ed.), *The Social Psychology of Identity and the Self Concept.* London: Academic Press and Surrey University Press, pp. 221–50.

Kleinig, J. (1982) *Philosophical Issues in Education.* London: Croom Helm.

Kline, P. (1988) *Psychology Exposed, or, the Emperor's New Clothes.* London: Routledge.

Komter, M. L. (1991) *Conflict and Cooperation in Job Interviews: A Study of Talk, Tasks and Ideas.* Amsterdam: Benjamins.

Koriat, A. and M. Goldsmith (1996) Memory metaphors and the real-life/laboratory controversy: correspondence versus storehouse conceptions of memory. *Behavioral and Brain Sciences* 19: 167–228.

Kress G. (1985) *Linguistic Processes in Sociocultural Practice.* Oxford: Oxford University Press.

Kusterer, K. C. (1978) *Know-how on the Job: The Important Working Knowledge of 'Unskilled' Workers.* Boulder: Westview Press.

Laclau, E. and C. Mouffe (1985) *Hegemony and Socialist Strategy.* London: Verso.

Lakoff, G. and M. Johnson (1980) *Metaphors We Live By.* Chicago: University of Chicago Press.

Law, J. and D. Lodge (1984) *Science for Social Scientists.* London: Macmillan.

Lazar, M. (1998) The narrative discourse of heterosexual sociality and the dynamics in the discourses of gender relations in Singapore's family life advertisements: a critical discourse analysis. Unpublished PhD thesis, Lancaster University.

LeCouteur, A. and M. Augoustinos (in press a) Apologizing to the Stolen Generations: argument, rhetoric, and identity in public reasoning. *Australian Psychologist.*

LeCouteur, A. and M. Augoustinos (in press b) The language of racism. In: M. Augoustinos and K. J. Reynolds (eds), *Understanding Prejudice, Racism and Social Conflict.* London: Sage.

LeCouteur, A., M. Rapley and M. Augoustinos (in press) 'This very difficult debate about Wik': stake, voice and the management of category memberships in race politics. *British Journal of Social Psychology* 39.

Lemke, J. (1995) *Textual Politics: Discourse and Social Dynamics.* London: Taylor and Francis.

Leudar, I. and P. Thomas (2000) *Voices of Reason, Voices of Insanity: Studies of Verbal Hallucinations.* London: Routledge.

Linell, P. and T. Luckman (1991) Asymmetries in dialogue: some conceptual preliminaries.

In: I. Markova and K. Foppa (eds), *Asymmetries in Dialogue*. Hemel Hempstead: Harvester Wheatsheaf, pp. 1–20.

Locke, A. J. C. and D. Edwards (forthcoming) *Bill and Monica: Motive and Emotion: Talk in Clinton's Grand Jury Testimony*.

Lovering, K. M. (1995) The bleeding body: adolescents talk about menstruation. In: S. Wilkinson and C. Kitzinger (eds), *Feminism and Discourse*. London: Sage, pp. 10–31.

Luff, P., J. Hindmarsh and C. Heath (2000) *Workplace Studies: Recovering Work Practice and Informing System Design*. Cambridge: Cambridge University Press.

Lynch, M. (1993) *Scientific Practice and Ordinary Action: Ethnomethodology and Social Studies of Science*. New York: Cambridge University Press.

Lynch, M. and D. Bogen (1994) Harvey Sacks' primitive science. *Theory, Culture and Society* 11: 169–86.

Lynch, M. and D. Bogen (1996) *The Spectacle of History: Speech, Text, and Memory at the Iran-Contra Hearings*. Durham: Duke University Press.

Lyotard, J.-F. (1986/1987) Rules and paradoxes and svelte appendix. *Cultural Critique* 5: 209–19.

McCreanor, T. (1989) Talking about race. In: H. Yensen, K. Hague and T. McCreanor (eds), *Honouring the Treaty*. Auckland: Penguin, pp. 90–118.

McCreanor, T. (1993) Settling grievances to deny sovereignty: trade goods for the year 2000. *Sites* 27: 45–73.

McHoul, A. (1978) The organization of turns at formal talk in the classroom. *Language in Society* 7: 183–213.

McHoul, A. (1987) Why there are no guarantees for interrogators. *Journal of Pragmatics* 11(4): 455–71.

McIllvenny, P. (1995) Seeing conversations: analyzing sign language talk. In: P. ten Have and G. Psathas (eds), *Situated Order: Studies in the Social Organization of Talk and Embodied Activities*. Washington, DC: University Press of America, pp. 129–50.

Mackay, R. (1974) Conceptions of children and models of socialization. In: R. Turner (ed.), *Ethnomethodology: Selected Readings*. Harmondsworth: Penguin, pp. 180–93.

McKinlay, A. and A. Dunnett (1998) How gun-owners accomplish being deadly average. In: C. Antaki and S. Widdicombe (eds), *Identities in Talk*. London: Sage, pp. 34–51.

MacMillan, K. and D. Edwards (1999) Who killed the princess? Description and blame in the British press. *Discourse Studies* 1(2): 151–74.

MacPherson, M. (1998) *The Black Box: Cockpit Voice Recorder Accounts of In-flight Accidents*. London: HarperCollins.

Malone, M. (1997) *Worlds of Talk: The Presentation of Self in Everyday Conversation*. Cambridge: Polity Press.

Maynard, D. (1989) Notes on the delivery and reception of diagnostic news regarding mental disabilities. In: D. T. Helm, W. T. Anderson, A. J. Meehan and A. W. Rawls (eds), *The Interactional Order: New Directions in the Study of Social Order*. New York: Irvington, pp. 54–67.

Maynard, D. (1991) The perspective display series and the delivery and receipt of diagnostic news. In: D. Boden and D. H. Zimmerman (eds), *Talk and Social Structure: Studies in Ethnomethodology and Conversation Analysis*. Cambridge: Polity Press, pp. 164–92.

Maynard, D. (1992) On clinicians co-implicating recipients' perspective in the delivery of diagnostic news. In: P. Drew and J. Heritage (eds), *Talk at Work: Interaction in Institutional Settings*. Cambridge: Cambridge University Press, pp. 331–58.

Maynard, D. and S. Clayman (1991) The diversity of ethnomethodology. *Annual Review of Sociology* 17: 385–418.

Maynard, D. and S. Clayman (1995) Ethnomethodology and conversation analysis. In: P. ten Have and G. Psathas (eds), *Situated Order: Studies in the Organisation of Conversational Interaction and Embodied Activities*. Washington, DC: University Press of America, pp. 1–30.

Mazeland, H. (1992) *Vraag/antwoordsequenties*. Amsterdam: Stichting Neerlandistiek VU.

Mazeland, H. and P. ten Have (1996) Essential tensions in (semi)open research interviews. In: I. Maso and F. Wester (eds), *The Deliberate Dialogue: Qualitative Perspectives on the Interview*. Brussels: VUB University Press, pp. 87–113.

Meehan, A. J. (1986) Assessing the 'police-worthiness' of citizen complaints to the police: accountability and the negotiation of 'facts'. *Zeitschrift für Soziologie* 15: 341–62.

Mehan, H. (1979) *Learning Lessons: Social Organization in the Classroom*. Cambridge: Harvard University Press.

Meier, C. (1997) *Arbeitsbesprechungen: Interaktionstruktur, Interaktionsdynamik und Konsequenzen einer sozialen Form*. [*Work Meetings: Interactional Structure, Interaction Dynamics, and Consequences of a Social Form*.] Opladen: Westdeutscher Verlag.

Middleton, D. and D. Edwards (eds) (1990) *Collective Remembering*. London: Sage.

Morgan, M., K. Tuffin, L. Frederikson, A. Lyons, and C. Stephens (1994) The health reform advertisements: what are they all about and what will they mean to you? *New Zealand Journal of Psychology* 23: 28–35.

Moscovici, S. (1984) The phenomenon of social representations. In: R. M. Farr and S. Moscovici (eds), *Social Representations*. Cambridge: Cambridge University Press, pp. 3–70.

Muhlhausler, P. and R. Harré (1990) *Pronouns and People: The Linguistic Construction of Social and Personal Identity*. Oxford: Blackwell.

Mulcahy, D. (1995) Performing competencies: of training protocols and vocational education practices. *Australian and New Zealand Journal of Vocational Education Research* 4(1): 35–67.

Myers, G. (1998) Displaying opinions: topics and disagreement in focus groups. *Language in Society* 27: 85–111.

Nairn, R. and T. McCreanor (1990) Insensitivity and hypersensitivity: an imbalance in Pakeha discourse on Maori/Pakeha accounts of racial conflict. *Journal of Language and Social Psychology* 9: 293–308.

Nairn, R. and T. McCreanor (1991) Race talk and common sense: ideological patterns in Pakeha talk about Maori/Pakeha relations. *Journal of Language and Social Psychology* 10: 245–62.

National Clerical-Administrative Competency Standards: Private Sector (1997) Melbourne: Australian National Training Authority.

Neisser, U. (1967) *Cognitive Psychology*. New York: Appleton-Century-Crofts.

Newnes, C., G. Holmes, and C. Dunn (eds) (1999) *This Is Madness: A Critical Look at Psychiatry and the Future of Mental Health Services*. Ross-on-Wye: PCCS Books.

Nisbett, R. E. and T. D. Wilson (1977) Telling more than we can know: verbal reports on mental processes. *Psychological Review* 84: 231–59.

Pêcheux, M. (1975) *Les Vérités de la police*. Paris: Maspero.

Peräkylä, A. (1995) *AIDS Counselling: Institutional Interaction and Clinical Practice*. Cambridge: Cambridge University Press.

Pollner, M. (1987) *Mundane Reason: Reality in Everyday and Sociological Discourse*. Cambridge: Cambridge University Press.

Pomerantz, A. (1978) Compliment responses: notes on the co-operation of multiple constraints. In: J. Schenkein (ed.), *Studies in the Organization of Conversational Interaction*. London: Academic Press, pp. 79–98.

Pomerantz, A. (1984) Agreeing and disagreeing with assessments: some features of preferred/dispreferred turn shapes. In: J. M. Atkinson and J. Heritage (eds), *Structures of Social Action: Studies in Conversation Analysis*. Cambridge: Cambridge University Press, pp. 57–101.

Pomerantz, A. (1986) Extreme case formulations: a way of legitimizing claims. *Human Studies* 9: 219–29.

Pope, J. A. (1995) Comparing accident reports: looking beyond causes to identify recurrent factors. *Flight Safety Digest* 14(5): 1–8.

Potter, J. (1996a) *Representing Reality: Discourse, Rhetoric and Social Construction*. London: Sage.

Potter, J. (1996b) Attitudes, social representations, and discursive psychology. In: M. Wetherell (ed.), *Identities, Groups and Social Issues*. London: Sage, pp. 119–73.

Potter, J. (1996c) Discourse analysis and constructionist approaches: theoretical background. In: J. T. E. Richardson (ed.), *Handbook of Qualitative Research Methods for Psychology and the Social Sciences*. Leicester: BPS Books, pp. 125–40.

Potter, J. (1998) Discursive social psychology: from attitudes to evaluations. *European Review of Social Psychology* 9: 233–66.

Potter, J., D. Edwards and M. Wetherell (1993) A model of discourse in action. *American Behavioural Scientist* 36: 383–401.

Potter, J. and M. Wetherell (1987) *Discourse and Social Psychology: Beyond Attitudes and Behaviour*. London: Sage.

Potter, J. and M. Wetherell (1988) Accomplishing attitudes: fact and evaluation in racist discourse. *Text* 8: 51–68.

Potter, J. and M. Wetherell (1994) Analyzing discourse. In: A. Bryman and R. G. Burgess (eds), *Analyzing Qualitative Data*. London: Routledge, pp. 47–66.

Psathas, G. (1990) Introduction: methodological issues and recent developments in the study of naturally occurring interaction. In: G. Psathas (ed.), *Interactional Competence*. Washington, DC: University Press of America, pp. 1–30.

Psathas, G. (1995) *Conversation Analysis: The Study of Talk-in-Interaction*. London: Sage.

Psychonomic Bulletin and Review (1997) Implicit learning: a symposium.

Puchta, C. and J. Potter (in press) Manufacturing individual opinions: market research focus groups and the discursive psychology of attitudes. *British Journal of Social Psychology*.

Quirk, R. and S. Greenbaum (1973) *A University Grammar of English*. London: Longman.

Rapley, M. (1998) 'Just an ordinary Australian': self-categorisation and the discursive construction of facticity in 'racist' political rhetoric. *British Journal of Social Psychology* 37: 325–44.

Riessman, C. K. (1993) *Narrative Analysis*. Newbury Park: Sage.

Roulston, K. J (1998a) Itinerant primary music teachers in Queensland: a report on a survey. *Australian Journal of Music Education* 1: 7–19.

Roulston, K. J. (1998b) Music teachers talk about itinerancy. *Queensland Journal of Educational Research* 14(1): 59–74.

Roulston, K. J. (1998c) The integral nature of extracurricular work. In: B. Baker, M. Tucker and C. Ng (eds), *Education's New Timespace: Visions from the Present*. Brisbane: Postpressed, pp. 74–80.

Roulston, K. J. (1999) Costing the 'worldly riches of extra time'. In: K. Chalmers, S. Bogitini and P. Renshaw (eds), *Educational Research in New Times: Imagining Communities for Diversity and Inclusiveness*. Brisbane: Postpressed, pp. 97–106.

Sacks, H. (1984) Notes on methodology. In: J. M. Atkinson and J. Heritage (eds), *Structures of Social Action: Studies in Conversation Analysis*. Cambridge: Cambridge University Press, pp. 2–17.

Sacks, H. (1992a) *Lectures on Conversation*, Vol. 1. Ed. G. Jefferson. Oxford: Blackwell.

Sacks, H. (1992b) *Lectures on Conversation*, Vol. 2. Ed. G. Jefferson. Oxford: Blackwell.

Sacks, H., E. A. Schegloff and G. Jefferson (1974) A simplest systematics for the organization of turn-taking for conversation. *Language* 50: 696–735.

Sacks, H., E. A. Schegloff and G. Jefferson (1978) A simplest systematics for the organization of turn taking for conversation. In: J. N. Schenkein (ed.), *Studies in the Organization of Conversational Interaction*. New York: Academic Press, pp. 7–55.

Said, E. W. (1993) *Culture and Imperialism*. London: Vintage.

Sampson, E. E. (1989) The deconstruction of the self. In: J. Shotter and K. Gergen (eds), *Texts of Identity*. London: Sage, pp. 1–19.

Sarangi, S. and S. Slembrouck (1996) *Language, Bureaucracy and Social Control*. London: Longman.

Sarbin, T. E. and J. Mancuso (1984) *Schizophrenia: Medical Diagnosis or Moral Verdict?* New York: Pergamon.

Schegloff, E. A. (1972) Notes on a conversational practice: formulating place. In: D. Sudnow (ed.), *Studies in Social Interaction*. New York: Free Press, pp. 75–119.

Schegloff, E. A. (1980) Preliminaries to preliminaries: 'Can I ask you a question?' *Sociological Inquiry* 50: 104–52.

Schegloff, E. A. (1986) The routine as achievement. *Human Studies* 9: 111–52.

Schegloff, E. A. (1989) Harvey Sacks – lectures 1964–65: an introduction/memoir. *Human Studies* 12(3/4): 185–209.

Schegloff, E. A. (1991) Reflections on talk and social structure. In: D. Boden and D. H. Zimmerman (eds), *Talk and Social Structure: Studies in Ethnomethodology and Conversation Analysis*. Cambridge: Polity Press, pp. 44–70.

Schegloff, E. A. (1992) On talk and its institutional occasions. In: P. Drew and J. Heritage (eds), *Talk at Work: Interaction in Institutional Settings*. Cambridge: Cambridge University Press, pp. 101–34.

Schegloff, E. A. (1996) Confirming allusions: towards an empirical account of action. *American Journal of Sociology* 104: 161–216.

Schegloff, E. A. (1997) Whose text? Whose context? *Discourse and Society* 8: 165–87.

Schegloff, E. A. (1998) Reply to Wetherell. *Discourse and Society* 9 (3): 413–16.

Schegloff, E. A. and H. Sacks (1973) Opening up closings. *Semiotica* 7: 289–327.

Scollon, R. (1998) *Mediated Discourse as Social Interaction: A Study of News Discourse*. London: Longman.

Searle, J. (1996) Language and literacy competencies. In: J. Stevenson (ed.), *Learning in the Workplace – Tourism and Hospitality: An Initial Examination of Critical Aspects of Small Business in the Tourism and Hospitality Industry*. Griffith University: Centre for Skill Formation Research and Development, pp. 22–50.

Shanks, D. R. and M. F. St John (1994) Characteristics of dissociable human memory systems. *Behavioral and Brain Sciences* 17: 367–447.

Sharrock, W. W. and R. Anderson (1986) *The Ethnomethodologists*. London: Tavistock.

Sharrock, W. W. and R. Turner (1978) On a conversational environment for equivocality.

In: J. N. Schenkien (ed.), *Studies in the Organization of Conversational Interaction*. New York: Academic Press, 173–97.

Silverman, D. (1987) *Communication and Medical Practice*. London: Sage.

Silverman, D. (1993) *Interpreting Qualitative Data: Methods for Analysing Talk, Text, and Interaction*. London: Sage.

Silverman, D. (1998) *Harvey Sacks: Social Science and Conversation Analysis*. Cambridge: Polity Press.

Silverstein, M. (1976) Shifters, linguistic categories, and cultural description. In: K. H. Basso and H. A. Selby (eds), *Meaning in Anthropology*. Albuquerque: University of New Mexico Press, pp. 11–55.

Smith, D. E. (1974) Social construction of documentary reality. *Sociological Inquiry* 44: 257–67.

Smith, D. E. (1978) K is mentally ill: the anatomy of a factual account. *Sociology* 12: 23–53.

Smith, D. E. (1984) Textually mediated social organization. *International Social Science Journal* 36(1): 59–75.

Smith, D. E. (1990a) *The Conceptual Practices of Power: A Feminist Sociology of Knowledge*. Boston: Northeastern University Press.

Smith, D. E. (1990b) *Texts, Facts and Femininity: Exploring the Relations of Ruling*. London: Routledge.

Spears, R. (1997) Introduction. In: T. Ibanez and L. Iniguez (eds), *Critical Social Psychology*. London: Sage, pp. 1–26.

Speer, S. and J. Potter (2000) The discursive construction of 'heterosexist' talk: participant resources in the management of (potentially) prejudiced claims. *Discourse and Society* 11: 543–72.

Speier, M. (1970) The everyday world of the child. In: J. Douglas (ed.), *Understanding Everyday Life: Toward the Reconstruction of Sociological Knowledge*. Chicago: Aldine, pp. 188–218.

Speier, M. (1976) The child as conversationalist: some cultural contact features of conversational interactions between adults and children. In: M. Hammersley and P. Woods (eds), *The Process of Schooling*. London: Routledge & Kegan Paul, pp. 98–103.

Spiegelberg, H. (1973) On the right to say 'we': a linguistic and phenomenological analysis. In: G. Psathas (ed.), *Phenomenological Sociology: Issues and Applications*. New York: Wiley, pp. 129–56.

Stadler, M. A. (1997) Distinguishing implicit and explicit learning. *Psychonomic Bulletin and Review* 4: 56–62.

Stephens, C. V. (1996) The impact of trauma on health and the moderating effects of social support: a study with the New Zealand police. Unpublished PhD thesis, Massey University.

Suchman, L. (1987) *Plans and Situated Action: The Problem of Human–Machine Communication*. Cambridge: Cambridge University Press.

Suchman, L. (1992) Technologies of accountability: of lizards and airplanes. In: G. Button (ed.), *Technology in Working Order: Studies of Work, Interaction and Technology*. London: Routledge, pp. 113–26.

Suchman, L. (1996) Constituting shared workspaces. In: Y. Engeström and D. Middleton (eds), *Cognition and Communication at Work*. Cambridge: Cambridge University Press, pp. 35–60.

Suchman, L. and B. Jordan (1990) Interactional troubles in face-to-face survey interviews. *Journal of the American Statistical Association* 85: 232–41.

Suchman, L. and R. H. Trigg (1991) Understanding practice: video as a medium for reflection and design. In: J. Greenbaum and M. Kyng (eds), *Design at Work: Cooperative Design of Computer Systems*. Hillsdale: Lawrence Erlbaum, pp. 65–89.

Suchman, L. and R. H. Trigg (1993) Artificial intelligence as craftwork. In: S. Chaiklin and J. Lave (eds), *Understanding Practice: Perspectives on Activities and Context*. New York: Cambridge University Press, pp. 144–78.

Talbot, M. (1998) *Language and Gender: An Introduction*. Cambridge: Polity Press.

Tapsell, L. (2000) Using applied conversation analysis to teach novice dieticians history taking skills. *Human Studies* 23: 281–307.

te Molder, H. (1999) Discourse of dilemmas: an analysis of communication planners' accounts. *British Journal of Social Psychology* 38: 245–63.

ten Have, P. (1989) The consultation as a genre. In: B. Torode (ed.), *Text and Talk as Social Practice*. Dordrecht: Foris, pp. 115–35.

ten Have, P. (1999) *Doing Conversation Analysis: A Practical Guide*. London: Sage.

Thiele, C. (1974) *Magpie Island*. Ringwood: Puffin Books.

Tyler, D. (1993) Making better children. In: D. Meredyth and D. Tyler (eds), *Child and Citizen: Genealogies of Schooling and Subjectivity*. Brisbane: Brisbane Institute for Cultural Policy Studies, pp. 35–59.

van Dijk, T. A. (1993) *Discourse and Elite Racism*. London: Sage.

van Leeuwen, T. (1993) Genre and field in critical discourse analysis: a synopsis. *Discourse and Society* 4(2): 193–223.

Watson, D. R. (1987) Interdisciplinary considerations in the analysis of pro-terms. In: G. Button and J. R. E. Lee (eds), *Talk and Social Organisation*. Clevedon: Multilingual Matters, pp. 261–89.

Watson, D. R. (1992) Ethnomethodology, conversation analysis and education: an overview. *International Review of Education* 38(3): 257–74.

Watson, D. R. (1995) Some potentialities and pitfalls in the analysis of process and personal change in counselling and therapeutic interaction. In: J. Siegfried (ed.), *Therapeutic and Everyday Discourse as Behaviour Change*. Norwood: Ablex, pp. 301–39.

Watson, D. R. (1997a) Ethnomethodology and textual analysis. In: D. Silverman (ed.), *Qualitative Research: Theory, Method and Practice*. London: Sage, pp. 80–98.

Watson, D. R. (1997b) Some general reflections on 'categorization' and 'sequence' in the analysis of conversation. In: S. Hester and P. Eglin (eds), *Culture in Action: Studies in Membership Categorizaton Analysis*. Washington, DC: University Press of America, pp. 49–76.

Watson, D. R. (1997c) The presentation of 'victim' and 'motive' in discourse: the case of police interrogations and interviews. In: M. Travers and J. F. Manzo (eds), *Law in Action*. Aldershot: Dartmouth Publishing, pp. 77–99.

Wearing, M. and R. Berreen (eds) (1994) *Welfare and Social Policy in Australia: The Distribution of Advantage*. Sydney: Harcourt Brace.

Wetherell, M. (1998) Positioning and interpretative repertoires: conversation analysis and post-structuralism in dialogue. *Discourse and Society* 9(3): 387–412.

Wetherell, M. and J. Potter (1992) *Mapping the Language of Racism: Discourse and the Legitimation of Exploitation*. Hemel Hempstead: Harvester Wheatsheaf.

Whalen, J. (1995) A technology of order production: computer-aided dispatch in public safety communications. In: P. ten Have and G. Psathas (eds), *Situated Order: Studies in the Social Organization of Talk and Embedded Activities*. Washington, DC: University Press of America, pp. 186–230.

Whalen, J., D. H. Zimmerman and M. Whalen (1988) When words fail: a single case analysis. *Social Problems* 35(4): 335–62.

Whalen, M. and D. H. Zimmerman (1987) Sequential and institutional contexts in calls for help. *Social Psychology Quarterly* 50: 172–85.

Whalen, M. and D. H. Zimmerman (1990) Describing trouble: practical epistemology in citizen calls to the police. *Language in Society* 19: 465–92.

White, H. (1978) *Tropics of Discourse*. Baltimore: The Johns Hopkins University Press.

Widdicombe, S. (1998) Identity as an analysts' and a participants' resource. In: C. Antaki and S. Widdicombe (eds), *Identities in Talk*. London: Sage, pp. 191–206.

Widdicombe, S. and R. Wooffitt (1995) *The Language of Youth Subcultures: Social Identity in Action*. Hemel Hempstead: Harvester Wheatsheaf.

Wieder, D. L. (1974a) *Language and Social Reality*. The Hague: Mouton.

Wieder, D. L. (1974b) Telling the code. In: R. Turner (ed.), *Ethnomethodology*. Harmondsworth: Penguin, pp. 144–72.

Wieder, D. L. (1988) From resource to topic: some aims of conversation analysis. In: J. Anderson (ed.), *Communication Yearbook*, Vol. 2. Thousand Oaks: Sage, pp. 444–54.

Williams, R. (1977) *Marxism and Literature*. Oxford: Oxford University Press.

Willig, C. (1997) The limitations of trust in intimate relationships: constructions of trust and sexual risk-taking. *British Journal of Social Psychology* 36: 211–21.

Wilson, J. (1990) *Politically Speaking: The Pragmatic Analysis of Political Language*. Oxford: Blackwell.

Wilson, T. P. (1991) Social structure and the sequential organization of interaction. In: D. Boden and D. H. Zimmerman (eds), *Talk and Social Structure: Studies in Ethnomethodology and Conversation Analysis*. Cambridge: Polity Press, pp. 22–43.

Wittgenstein, L. (1953) *Philosophical Investigations*. Oxford: Blackwell.

Wittgenstein, L. (1969) *The Blue and Brown Books*, 2nd edn. Oxford: Blackwell.

Wodak, R. (1996) *Disorders of Discourse*. London: Longman.

Wooffitt, R. (1992) *Telling Tales of the Unexpected: The Organization of Factual Discourse*. Hemel Hempstead: Harvester Wheatsheaf.

Wooffitt, R. (1993) Analyzing accounts. In: N. Gilbert (ed.), *Researching Social Life*. London: Sage, pp. 287–305.

Wortham, S. E. F. (1994) *Acting out Participant Examples in the Classroom*. Amsterdam: Benjamins.

Zimmerman, D. H. (1984) Talk and its occasion: the case of calling the police. In: D. Schiffrin (ed.), *Meaning, Form, and Use in Context: Linguistic Applications*. Washington, DC: Georgetown University Press, pp. 210–28.

Zimmerman, D. H. (1992a) Achieving context: openings in emergency calls. In: G. Watson and R. M. Seiler (eds), *Text in Context: Contributions to Ethnomethodology*. London: Newbury Park, pp. 35–51.

Zimmerman, D. H. (1992b) The interactional organization of calls for emergency assistance. In: P. Drew and J. Heritage (eds), *Talk at Work: Interaction in Institutional Settings*. Cambridge: Cambridge University Press, pp. 418–69.

Zimmerman, D. H. and D. Boden (1991) Structure-in-action. In: D. Boden and D. H. Zimmerman (eds), *Talk and Social Structure: Studies in Ethnomethodology and Conversation Analysis*. Cambridge: Polity Press, pp. 3–21.

Index